Influential
Writing

Influential Writing

William Connor
University of Alberta

Maurice Legris
University of Alberta

McGraw-Hill Ryerson Limited

Toronto Montreal New York Auckland
Bogota Caracas Lisbon London
Madrid Mexico Milan New Delhi
San Juan Singapore Sydney Tokyo

INFLUENTIAL WRITING

ISBN: 0-07-552520-8

1 2 3 4 5 6 7 8 9 10 BBM 4 3 2 1 0 9 8 7 6 5

Printed and bound in Canada

Sponsoring Editor: David Ward
Developmental Editor: Laurie Graham
Supervising Editor: Margaret Henderson
Production Editor: Andrea Gallagher Ellis
Page Makeup: McGraphics Desktop Publishing Ltd.
Cover Design: Dianna Little
Cover Photo: Don Mason/Masterfile
Printer: Best Book Manufacturers

Canadian Cataloguing in Publication Data

Connor, William
   Influential writing

ISBN 0-07-552520-8

1. College readers.   I. Legris, Maurice.   II. Title.

PE1417.C65 1995   808'.0427   C94-932765-4

Contents

Alternative List of Readings: Types of Writing   ix

Preface   xvii

Acknowledgements   xix

Introduction   1

Readings

AMIEL, BARBARA. *Another Threat to Freedom in Ontario*   11

AMIEL, BARBARA. *The Frightening Tyranny of Language*   14

AMIEL, BARBARA. *Ontario and Gays: A New Frontier?*   17

ATWOOD, MARGARET. *Canadians: What Do They Want?*   20

BAKER, RUSSELL. *Any Humans There?*   24

BAKER, RUSSELL. *Beastly Manhattan*   27

BOK, SISSELA. *To Lie, or Not to Lie? — I:*
The Doctors' Dilemma   30

BOK, SISSELA. *To Lie, or Not to Lie?— II:*
Here a Pseudo —, There a Pseudo —   33

BOK, SISSELA. *To Lie, or Not to Lie?— III:*
Bricks and Mortar and Deceit   36

BRENNAN, ANNE. *The Creationism Controversy:*
The Religious Issues   39

BRUCE, HARRY. *Suit, Ties Give Way to Polo Shirts, Loafers*   45

DAVIES, ROBERTSON. *A Few Kind Words for Superstition*   48

EPHRON, NORA. *The Hurled Ashtray*   51

EPHRON, NORA. *Revision and Life*   55

FRYE, NORTHROP. *The Motive for Metaphor*   59

FULFORD, ROBERT. *By the Book*   68

GILBERT, BIL. *Fast As an Elephant, Strong As an Ant*   73

GOYETTE, LINDA. *Loosening the Ties That Bind*   78

IYER, PICO. *In Praise of the Humble Comma*   81

JILES, PAULETTE. *Born Free? The Poetry Beast in the Classroom*   84

JONAS, GEORGE. *Legally Bombed*   99

KING, MARTIN LUTHER, JR. *Where Do We Go from Here?*   110

KOCH, EDWARD I. *Death and Justice: How Capital Punishment Affirms Life*   115

LEITCH, CAROLYN. *Big Blue Goes Plaid*   121

LUNDBERG, NORMA. *Making Sense of War: Demythologizing the Male Warrior*   124

McCALL, CHRISTINA. *How the Sour Sounds of Bitchery Undermine the Sisterly Cause*   135

McCLUNG, NELLIE L. *The War That Ends in Exhaustion Sometimes Mistaken for Peace*   138

McCULLOUGH, E. J. *On Euthanasia and Dying Well*   144

MacLENNAN, HUGH. *French Is a Must for Canadians*   150

MERCREDI, OVIDE. *Indian Self-Government and Sovereignty in Canada*   155

MITFORD, JESSICA. *The Story of Service*   161

MORRIS, RUTH. *The Noose, the Chair and the Needle*   172

MOWAT, FARLEY. *Swiftwings*   178

NELSON, JOYCE. *The Temple of Fashion*   189

NEWMAN, PETER C. *To Kill a People — Dash Their Dream*   194

NOWELL-SMITH, PATRICK. *Do We Have the Right to Die?*   197

ORWELL, GEORGE. *A Hanging*   204

PAGLIA, CAMILLE. *Rock As Art*   209

PARKER, JO GOODWIN. *What Is Poverty?*   212

RANDO, THERESE A. *American Socio-Cultural Attitudes Towards Death*   217

RICHLER, MORDECAI. *In the Eye of the Storm*   223

SAGAN, CARL. *One Voice in the Cosmic Fugue* 228

SMYTH, DONNA E. *On Not Seeing: Vincent van Gogh
and the Birth of Cloisonism* 236

SUZUKI, DAVID. *The Pain of Animals* 240

THOMAS, LEWIS. *Late Night Thoughts on Listening
to Mahler's Ninth Symphony* 245

THOMAS, LEWIS. *Nurses* 248

WIESEL, ELIE. *The Shame of Hunger* 253

WOODCOCK, GEORGE. *The Tyranny of the Clock* 258

Appendix 1: Guiding Questions 263

Appendix 2: Biographical Notes 269

Alternative List of Readings: Types of Writing

ANALYSIS

AMIEL, BARBARA. *The Frightening Tyranny of Language*   14

AMIEL, BARBARA. *Ontario and Gays: A New Frontier?*   17

ATWOOD, MARGARET. *Canadians: What Do They Want?*   20

BOK, SISSELA. *To Lie, or Not To Lie?— II: Here a Psuedo —, There a Pseudo —*   33

BRENNAN, ANNE. *The Creationism Controversy: The Religious Issues*   39

EPHRON, NORA. *The Hurled Ashtray*   51

FRYE, NORTHROP. *The Motive for Metaphor*   59

FULFORD, ROBERT. *By the Book*   68

JILES, PAULETTE. *Born Free? The Poetry Beast in the Classroom*   84

JONAS, GEORGE. *Legally Bombed*   99

KING, MARTIN LUTHER, JR. *Where Do We Go from Here?*   110

KOCH, EDWARD I. *Death and Justice: How Capital Punishment Affirms Life*   115

LUNDBERG, NORMA. *Making Sense of War: Demythologizing the Male Warrior*   124

McCULLOUGH, E. J. *On Euthanasia and Dying Well*   144

MERCREDI, OVIDE. *Indian Self-Government and Sovereignty in Canada*   155

MITFORD, JESSICA. *The Story of Service*   161

MORRIS, RUTH. *The Noose, the Chair and the Needle*   172

NEWMAN, PETER C. *To Kill A People — Dash Their Dream*   194

NOWELL-SMITH, PATRICK. *Do We Have the Right to Die?* — 197

SMYTH, DONNA E. *On Not Seeing: Vincent van Gogh and the Birth of Cloisonism* — 236

CAUSE AND EFFECT

BOK, SISSELA. *To Lie, or Not to Lie? — III: Bricks and Mortar and Deceit* — 36

BRUCE, HARRY. *Suit, Ties Give Way to Polo Shirts, Loafers* — 45

JONAS, GEORGE. *Legally Bombed* — 99

KING, MARTIN LUTHER, JR. *Where Do We Go from Here?* — 110

McCLUNG, NELLIE L. *The War That Ends in Exhaustion Sometimes Mistaken for Peace* — 138

McCULLOUGH, E. J. *On Euthanasia and Dying Well* — 144

MOWAT, FARLEY. *Swiftwings* — 178

PAGLIA, CAMILLE. *Rock As Art* — 209

PARKER, JO GOODWIN. *What Is Poverty?* — 212

RANDO, THERESE A. *American Socio-Cultural Attitudes Towards Death* — 217

SAGAN, CARL. *One Voice in the Cosmic Fugue* — 228

WOODCOCK, GEORGE. *The Tyranny of the Clock* — 258

CLASSIFICATION

DAVIES, ROBERTSON. *A Few Kind Words for Superstition* — 48

FRYE, NORTHROP. *The Motive for Metaphor* — 59

KING, MARTIN LUTHER, JR. *Where Do We Go from Here?* — 110

MORRIS, RUTH. *The Noose, the Chair and the Needle* — 172

RANDO, THERESE A. *American Socio-Cultural Attitudes Towards Death* — 217

COMPARISON, ANALOGY

AMIEL, BARBARA. *Another Threat to Freedom in Ontario*   11

BAKER, RUSSELL. *Any Humans There?*   24

BRENNAN, ANNE. *The Creationism Controversy:*
The Religious Issues   39

FRYE, NORTHROP. *The Motive for Metaphor*   59

JILES, PAULETTE. *Born Free? The Poetry Beast in the*
Classroom   84

JONAS, GEORGE. *Legally Bombed*   99

MacLENNAN, HUGH. *French Is a* Must *for Canadians*   150

NELSON, JOYCE. *The Temple of Fashion*   189

RANDO, THERESE A. *American Socio-Cultural Attitudes*
Towards Death   217

THOMAS, LEWIS. *Nurses*   248

DEFINITION

BRENNAN, ANNE. *The Creationism Controversy:*
The Religious Issues   39

DAVIES, ROBERTSON. *A Few Kind Words for Superstition*   48

KING, MARTIN LUTHER, JR. *Where Do We Go from Here?*   110

McCULLOUGH, E. J. *On Euthanasia and Dying Well*   144

MERCREDI, OVIDE. *Indian Self-Government and*
Sovereignty in Canada   155

MOWAT, FARLEY. *Swiftwings*   178

NOWELL-SMITH, PATRICK. *Do We Have the Right*
to Die?   197

PARKER, JO GOODWIN. *What Is Poverty?*   212

RANDO, THERESE A. *American Socio-Cultural Attitudes*
Towards Death   217

WIESEL, ELIE. *The Shame of Hunger*   253

DESCRIPTION

BAKER, RUSSELL. *Beastly Manhattan*   27

JILES, PAULETTE. *Born Free? The Poetry Beast in the Classroom*   84

MITFORD, JESSICA. *The Story of Service*   161

MOWAT, FARLEY. *Swiftwings*   178

NELSON, JOYCE. *The Temple of Fashion*   189

ORWELL, GEORGE. *A Hanging*   204

PARKER, JO GOODWIN. *What Is Poverty?*   212

SMYTH, DONNA E. *On Not Seeing: Vincent van Gogh and the Birth of Cloisonism*   236

SUZUKI, DAVID. *The Pain of Animals*   240

THOMAS, LEWIS. *Late Night Thoughts on Listening to Mahler's Ninth Symphony*   245

THOMAS, LEWIS. *Nurses*   248

WIESEL, ELIE. *The Shame of Hunger*   253

WOODCOCK, GEORGE. *The Tyranny of the Clock*   258

DIRECT ARGUMENT

AMIEL, BARBARA. *Another Threat to Freedom in Ontario*   11

AMIEL, BARBARA. *The Frightening Tyranny of Language*   14

AMIEL, BARBARA. *Ontario and Gays: A New Frontier?*   17

BOK, SISSELA. *To Lie, or Not to Lie? — I: The Doctors' Dilemma*   30

BOK, SISSELA. *To Lie, or Not to Lie? — II: Here a Pseudo —, There a Pseudo —*   33

BOK, SISSELA. *To Lie, or Not to Lie? — III: Bricks and Mortar and Deceit*   36

BRENNAN, ANNE. *The Creationism Controversy: The Religious Issues*   39

FULFORD, ROBERT. *By the Book*   68

GOYETTE, LINDA. *Loosening the Ties That Bind*   78

JONAS, GEORGE. *Legally Bombed* 99

KING, MARTIN LUTHER, JR. *Where Do We Go from Here?* 110

KOCH, EDWARD I. *Death and Justice: How Capital Punishment Affirms Life* 115

LUNDBERG, NORMA. *Making Sense of War: Demythologizing the Male Warrior* 124

McCLUNG, NELLIE L. *The War That Ends in Exhaustion Sometimes Mistaken for Peace* 138

McCULLOUGH, E. J. *On Euthanasia and Dying Well* 144

MacLENNAN, HUGH. *French Is a Must for Canadians* 150

MERCREDI, OVIDE. *Indian Self-Government and Sovereignty in Canada* 155

MORRIS, RUTH. *The Noose, the Chair and the Needle* 172

NEWMAN, PETER C. *To Kill a People — Dash Their Dream* 194

PAGLIA, CAMILLE. *Rock As Art* 209

RICHLER, MORDECAI. *In the Eye of the Storm* 223

EXAMPLE/ILLUSTRATION, ALLUSION

AMIEL, BARBARA. *Another Threat to Freedom in Ontario* 11

AMIEL, BARBARA. *The Frightening Tyranny of Language* 14

ATWOOD, MARGARET. *Canadians: What Do They Want?* 20

BAKER, RUSSELL. *Any Humans There?* 24

BOK, SISSELA. *To Lie, or Not to Lie?— I: The Doctors' Dilemma* 30

BOK, SISSELA. *To Lie, or Not to Lie? — II: Here a Pseudo —, There a Pseudo —* 33

BRUCE, HARRY. *Suit, Ties Give Way to Polo Shirts, Loafers* 45

DAVIES, ROBERTSON. *A Few Kind Words for Superstition* 48

EPHRON, NORA. *Revision and Life* 55

FRYE, NORTHROP. *The Motive for Metaphor* 59

FULFORD, ROBERT. *By the Book* 68

GILBERT, BIL. *Fast As an Elephant, Strong As an Ant* 73

IYER, PICO. *In Praise of the Humble Comma*   81

JILES, PAULETTE. *Born Free? The Poetry Beast in*
   the Classroom   84

KING, MARTIN LUTHER, JR. *Where Do We Go from Here?*   110

KOCH, EDWARD I. *Death and Justice: How Capital*
   Punishment Affirms Life   115

LEITCH, CAROLYN. *Big Blue Goes Plaid*   121

McCALL, CHRISTINA. *How the Sour Sounds of Bitchery*
   Undermine the Sisterly Cause   135

McCLUNG, NELLIE L. *The War That Ends in Exhaustion*
   Sometimes Mistaken for Peace   138

MITFORD, JESSICA. *The Story of Service*   161

MOWAT, FARLEY. *Swiftwings*   178

NELSON, JOYCE. *The Temple of Fashion*   189

PARKER, JO GOODWIN. *What Is Poverty?*   212

SAGAN, CARL. *One Voice in the Cosmic Fugue*   228

SUZUKI, DAVID. *The Pain of Animals*   240

THOMAS, LEWIS. *Nurses*   248

HUMOUR

BAKER, RUSSELL. *Any Humans There?*   24

BAKER, RUSSELL. *Beastly Manhattan*   27

BRUCE, HARRY. *Suit, Ties Give Way to Polo Shirts, Loafers*   45

DAVIES, ROBERTSON. *A Few Kind Words for Superstition*   48

EPHRON, NORA. *The Hurled Ashtray*   51

GILBERT, BIL. *Fast As an Elephant, Strong As an Ant*   73

GOYETTE, LINDA. *Loosening the Ties That Bind*   78

IYER, PICO. *In Praise of the Humble Comma*   81

JILES, PAULETTE. *Born Free? The Poetry Beast in*
   the Classroom   84

MITFORD, JESSICA. *The Story of Service*   161

NARRATION

BAKER, RUSSELL. *Any Humans There?*   24

BAKER, RUSSELL. *Beastly Manhattan*   27

EPHRON, NORA. *The Hurled Ashtray*   51

JILES, PAULETTE. *Born Free? The Poetry Beast in the Classroom*   84

McCALL, CHRISTINA. *How the Sour Sounds of Bitchery Undermine the Sisterly Cause*   135

MITFORD, JESSICA. *The Story of Service*   161

MOWAT, FARLEY. *Swiftwings*   178

ORWELL, GEORGE. *A Hanging*   204

SAGAN, CARL. *One Voice in the Cosmic Fugue*   228

PERSONAL EXPERIENCE

ATWOOD, MARGARET. *Canadians: What Do They Want?*   20

EPHRON, NORA. *The Hurled Ashtray*   51

EPHRON, NORA. *Revision and Life*   55

JILES, PAULETTE. *Born Free? The Poetry Beast in the Classroom*   84

McCALL, CHRISTINA. *How the Sour Sounds of Bitchery Undermine the Sisterly Cause*   135

McCULLOUGH, E. J. *On Euthanasia and Dying Well*   144

MacLENNAN, HUGH. *French Is a Must for Canadians*   150

ORWELL, GEORGE. *A Hanging*   204

PARKER, JO GOODWIN. *What Is Poverty?*   212

RICHLER, MORDECAI. *In the Eye of the Storm*   223

SAGAN, CARL. *One Voice in the Cosmic Fugue*   228

SMYTH, DONNA E. *On Not Seeing: Vincent van Gogh and the Birth of Cloisonism*   236

SUZUKI, DAVID. *The Pain of Animals*   240

THOMAS, LEWIS. *Late Night Thoughts on Listening to Mahler's Ninth Symphony*   245

THOMAS, LEWIS. *Nurses* 248

WIESEL, ELIE. *The Shame of Hunger* 253

Preface

The word "influential," as we use it in this anthology, identifies an emphasis rather than a category of writing. Writing in all the standard forms — narration, description, exposition in its various patterns, and argumentation (sometimes differentiated from persuasion) — can be influential, and influential power is treated here less as a defining characteristic than as an important measure of success. Thus, while all the pieces included in *Influential Writing* promote action or challenge opinions, they represent a broader range of writing than would normally be classed as persuasive.

In preparing *Influential Writing*, we concentrated on offering a new, more flexible, approach in an anthology of model writing, one that could readily be adapted for use in traditionally organized composition courses. We wanted to avoid the simplistic implication, inherent in texts that group selections according to the standard classifications, that most writing belongs exclusively to a single mode. On the other hand, we did not want to sacrifice the advantages of studying writing in terms of modes. In the end, we chose to arrange the essays simply, in alphabetical order by the authors' names, and, rather than using modes as an organizing principle, we have identified in an alternative listing of the essays the various types of writing that the selections can be used to represent. While our focus on influence naturally diminishes to some extent the significance of traditional classifications, we view this approach as a supplement to, rather than as a replacement for, more commonly studied structural and stylistic matters. In recognition of the many approaches to teaching writing, we have designed *Influential Writing* to be adaptable; thus instructors may choose to organize their courses according to authors, to themes, or, using the alternative list of essays, to forms of writing. The focus in *Influential Writing* should affect the organization of writing courses only to the extent that teachers want it to.

In addition to avoiding oversimplified classification, focusing on influence provides secondary advantages, not the least of which is motivation. Most students will use this text in college or university, where one of their primary goals will be preparing themselves to function effectively in society, particularly at work. Early along, however, when most students encounter writing courses, usually required, few have any idea of how enormously valuable an asset writing well can be. In consequence, they approach writing courses as less important than others competing for their time and fail to commit themselves until their opportunity to study writing formally has passed. An awareness of writing's influential power will increase commitment and, in doing so, make both teaching and learning easier.

Focusing on influence also helps students grasp the practical point of the technical skills they practice in writing courses. Most writing texts routinely advocate an awareness of audience, but link the discussion of audience more to appropriateness of tone, style, and level of diction than to the question of whether an intended audience will be receptive to the ideas presented. It is all too easy to ignore the fact that, outside of classrooms, an audience, even a receptive one, can rarely be taken for granted. Concentrating on influence entails relating basic stylistic concerns to structure, content, and emphasis, as well as to the fundamental question on which all the others depend: whether or not the intended audience will read the piece.

Each of the selections in this text is followed by a number of questions and topics for discussion, few of which suggest a single neat answer. Our aim is to encourage precise, thoughtful reading while focusing attention particularly on the power of the selections to influence readers. Our suggestions will provide starting points for exploration, but they are, of course, less important than the questions and insights that develop from the students' own explorations of texts, and answering the questions provided should not be viewed as an end in itself. The headings "Topics for Discussion" and "Topics for Writing" should be taken as suggestions only; some topics that we consider appropriate for writing will also serve to generate class discussion, while topics for discussion may well be adapted for writing.

An instructor's manual to accompany this text will be provided on request.

Acknowledgements

We wish to acknowledge, with gratitude, the comments — witty, wry, at times almost acerbic, but always detailed and thoughtful — of those who read this text while it was still in manuscript form; Adele Ashby, Centennial College; Stephen Campbell, University of New Brunswick; Greg Chan, University of British Columbia; Gary Corscadden, New Brunswick Community College; Christine Grotefeld, Mount Royal College; Jim Howard, Selkirk College; Ingrid Hutchinson, Fanshawe College; Diana Patterson, Mount Royal College; Joan Pilz, Humber College; Andrea Westcott, Capilano College; Sharon Winstanley, Seneca College.

We also owe thanks to Andrea Gallagher Ellis, Margaret Henderson, Laurie Graham, and Dave Ward, of McGraw-Hill Ryerson, whose hard work and sound advice helped us over many of the obstacles to publication.

For permission to use copyrighted material grateful acknowledgement is made to the following authors and publishers:

Barbara Amiel: "Another Threat to Freedom in Ontario," *Maclean's* magazine, July 20, 1992. Reprinted by permission of Maclean Hunter Ltd.

Barbara Amiel: "The Frightening Tyranny of Language," from *Maclean's* magazine, December 31, 1990. Reprinted by permission of Maclean Hunter Ltd.

Barbara Amiel: "Ontario and Gays: A New Frontier?" from *Maclean's* magazine, June 6, 1994. Reprinted by permission of Maclean Hunter Ltd.

Margaret Atwood: "Canadians: What Do They Want?" from *Mother Jones* magazine, January 1982. Reprinted by permission of *Mother Jones* magazine, copyright © 1982, Foundation for National Progress.

Russell Baker: "Any Humans There?" from *The Rescue of Miss Yaskell*. Copyright © 1983, by Russell Baker. Reprinted by permission of Don Congdon Associates, Inc.

Russell Baker: "Beastly Manhattan," from *The Rescue of Miss Yaskell*. Copyright © 1983, by Russell Baker. Reprinted by permission of Don Congdon Associates, Inc.

Sissela Bok: "To Lie, Or Not To Lie? — I: The Doctors' Dilemma," from *The New York Times*, April 18, 1978. Copyright © 1978. Reprinted by permission of The New York Times Company.

Sissela Bok: "To Lie, Or Not To Lie? — II: Here a Pseudo —, There a Pseudo —," from *The New York Times*, April 19, 1978. Copyright © 1978. Reprinted by permission of The New York Times Company.

Sissela Bok: "To Lie, Or Not To Lie? — III: Bricks and Mortar and Deceit," from *The New York Times*, April 20, 1978. Copyright © 1978. Reprinted by permission of The New York Times Company.

E. J. McCullough: "On Euthanasia and Dying Well," from *The Canadian Catholic Review*, October, 1991. Reprinted by permission of the author.

Hugh MacLennan: "French is a *Must* for Canadians," from *The Other Side of Hugh MacLennan: Selected Essays Old and New*, ed. Elspeth Cameron. Copyright © 1978, Macmillan Canada. Reprinted by permission of Macmillan Canada.

Ovide Mercredi: "Indian Self-Government and Sovereignty in Canada,"from *Humanist in Canada* magazine, vol. 23, no. 3, Autumn, 1990. Reprinted by permission of the author, The Assembly of First Nations, and *Humanist in Canada* magazine.

Jessica Mitford: "The Story of Service," from *The American Way of Death*, by Jessica Mitford, London: Hutchinson, 1963. Copyright © 1963, 1978 by Jessica Mitford, all rights reserved. Reprinted by permission of the author.

Ruth Morris: "The Noose, the Chair and the Needle," from *Canadian Dimension* magazine, vol. 20, no. 3, May, 1986. Reprinted by permission of the author.

Farley Mowat: "Swiftwings," from *Sea of Slaughter*, pp. 41–52, by Farley Mowat, McClelland & Stewart, 1982. Reprinted by permission of McClelland & Stewart, Toronto.

Joyce Nelson: "The Temple of Fashion," from *Sign Crimes/Road Kill*, pp. 165–169, Between The Lines, 1992. Copyright © Joyce Nelson. Reprinted by permission of Between The Lines.

Peter C. Newman "To Kill a People — Dash Their Dream," from *Maclean's* magazine, April 25, 1994. Reprinted by permission of Maclean Hunter Ltd.

Patrick Nowell-Smith: "Do We Have the Right to Die?" from *Canadian Forum*, December/January, 1981. Reprinted by permission of the author.

George Orwell: "A Hanging," from *The Collected Essays, Journalism and Letters of George Orwell. Volume 1: An Age Like This. 1920–1940*, eds. Sonia Orwell and Ian Angus. London: Secker & Warburg, 1968. Reprinted by permission of the estate of the late Sonia Brownell Orwell, and Martin Secker & Warburg.

Camille Paglia: "Rock As Art," from *Sex, Art and American Culture*, by Camille Paglia. Copyright © 1992 by Camille Paglia. Reprinted by permission of Vintage Books, a Division of Random House Inc.

Jo Goodwin Parker: "What Is Poverty?" from *America's Other Children: Public Schools Outside Suburbia*, ed. George Henderson. Copyright © 1971, University of Oklahoma Press. Reprinted by permission of University of Oklahoma Press.

Therese A. Rando: "American Socio-Cultural Attitudes Towards Death,"from *Grief, Dying and Death: Clinical Interventions for Caregivers*, by Therese A. Rando. Research Press, Champaign, Illinois, 1984. Copyright © 1984, by Therese A. Rando. Reprinted by permission of Research Press.

Mordecai Richler: "In the Eye of the Storm," from *Maclean's* magazine, April 13, 1992. Reprinted by permission of Maclean Hunter Ltd.

Carl Sagan: "One Voice in the Cosmic Fugue," excerpted from *Cosmos*, by Carl Sagan. Copyright © 1980 by Carl Sagan. Reproduced by permission of the author.

Donna E. Smyth: "On Not Seeing: Vincent van Gogh and the Birth of Cloisonism," from *This Magazine*, vol. 15, no. 2, May-June, 1981. Reprinted by permission of the author.

David Suzuki: "The Pain of Animals," from *Inventing the Future: Reflections on Science, Technology and Nature*, by David Suzuki. Stoddart Publishing Company, 1989. Reprinted by permission of the author.

Introduction

The writings collected in this text represent a wide range of forms, attitudes, and stylistic approaches, but they are all, in varying degrees, influential. Why influential? Because influence is an important, although often neglected, aspect of writing, one that it is especially useful for students to understand. You live in a democratic society, a society in which citizens are convinced rather than coerced to consent. Your ability to function effectively in such a society will depend to a large extent both on your ability to exert influence through language and on your related capacity to recognize and resist manipulation.

In studying these writings, you will see that different kinds of writing influence in different ways, and that writing that openly solicits a change of opinion is sometimes less effective than less direct persuasion. What follows is a general discussion of the main influential advantages and disadvantages of the four primary modes of writing — argument, exposition, narration, and description. It will suggest approaches to the individual selections, and to some extent prepare you to deal with the questions that accompany these pieces, but it should be viewed only as a simple overview of a subtle subject. Your real understanding of influence in writing will come from carefully analyzing individual examples and practicing the techniques of influence so learned in your own writing.

ARGUMENT VERSUS INFLUENCE

Of the traditional modes of writing, argument is the one most obviously related to influence, yet the relationship between argument and influence and indeed the nature of argument itself are often misunderstood. When inexperienced writers set out to influence readers through argument, the result all too often barely reflects the intention. They commonly make the mistake of confusing formal argument, which, strictly speaking, refers to an effort to arrive at the truth about a subject through the use of formal logic, with the popular idea of an argument as a heated verbal disagreement. In consequence, their argumentative writing becomes tru-

1

culent writing, more likely to offend than to convince those who do not share the writer's views. Remember that adopting an aggressive, all-or-nothing stance on a controversial topic will usually do your cause more harm than good in that it will harden the resistance of those readers who disagree and prod them to form counter-arguments in defence of the position you are attacking. An aggressive, one-sided argument will rarely hold readers who do not already strongly agree with it, and you obviously cannot influence an audience that refuses to read what you have written.

Remember also that in seeking to influence readers you are asking them, first, to do a good deal of hard thinking in order to reconcile the intended change of opinion with their established beliefs and, second, to face the threat to personal pride involved in admitting that they were mistaken. You are asking them to trust your sincerity and good intentions and to approach what you have to say with an open mind. Will treating views opposed to yours with anger and contempt accomplish this? The answer is obvious here but often forgotten in the heat of argument.

The importance of tact and restraint in influential writing cannot be over-stressed. The more controversial the issue you are addressing, the more tactful you have to be, and the more vital it is to ask yourself what your intended audience will stand for being told. Consider carefully: what is your target audience's attitude toward the subject? Why will this audience read what you have written: out of curiosity? for entertainment? because of its special interest in the subject? Will your approach make a desired audience read defensively — or, worse still, stop reading altogether? Will the position you are defending be perceived as threatening? Will it seem offensive in any way? There are many obstacles to effective persuasion, and the essential challenge you face as an influential writer is to keep your intended audience reading, as sympathetically and receptively as possible.

One of the surest ways to gain the confidence and interest of the unconvinced is to demonstrate a thorough understanding of alternative outlooks. Nothing will encourage a defensive audience to take your views on a subject seriously as much as demonstrating that you have genuinely tried to understand alternative views. This is not easily faked; it usually requires a thorough, honest reconsideration of your thinking and motives, which may be an unsettling experience to the extent that it puts your own position at risk of change. But do you have a right to ask others to think about changing their opinions if you are unwilling to consider changing your own?

Patience is vital to influential writing because individual opinions usually change gradually in association with collective changes in the attitudes of groups with which individuals identify. Experienced writers know that a single piece of influential writing, however brilliantly marshalled its arguments may be, will seldom bring about anything approaching a complete reversal of opinion. Lasting, significant changes of opinion take time; therefore, those genuinely concerned with exerting influence, rather than with scoring points against the opposition, proceed tactfully, resisting the temptation to try to gain too much too fast. By not attempting immediate change, they often accomplish much more in the long run. So be patient. Be polite. Be determined. In order to bring about substantial changes in opinions, you have to believe strongly enough in the worthiness of your position to defend it over time.

One further caution is necessary about the use of formal argument in influential writing. The most serious problems stem from misunderstanding the nature of argument, and a sound understanding of logical argument can be extremely valuable in developing your own ideas and analyzing counter-arguments. However, the traditional importance assigned to logic in many writing textbooks may lead you to forget that modern readers in general cannot be depended upon to abide by logical rules. In order to appreciate a formal logical argument they need to have studied logic, and they must also agree that logic is a legitimate means of arriving at truth. Today, the average person you will want to influence will not be schooled in formal logic and may very well lose patience with an argument based entirely or even mainly on logic. Formal logic works according to a set of rules — like mathematics or chess. The rules of logic, and the ways of breaking them, are too complex to be dealt with here; detailed treatments are to be found in many rhetorics and writing handbooks. It is enough to say here that logical argument emphasizes appeals to reason and downplays appeals to emotion. In formal logic, an appeal to pity or an attack on the character of one's opponents is considered a fallacy — a sort of unsportsmanlike departure from the rules of the game. You do not have to be a social scientist, however, to know how widespread and forceful these and other appeals to emotion are in shaping public opinion. Few in the twentieth century think like *Star Trek*'s Mr. Spock.

This is not to say that logic cannot be extremely useful in presenting an argument; it does mean that you cannot rely entirely on logic in making a case. For example, Edward Koch's essay, "Death and Justice: How Capital Punishment Affirms Life," relies heavily on logic in disposing of arguments against the death penalty. But you will also find many instances of emotionally charged language in Koch's essay, and for all but a very select audience of logicians, his logic is more compelling because it is not purely detached from emotions. For many, in fact, the emotional appeal beneath the surface of Koch's reasoning would prove more forceful than the reasoning itself. The point is that for most modern readers an argument based entirely on reason will be even more limited in its appeal than one based entirely on emotion.

INFLUENTIAL EXPOSITION

Among the responsibilities of living in a free society, in which we have access to a tremendous variety of information and ideas, is the necessity of choosing what to accept as true and worthwhile. Growing up, we learn to resist propaganda and advertising and to test the advice, claims, and assumptions that are thrust upon us from all sides against our own experience. The sceptical habit of mind, which is one of the characteristics of our time, is necessary to each of us if we are not to be deluded by advertisers and propagandists. At the same time, however, this scepticism in others can be frustrating because it makes exerting influence so challenging. This is especially true in writing because reading is characteristically a private act, in which the reader engages without obligation either to the writer or to any rules of fair play governing how she deals with the writer's views. Readers pose questions and counter-arguments to defend their positions against change, but the writer who has not anticipated these has no opportunity to reply. Readers are free to misjudge motives, misinterpret information, or attack the writer's character — and the writer has no forum to correct wrong ideas or insist on fair play. At any time, readers can win the mental debate involved in reviewing a written argument simply by ceasing to read. Thus, in a forthright attempt to change beliefs, the writer is at a serious disadvantage.

One of the simplest ways around the natural defensiveness most readers feel about having their views changed is to exert influence through types of writing not commonly associated with persuasion. By definition, expository writing explains, clarifies, and illuminates, but exposition is not limited to these fundamental functions with which it has traditionally been identified. For a modern audience, inclined to defensive scepticism, exposition can often be more effective than direct argument.

Exposition is a broad category that includes a range of subsidiary forms, each with its own function and characteristic patterns of organization, and it can also include narration and description when they are employed primarily to explain. The daily newspaper, many magazines, statements of government policy, corporate reports, legal documents, the innumerable pieces of correspondence necessary to keep our vast economic and social system functioning, textbooks, the manuals that explain the computer this is being written on — all are primarily expository prose. You are reading expository prose now. Like most exposition, this introduction avoids clutter, whimsy, and rhetorical frills and concentrates on presenting information with as little appearance of bias as possible, but it is also intended to influence the way you understand writing. It is expository in that it attempts to share understanding — to convey truth understandably. But whose truth? Like most writing that explains a complex subject, this introduction is designed not only to inform but to shape understanding — to influence the way those who read it think about the subject it presents. Does this admission make you read more sceptically? If not, it should — not only this introduction but the rest of the expository writing you encounter as well. Whether or not an explanation includes an acknowledgment that it represents an opinion, the truth remains: in presenting information about a subject, expository writing shapes the way receptive readers think about that subject.

Writing that explains offers the reader a kind of trade, a sounder, more complete understanding of a subject in return for willingness to at least consider change. In a complex society such as ours, one that depends as much on exchanging vast amounts of information as it does on the exchange of tangible commodities, convenience in the transfer of information is essential, and convenience requires simplification. Writers know, and readers accept, consciously or subconsciously, that explanations must concentrate on one or a limited number of alternative approaches and can rarely even come close to presenting the complete truth of a subject. As readers, we have become used to the necessity for writers to make selections in the interests of simplification and accessibility, and, in the absence of obvious evidence of manipulation, we tend to accept the inevitability of such selectivity. In effect, we consent to be influenced in exchange for convenient understanding. The inevitability, the variety, and the pervasiveness of information exchange in our society, together with our widespread cultural habit of accepting simplified information willingly, give exposition a potential for exerting influence far exceeding that of direct argument. The lesson is clear: when your subject is important to an audience, that audience will approach any overt attempt to change its views with scepticism — and may refuse to read the piece at all; if, on the other hand, what you write about a subject offers an opportunity to obtain information, those who consider the subject important will usually read what you write receptively, with interest. Therefore, influencing opinion gradually through information is an ideal way of overcoming prejudice.

Not only does the information provided by exposition give readers an incentive to continue reading, it also assists them in changing their opinions in a way that an argument rarely can. Why is assistance needed? Because opinions do not exist in isolation: changes of opinion involving one subject require reconciliation with views about related topics. This is why targeting an audience and understanding as much as you can about it are so vital in influential writing. Integrating changes in belief takes time and hard mental effort, so as a writer you can promote specific changes by considering how they relate to the collective values and beliefs of your targeted audience and guiding the process of reconciliation. The more you think about it, the more you will see that the dual goals of promoting understanding and winning consent are not at odds: the thoughtful organization, precise wording, and freedom from clutter standard in sound expository prose naturally win the confidence of readers. Achieving a comfortable understanding of ideas and accepting them as true are often connected. Because the various forms of exposition reflect the ways people understand and organize information, they shape belief. So when you as a writer succeed in making sense of a subject through one or more of the expository forms, you will be well on your way to winning agreement from your readers.

Take analysis, for example, which is fundamental to most exposition. Although analysis is commonly associated with science, it is also fundamental in less formal understanding when it involves dividing information into parts and then grouping and ordering the results in ways that will aid understanding. In addition to making the subject more accessible, the arrangements that emerge from analysis both simplify and shape meaning. In analyzing a process by breaking it down into steps, for example, you necessarily simplify and to some extent personalize. Although a process of doing something, when explained well, may influence readers to accept that it is the best or most natural way of proceeding, it is still only one account of the subject. How many books have been written on how to hit a golf ball, for example? What seems to be a simple, almost continuous action can be analyzed again and again without exhausting the topic, provided the interest is there. How much more so is there room for influential differences of opinion in analyzing the causes and effects of social situations and political events. In writing texts, causal analysis is generally considered exposition, but it also very often provides the foundation on which persuasive essays are constructed.

Another common form of exposition that has enormous potential for influence is comparison, which consists essentially of identifying and organizing points of similarity and difference. If the subject is straightforward, perhaps focusing on clearly definable and quantifiable specifications, comparison can be mainly expository. However, even when scientific objectivity is observed in making a comparison, the result is still often very influential. Publications aimed at evaluating products for consumers, for example, usually represent a much more honest effort to inform than do comparisons devised by advertisers, but precisely for that reason, the objective evaluations have far more potential for influence.

The more personal the comparison — an essay is more personal than a table of technical points, for example — the more subjective the comparison is likely to be. Depending on individual intention and perception of a subject, one writer will include points another will omit. Writers will give different points of comparison different degrees of emphasis by covering them in greater or less detail. Such choices influence the way in which readers perceive what is being compared. Even the order in which points of comparison are presented will be influential in that the first and last points will usually be the most memorable. Thus, both in writing and in reading, you will be wise to keep in mind that, in comparison, influence is far more difficult to avoid than to achieve. Whether a comparison is designed simply to present information about similarities and differences or to imply superiority, it will inevitably represent only one of many possible approaches. One comparative analysis may be more useful than another, or more accurate in some respects, or more free from bias, but no comparison will be more than a respectable attempt to represent truth. But representations of truth, particularly those that appear to be unbiased and informed, can be influential indeed.

Classification and definition are often more subtle and pervasive in the ways they shape perception. Definition locates the term to be defined in a familiar class or group with which it shares common characteristics and then explains why or how the thing represented by the term is unique; classification groups things according to defining characteristics. These two forms of writing are interdependent and exert influence in similar ways — through association, and by emphasizing similarities and differences — to shape the manner in which readers perceive subjects. The influential effects of definition and classification are often harder to resist than those of comparative analysis because most people, in forming their opinions, rely heavily on commonly accepted terms and commonly assumed relationships, whose validity they take for granted. Those in the business of influencing large numbers of people know this well. Advertising — for everything from breakfast cereal to political parties — relies heavily on the influential effects of association, both positive and negative. A breakfast cereal may be characterized as "high-fibre" or more "natural" than its competitors. A political opponent may be depicted as a member of an elite, wealthy group, to which by implication she owes more loyalty than to the electorate as a whole. Lacking the time or training required to analyze the connotations of language contrived by experts in public relations and advertising, the average person is vulnerable to manipulation.

One particularly effective way of influencing readers who have given little thought to the implications of a term is to explore its meaning at length in an essay. Martin Luther King, Jr.'s, treatment of reactions to oppression in "Where Do We Go from Here?" for example, offers specialized definitions of the terms "acquiescence," "violence," and "nonviolent resistance" in forming a classification of reactions to oppression. With the implications of the alternatives examined, King's appeal that nonviolent resistance is the only right and practical response becomes compelling indeed. King uses specific examples and figurative language to make his explanation clear and forceful, but his essay is still fairly abstract. In "What Is Poverty?" Jo Goodwin Parker demonstrates the advantage of moving further away from abstraction to show readers the detailed reality behind a common general term. The influential force Parker achieves by making the concept of poverty real would be extremely difficult to duplicate in a logical argument, however brilliantly conceived.

The essential point to understand is that any form of expository writing (not just those discussed here) can also be influential. In fact, even with serious journalism, government reports, research papers, textbooks, and other kinds of writing in which fairness and objectivity are fundamental goals, influence is impossible to avoid and may actually be greater than the influence of overt attempts to persuade, which usually reach smaller, less receptive audiences. All forms of prose can influence.

INFLUENCE THROUGH CREATIVE WRITING: NARRATION, DESCRIPTION, AND HUMOUR

Just as writers of expository prose reach audiences that are more willing to have their views expanded than altered directly, so creative writers avoid the defensive reading they would face if the views behind what they depict were stated as arguments. The simple fact that readers are unlikely to associate creative forms with influence offers writers an important advantage in using these forms, rather than direct persuasion, for influence. But creative writing offers an added advantage over exposition or direct persuasion in that it not only avoids resistance but encourages the reader's active involvement. Our cultural addiction to being entertained, and the attendant mental habit of giving ourselves up noncritically to creative writing and forms of entertainment based on creative writing, give narration, description, and humour tremendous potential for influence.

Although narration and description are commonly used for expository purposes, and humour is certainly not at odds with the goals of informative writing, we usually think of these forms as more imaginative than expository, and we value them primarily as entertainment or for their aesthetic appeal. Used imaginatively, narration and description are the basic elements from which fiction is created, and prose fiction, in spite of increasing competition from movies and television, continues to be a major form of both art and entertainment, reaching and influencing many millions of people each year. Moreover, narration, description, and humour provide the foundation for the more technologically dependent media that influence virtually everyone in our society.

Few students using this textbook will write publishable fiction and fewer still will find themselves writing scripts for movies or the broadcast media, but they can handle creative forms of writing well enough to use them for effective influential writing. Creative forms are essential for presenting the illustrations and examples that make ideas more real, more accessible, and more moving, and they add an extra element of interest that catches and holds readers. George Orwell's evocative description in "A Hanging" is as influential in its own way as Edward Koch's much more carefully marshalled arguments in favour of capital punishment in "Death and Justice," in that Orwell forces readers to deal with the fact of execution at an emotional, experiential level rather than at the primarily rational level of Koch's essay. An emotional reaction to a situation will rarely accomplish lasting change by itself; however, if it is accompanied by a more rational consideration of the same subject, the vivid representation of ideas that touch readers at an emotional level can produce more profound and long-lasting commitment than can the most brilliant rational persuasion alone.

Influence though narration and description depends of course on a writer's ability to use these forms well, so that the sort of advice that will help you write successful narration or description — such as remembering the five senses in creating imagery, and concentrating on specific, physical details rather than abstract generalizations — will also serve indirectly to make writing influential. The influential advantage of creative writing is gained through careful craftsmanship. The advantage of showing readers what you want them to understand rather than explaining it to them in general terms requires creating, however briefly, an illusion of experience. Readers must use their imaginations, and if you are successful they will do so with little or no effort. Your success will depend in large part on attention to detail — care and craftsmanship.

Using humour as an influential strategy involves many of the same sorts of risks and tactical considerations as using description and narration, but the types of subjects for which humour is appropriate are more limited. For example, an average audience will likely consider a comical treatment of a serious issue, such as abortion or capital punishment, in bad taste. But for less important questions of morality or manners — Russell Baker's treatment of irresponsible pet ownership in "Beastly Manhattan," for example — from which readers can easily distance themselves, humour can be an extremely effective tool both for generating interest and for shaping attitudes. In revealing a sense of humour, writers also reveal their humanity, thereby diminishing the reader's defensiveness, striking a common bond, and providing an incentive — amusement — for continuing to read.

USING THIS BOOK

You will almost certainly be using this text in combination with more detailed instructional material provided either by other textbooks or your teacher; such material should be viewed as a supplement to the explanations and questions provided here. Even if your other textbooks pay little attention to influence, they will help you to understand the techniques necessary to catch and hold an audience and to appreciate other goals in writing. Keep in mind that although in this book we explore writing chiefly as a means of influencing people, the act of writing can also be approached as communication, as self-exploration, as a tool for learning and analyzing ideas, as a means of recording information and experience, or in a number of other ways. Each approach yields its special insights, and none should be emphasized to the exclusion of the others.

Much more can be learned from considering examples of writing in detail than from general explanations, but you should keep the general points above in mind as you work with the essays. You will find an appendix of questions following the essays which will guide you in approaching influence as a characteristic of any of the essays in this text, or, for that matter, of almost any essay you come across in your daily reading. In addition, the critical apparatus that follows each essay is designed to help you appreciate the influential force of various kinds of writing by relating the general ideas developed in this introduction to specific examples. Answering the questions and exploring the suggested topics should be just the beginning; you should approach these suggestions for learning as starting points. From them you will develop your personal awareness of how the individual pieces work; thus you will soon be able to apply what you learn in order to test the success or failure of anything you read — or write.

Another Threat to Freedom in Ontario

Barbara Amiel

I don't know whether George Orwell's *Animal Farm* is compulsory read- 1
ing in Ontario high schools. I rather suspect not. If it were, perhaps the
citizens of Ontario — black and white, male and female, handicapped
and able-bodied, old, middle-aged, clever, ordinary, wealthy, poor, of
Indian, European, Middle Eastern and Oriental extraction — might show a
bit of backbone in fighting the virus that has infected their province.

That virus has two nasty strands: divisive envy and pressure-group 2
politics. The latest outbreak comes with the Ontario government's proposed employment equity legislation, which requires any business with
over 50 employees to draw up a plan to make sure the correct number of
"aboriginal people, people with disabilities, members of racial minorities
and women in the community" are reflected in the workplace. As the
Toronto *Globe and Mail* pointed out in a recent editorial, the definitions
and fine-tuning opportunities here for our bureaucrats are marvellous:
how do dark-skinned Turks rate as a minority compared with dark-
skinned Israelis or Palestinians? Two points for being a Moslem and one
point for being a Jew, perhaps?

The bill would bring into being an employment equity commission 3
to monitor the plans and to take complaints from disgruntled people.
(Encouraging citizens to become resentful crybabies is a symptom of the
virus.) The stand all decent people ought to take is clear. Every Ontarian,
upon being asked to become collaborators in this, the extinction of equality in their province, should refuse to fill out the forms that the new act
will require. Since filling out the forms is voluntary, this one moment of
defiance will not even incur a penalty.

Let me return to *Animal Farm* for a moment. The book begins with 4
the dream of an old boar named Major, who sees a golden future in
which man the oppressor is thrown out, all animals unite and are equal.
His vision inspires the animals to drive the farmers and human beings
off their farm.

But power gradually becomes centralized in the hands of the pigs, 5
who become a bureaucracy cushioned with perks and distanced from
the ordinary lives of the other animals. At the conclusion of the book, the
pigs end up as the new oppressors in a puritanical, sexless society, killing dissidents and liberty in the name of social justice. As for all the
ethical precepts that were behind the revolution, the terrorized animals
are faced with only one single commandment: "All animals are equal.
But some animals are more equal than others."

The parallel with what is happening in Ontario cannot be lost on 6
anyone reading the employment equity bill. Equality is indivisible —
people cannot have a little equality, or even greater equality than other
people. You are either equal or unequal. And because human beings are

11

intrinsically unequal in terms of their gifts, aspirations, goals and values, all a decent society can do is make sure every human being has equality of opportunity.

7   If you are not blinded by racism, you will see immediately that one cannot expect the ethnic and racial composition of society to be mirrored in jobs and achievement. People are individuals first, not members of a group. They do well or badly according to their own personal qualities, not the pigment of their skin. The idiocy of the bill becomes clear if we look at school exams: everyone writes the same exam paper, but unless you put a fix in, people will end up with different exam results. There is no way to guarantee equality of result without being unfair to the person that got the best result fairly.

8   For me, arguing against employment equity is rather like arguing against anti-Semitism. To ask citizens to register their race, gender, ethnic origins and handicap so that promotions, layoffs, part-time work, contract work, terminations and hiring correctly reflect the number of status Indians, non-status Indians, Inuits, blacks, blind people and so on — not to mention all other categories — makes the Third Reich's Nuremberg laws look benign.

9   This proposed act is true racism. It proceeds from an entirely false premise and utter ignorance of the world of real work: namely, the notion that business would operate against its own interests and ignore a talented or able workforce because of prejudice. If some businesses are silly enough to ignore hiring good workers because they are black or female, they will pay the price and be outdone by the competition. No business wants to self-destruct.

10   The proposed legislation tries to cover its attack on individual liberty, and the right of employers to run their businesses as they see fit, with the excuse that it is only establishing voluntary "goals," not quotas. But attached to this is the stick of contract compliance. The tragedy of all this is evident. Businesses in Ontario are already suffering under the combined horror of the NDP's labor and taxation policies as well as the recession. If we now create an entirely new layer of bureaucracy and force business to enact this more recent bit of political correctness, we will further cripple (oops, handicap) those companies trying to survive in Ontario and discourage new business from coming.

11   But the real fallacy behind the NDP world-view is the following: people are not simply aboriginals or women, blacks or wheelchair occupants. They live many lives in one. They are wives, husbands and daughters as well as ethnic-group members. The black woman whose white husband is turned down for a promotion loses; the wife whose husband's business is ruined by this expensive program loses; the wheelchair occupant who replaces a female receptionist with three children creates another injustice and set of victims. These terrible NDP commissars seem not to care a damn about replacing one wrong with another. They have their dream, their vision of social justice in which, yup, some people are more equal than others.

It will all come to tears, group against group, resentment and institu- 12 tionalized inequality. And as for Bob Rae's government, well, Orwell's last lines in *Animal Farm* deal with that. The browbeaten barnyard inhabitants look at their leaders, the pigs, "from pig to man, and from man to pig, and from pig to man again; but already it was impossible to say which was which."

TYPES OF WRITING: allusion, analogy, direct argument

Topics for Discussion

1. Amiel begins this essay with a challenge that is almost insulting: "perhaps the citizens of Ontario . . . might show a bit of backbone." What are the advantages, and disadvantages, of such an introduction?
2. What do you think Amiel is trying to achieve with the long series in the first paragraph?
3. In paragraph 2 Amiel points out that the virus she is describing has "two nasty strands: divisive envy and pressure-group politics." Does Amiel deal adequately with each of these two "strands"?
4. Comment on paragraph 9 with regard to its accuracy in representing the way businesses operate and its effectiveness as persuasive technique.
5. Explain how the parenthetical expression in paragraph 10 might influence some readers.
6. Does Amiel's attitude toward her readers seem to change in the course of her essay? If so, how? And how might any change affect the influential force of her essay?

Topic for Writing

1. Write an essay that either supports or opposes legislation to promote employment equity. Focus your argument by referring to an area of employment with which you are familiar.

The Frightening Tyranny of Language

Barbara Amiel

1   On Monday, Dec. 10, the *Globe and Mail* published a new stylebook, its first since 1976. Normally, stylebooks are used to check idiosyncrasies. Are reporters permitted, for example, to use an ampersand ("&") in their copy? However, the front-page story that trumpeted the new edition of the *Globe*'s stylebook explained that changes to actual rules and spelling were relatively small. What then, I wondered, was the need for a new book.

2   The *Globe* was pleased to inform me. The changes "are the book's detailed policies on women and language, reflecting the *Globe*'s desire to avoid sexist language; on obscene language; on foreign and French words; on the handling of quotations; and on expressions dealing with disabled people." The *Globe* invited "interested members of the public" to purchase a copy of the book. I couldn't wait.

3   In the book, the *Globe* assures readers that it has taken special care *"not to sacrifice clarity and precision on the altar of trendiness."* Alas, if this was the pitfall the stylebook editors wished to avoid, I regret to inform them that they have failed — miserably.

4   Skipping through the book, my eyes came to rest on the entry for the phrase "Iron Curtain, the." Here is what the *Globe* had to say: "Use only in direct quotes. Whether the term described reality or actually helped to shape it is open to argument, but the new levels of travel and commerce among European countries certainly make it inaccurate today."

5   The newsroom of the *Globe and Mail*, it seems, regards the 1945 speech of Winston Churchill, in which the phrase "Iron Curtain" was first used, as simply a policy tip to the Soviets. Perhaps, the *Globe* editors visualized Stalin listening to Churchill and leaping from his bath exclaiming "Eureka," or the Russian equivalent, as he went about making reality conform to Churchill's metaphor.

6   What this reveals is that the *Globe* has a mind-set that in 1990 doubts matters which the present Central Committee of the Soviet Communist party has not doubted for several years — namely, that they have lived under a tyranny for the past 70 years. I don't think one needs to analyse this further, but it ought to be noted, particularly by any schools planning to use the thoughts of Chairman *Globe and Mail* as "resource" material.

7   This mind-set is important, however, because it tells us a great deal about the rest of the book. The problem is not a matter of whether the editors are too left-wing or too right-wing. The error is far more basic. What is revealed is that regardless of how you feel about such matters as "women's issues" or "race" or any contentious issue, the *Globe*'s editors are in thrall to one serious misunderstanding.

8   Essentially, they follow a very primitive type of belief that judgment follows words. They think that the renaming of something they judge

14

bad or undesirable will cause people to change their judgment of it. By using euphemisms for disapproved ideas, the *Globe* believes that you can make the bad idea disappear.

A perfect example of this is the use of the word "crippled." This word, as the *Globe* explains, is now in disfavor. Since the days of "crippled," we have substituted "handicapped," which the *Globe* tells us is now also a no-no. The preferred word is "disabled." Crippled, handicapped, disabled: it will all give off the same negativism since human beings have a natural fear and aversion to the state of being less than whole in body.   9

I could have chosen dozens of other entries to make the point. The section on "Women" would be hilarious were it not so lunatic. *Globe* writers must avoid words like "manpower," "the common man" and "man in the street." They are reminded that this does not have to be carried to "extremes," so diligent *Globe* writers need not worry about using "boycott" and "manufactured." The editors are worried about terms like "manmade" and draw the line at fireman or postman. Writers must use gender-free words such as "letter carrier." "Hackneyed" and "stereotyped" expressions like "old wives' tales" must be replaced by such fresh, original phrases as the *Globe*'s suggestion of "superstition" or "popular misconception." This would simply be laughable were it not that the substitute phrase is inaccurate and that old wives' tales are by common acknowledgment most often true. Unfortunately, adds the stylebook, "words such as harbor master and taskmaster pose a problem with no easy solution."   10

Under the entry for race, while there is a great deal with which I would agree, I find it ludicrous to say that it is wrong to describe somebody as "part Indian" or "part black" on grounds that this suggests that white is the standard. In itself, the phrase "part Indian" carries no such connotation whatsoever. But the fact remains that just as in Africa the standard, numerically speaking, is black, or in the Orient the standard, numerically speaking, is Oriental, in Europe and North America the numerical standard is in fact white. What on earth is wrong with stating that? It is simply an observation of plain fact.   11

But there is a more fundamental objection to this stylebook. The *Globe* has decided that the phobias of the most hypersensitive, intolerant, humorless and narrowly ideological segment of the population will determine its language. The plain fact is that you could count on the fingers of one hand the people who worry about the use of the word "harbor master."   12

More importantly, having such a stylebook makes a mockery of a free press. This is a stylebook that goes far beyond the legitimate areas of spelling or policies on obscenity: this book seeks to put its ideological stamp on reporting. This is profoundly anti-intellectual and would be so even if I agreed with every entry. The whole point about writing is that one seeks the mot juste, and the mot juste is one that no style writer can   13 decide ahead of time. And while it can be argued that editors and writers will always be free to employ their own words when justified, in spite of the stylebook, the onus will be on them to justify their departure. A stylebook that goes beyond spelling or punctuation or notions of that kind is antithetical to both good and free journalism. The *Globe and Mail* — and Canada — can ill-afford this nonsense.

TYPES OF WRITING: analysis, direct argument, example/illustration

Topics for Discussion

1. How does the final sentence of the first paragraph serve both as a transition to the following paragraph and as an introduction to the whole essay?
2. What is the function of the last sentence in each of the first three paragraphs?
3. Since Amiel's column in *Maclean's* is restricted to only one page, she has to make her persuasive points rapidly and succinctly. Is there any part of her essay that you think needs more development? If so, explain why, and demonstrate what kind of development it needs.
4. In criticizing efforts to eliminate sexism in language, among other things, what advantage might Amiel gain from being a woman? To what extent does she draw on this potential advantage in her essay?
5. The three essays by Amiel are virtually the same length, intended as each is to fit onto a single page in *Maclean's*. Compare the structure of these three essays. Are there similarities that suggest Amiel is writing according to a structural formula as well as to a prescribed length?

Topics for Writing

1. According to Amiel, writers for the *Globe and Mail* must avoid using expressions such as "manpower" and "man in the street." Would you use such expressions? Your reply should deal with the terms you would use and those you would not, as well as with the reasons for your choices.
2. "The whole point about writing is that one seeks the mot juste, and the mot juste is one that no style writer can decide ahead of time." In an essay, discuss what reply a committed feminist might make to such a statement.

Ontario and Gays: A New Frontier?

Barbara Amiel

If the Ontario government gives homosexual couples the same recogni- 1
tion as heterosexual marriages, it will cross a new frontier. The implications are enormous: this action — which has passed first reading in the
Ontario legislature but faces a stiff fight — would redefine human relationships as we have known them since the beginning of recorded history,
as well as contradicting all we know about the way our society perpetuates itself. Why, I wondered, is Bob Rae trying to do this?

The benign reason is simply that the Ontario government wishes, for 2
emotional and symbolic reasons, to give a seal of approval to some of its
citizens who have a different sexuality from society's norm. Till now,
homosexuals have been free to follow their sexual predilections, but that
freedom is clearly emotionally insufficient. Homosexual couples want
not simply the freedom to do whatever they do, but society's full approval
and official recognition. If this is a bit costly — entailing as it would all
sorts of economic and social implications — well, the argument might
go, it is presumably no more than society can tolerate when trying to
make all its members happier.

The second reason is a more utilitarian one. Rae is in a peculiar 3
position. He has lost a great deal of his traditional support because financial difficulties have forced him to clamp down on the bloated civil
service and his own economic agenda. He has been unable to go whole
hog on what his featherbedding, syndicalist, Waffle pals in the NDP
would want him to do. He can't tax the middle- and upper-income earners
any more, nor can he redistribute much wealth around because Ontario
has so little wealth left. So, in lieu of his economic agenda, he is trying to
salvage support from his natural allies by implementing his social agenda,
which includes the standard feminist-eco-gays axis. Of course, this agenda
will have an economic impact, but it is primarily seen as social legislation.

Rae must believe that around three to five per cent of his constituency 4
will support this move; that percentage may be lower than the actual
number of homosexuals in the population but reflects my belief that not
all lesbians and gay men vote according to sexual politics.

The third reason is my special nightmare. These amendments to 5
Ontario's Human Rights Code and other legislation changing the definition of a spouse underline the power of the state in a new and terrifying
way. If the state can, by a stroke of the pen, fundamentally redefine the
old allocation of human roles — roles such as the heterosexual union,
femaleness, maleness and the family, which have been reaffirmed in
every historical period known to us — if it can redefine them willy-nilly
without any indication that there has been the slightest change in real
human behavior, then we are in Big Brother land. Two plus two does
equal five when spouses can be of the same gender. The notion is utter

lunacy and every thinking person knows so, but we have reached the point where the state can say it is so.

6   If these amendments pass, the state will prove it has the power to tell us how human beings behave rather than letting human behavior tell us. There has been no change in the amount of homosexual behavior in our society — it remains a minor sexual variation. The family has been strenuously attacked, but as yet we have not come up with a better alternative for raising children and perpetuating our species. Still, these observations are thrown to the wind: the state wants to change what is a family, what is normal or abnormal, and we must change our basic human instincts to conform with their political definitions. Previous states, even the most tyrannical or authoritarian ones, drew certain lines based on human experience and the basic habits of our species.

7   We have come full circle. One remembers the great battles to give ordinary people a voice through Parliament. Parliamentary supremacy was seen as the counterbalance to liege lords. When these great debates were going on and the voices of such constitutional experts as Albert Dicey and Walter Bagehot were to be heard, the optimistic assertion was made that Parliament could do anything save make a man a woman. Many laughed, because even those people caught up in the fervor of remaking the state in a democratic tradition realized there were certain limits. But we are now in the post-totalitarian age, Nazism and communism have been defeated, and we are entering the era of the limitless state. Here in the parliament of the limitless state there is nothing it cannot alter. When Caligula made a horse a consul, he did not do so because he thought his horse would be a good consul — he did it to show his power knew no limits. Ontario has declared two spouses can be of the same gender and by so doing they have imitated Caligula.

8   The incidental result of this is that the legitimacy of the family will be diminished. Homosexual unions can be called "families" but they cannot create children. The point is this: the family is the biological unit designed to propagate the species. Homosexual couples may occasionally adopt children and I have no doubt that some of them could bring up children as well or better than heterosexual families. But this does not forfeit the generality of the proposition that marriage has been designed for the raising of families and the biological continuation of our species. The family is not only weakened by all the restrictions we place on it (parents restrained in their disciplinary methods, schools teaching values to which parents object, and so on), it is weakened when the advantages of the family are given away to non-families. You cannot retain the meaningfulness of the true biological family as an institution when you extend its advantages, such as spousal benefit packages, to outsiders.

9   No doubt society will manage these changes. We have organized ourselves in a thousand ways before and there is no reason, I suppose, why a society organized along left-liberal lines cannot survive for a while — nothing lasts forever. All I can do is identify what is gained and what

is lost. We lose individual freedom and responsibility and gain a state that takes over more and more of the family's role. I think it's a great pity, but Canadians don't seem to agree.

TYPES OF WRITING:
analysis, direct argument

Topics for Discussion

1. What persuasive aim does the title of this essay suggest? What is the effect of using a question rather than a direct statement?
2. In her introductory paragraph Amiel makes two sweeping statements: "this action . . . would redefine human relationships as we have known them since the beginning of recorded history," and "contradicting all we know about the way our society perpetuates itself." Do such broad generalizations help, or hinder, the persuasive case she is trying to make?
3. In paragraph 5 Amiel states: "The notion is utter lunacy and every thinking person knows so, but we have reached the point where the state can say it is so." Comment on both the logic and the persuasive force — or lack of it — of this sentence.
4. How effective is Amiel's concluding paragraph in summing up her position? How well does it serve to unify the points she raises in her essay?
5. Did this essay change your mind about the problem? Did it help to clarify the issues involved?
6. The three essays included in this text represent Amiel's characteristically conservative views. What influential advantages does she gain from having established her general perspective on issues in a recurring column?

Topics for Writing

1. How do you feel about homosexual marriages? In approaching this controversial topic, be sure to present yourself as a fair-minded person who is attempting to provide a reasonable review of the issues involved before explaining your conclusions about the subject.
2. Whether or not you agree with Amiel, write a critical reply to her essay, pointing out where her generalizations are too broad, where her personal opinions are presented as universal truths, where her argument contains gaps, and any other flaws you see.
3. Write an essay considering the influential advantages of having established a public persona. Illustrate your views by referring to several examples. You should focus on writers, but you may also want to consider well-known figures from other media, such as talk-show hosts, comedians, or proponents of particular areas of public concern such as David Suzuki or Jacques Cousteau.

Canadians: What Do They Want?

Margaret Atwood

1   Last month, during a poetry reading, I tried out a short prose poem called "How to Like Men." It began by suggesting that one start with the feet. Unfortunately, the question of jackboots soon arose, and things went on from there. After the reading I had a conversation with a young man who thought I had been unfair to men. He wanted men to be liked totally, not just from the heels to the knees, and not just as individuals but as a group; and he thought it negative and inegalitarian of me to have alluded to war and rape. I pointed out that as far as any of us knew these were two activities not widely engaged in by women, but he was still upset. "We're both in this together," he protested. I admitted that this was so; but could he, maybe, see that our relative positions might be a little different.

2   This is the conversation one has with Americans, even, uh, *good* Americans, when the dinner-table conversation veers round to Canadian-American relations. "We're in this together," they like to say, especially when it comes to continental energy reserves. How do you *explain* to them, as delicately as possible, why they are not categorically beloved? It gets like the old Lifebuoy ads: even their best friends won't tell them. And Canadians are supposed to be their best friends, right? Members of the family?

3   Well, sort of. Across the river from Michigan, so near and yet so far, there I was at the age of eight, reading *their* Donald Duck comic books (originated, however, by one of *ours*; yes, Walt Disney's parents were Canadian) and coming at the end to Popsicle Pete, who promised me the earth if only I would save wrappers, but took it all away from me again with a single asterisk: Offer Good Only in the United States. Some cynical members of the world community may be forgiven for thinking that the same asterisk is there, in invisible ink, on the Constitution and the Bill of Rights.

4   But quibbles like that aside, and good will assumed, how does one go about liking Americans? Where does one begin? Or, to put it another way, why did the Canadian women lock themselves in the john during a '70s "international" feminist conference being held in Toronto? Because the American sisters were being "imperialist," that's why.

5   But then, it's always a little naive of Canadians to expect that Americans, of whatever political stamp, should stop being imperious. How can they? The fact is that the United States is an empire and Canada is to it as Gaul was to Rome.

6   It's hard to explain to Americans what it feels like to be a Canadian. Pessimists among us would say that one has to translate the experience into their own terms and that this is necessary because Americans are incapable of thinking in any other terms — and this in itself is part of the problem. (Witness all those draft dodgers who went into culture shock when they discovered to their horror that Toronto was not Syracuse.)

Here is a translation: Picture a Mexico with a population ten times 7
larger than that of the United States. That would put it at about two
billion. Now suppose that the official American language is Spanish, that
75 percent of the books Americans buy and 90 percent of the movies
they see are Mexican, and that the profits flow across the border to
Mexico. If an American does scrape it together to make a movie, the
Mexicans won't let him show it in the States, because they own the
distribution outlets. If anyone tries to change this ratio, not only the
Mexicans but many fellow Americans cry "National chauvinism," or,
even more effectively, "National socialism." After all, the American public
prefers the Mexican product. It's what they're used to.

Retranslate and you have the current American-Canadian picture. 8
It's changed a little recently, not only on the cultural front. For instance,
Canada, some think a trifle late, is attempting to regain control of its
own petroleum industry. Americans are predictably angry. They think
of Canadian oil as *theirs*.

"What's mine is yours," they have said for years, meaning exports; 9
"What's yours is mine" meaning ownership and profits. Canadians are
supposed to do retail buying, not controlling, or what's an empire for?
One could always refer Americans to history, particularly that of their
own revolution. They objected to the colonial situation when they themselves were a colony; but then, revolution is considered one of a very
few home-grown American products that definitely are not for export.

Objectively, one cannot become too self-righteous about this state of 10
affairs. Canadians owned lots of things, including their souls, before
World War II. After that they sold, some say because they had put too much
into financing the war, which created a capital vacuum (a position they
would not have been forced into if the Americans hadn't kept out of the
fighting for so long, say the sore losers). But for whatever reason, capital
flowed across the border in the '50s, and Canadians, traditionally sock-
under-the-mattress hoarders, were reluctant to invest in their own country.
Americans did it for them and ended up with a large part of it, which they
retain to this day. In every sellout there's a seller as well as a buyer, and
the Canadians did a thorough job of trading their birthright for a mess.

That's on the capitalist end, but when you turn to the trade union 11
side of things you find much the same story, except that the sellout
happened in the '30s under the banner of the United Front. Now Canadian
workers are finding that in any empire the colonial branch plants are the
first to close, and what could be a truly progressive labor movement has
been weakened by compromised bargains made in international union
headquarters south of the border.

Canadians are sometimes snippy to Americans at cocktail parties. 12
They don't like to feel owned and they don't like having been sold. But
what really bothers them — and it's at this point that the United States
and Rome part company — is the wide-eyed innocence with which their
snippiness is greeted.

13   Innocence becomes ignorance when seen in the light of international affairs, and though ignorance is one of the spoils of conquest — the Gauls always knew more about the Romans than the Romans knew about them — the world can no longer afford America's ignorance. Its ignorance of Canada, though it makes Canadians bristle, is a minor and relatively harmless example. More dangerous is the fact that individual Americans seem not to know that the United States is an imperial power and is behaving like one. They don't want to admit that empires dominate, invade and subjugate — and live on the proceeds — or, if they do admit it, they believe in their divine right to do so. The export of divine right is much more harmful than the export of Coca-Cola, though they may turn out to be much the same thing in the end.

14   Other empires have behaved similarly (the British somewhat better, Genghis Khan decidedly worse); but they have not expected to be *liked* for it. It's the final Americanism, this passion for being liked. Alas, many Americans are indeed likable; they are often more generous, more welcoming, more enthusiastic, less picky and sardonic than Canadians, and it's not enough to say it's only because they can afford it. Some of that revolutionary spirit still remains: the optimism, the 18th-century belief in the fixability of almost anything, the conviction of the possibility of change. However, at cocktail parties and elsewhere one must be able to tell the difference between an individual and a foreign policy. Canadians can no longer afford to think of Americans as only a spectator sport. If Reagan blows up the world, we will unfortunately be doing more than watching it on television. "No annihilation without representation" sounds good as a slogan, but if we run it up the flagpole, who's going to salute?

15   We *are* all in this together. For Canadians, the question is how to survive it. For Americans there is no question, because there does not have to be. Canada is just that vague, cold place where their uncle used to go fishing, before the lakes went dead from acid rain.

16   How do you like Americans? Individually, it's easier. Your average American is no more responsible for the state of affairs than your average man is for war and rape. Any Canadian who is so narrow-minded as to dislike Americans merely on principle is missing out on one of the good things in life. The same might be said, to women, of men. As a group, as a foreign policy, it's harder. But if you like men, you can like Americans. Cautiously. Selectively. Beginning with the feet. One at a time.

TYPES OF WRITING:
analysis, example/illustration, personal experience

Topics for Discussion

1. Given that Atwood's primary concern in this essay is Canadian-American relations, why would she risk putting half her potential audience — men — on the defensive in her opening?
2. "Canadians are sometimes snippy to Americans … They don't like to feel owned and they don't like having been sold. But what really bothers them . . . is that wide-eyed innocence with which their snippiness is greeted." Has this been your experience with Americans?
3. In paragraph 1 Atwood refers to men "from the heels to the knees," and in paragraph 5 she mentions that "the United States is an empire and Canada is to it as Gaul was to Rome." How does she further develop these two points? To what extent do they help her achieve her persuasive objectives?
4. The persuasiveness of Atwood's views derives more from apt perceptions and telling illustrations than from a logically ordered argument. Would a more formally organized argument have been more persuasive? Explain.

Topics for Writing

1. Drawing on Atwood's informal, personal approach as a model, write an essay explaining the position of some group with which you are familiar. Your essay might have a title such as "Engineering Students: What Do They Want?" or "University Athletes: What Do They Want?"
2. Many Canadians have had roughly the same kind of experience with American attitudes as that described by Atwood. Basing your essay at least in part on your own experience, explain some aspect of how Americans in general appear to misunderstand Canada and Canadians.

Any Humans There?

Russell Baker

1 A machine purporting to be the Rev. Jerry Falwell had written a strident letter asking me to send it $5, $10 or $25 immediately, and signed itself breezily as "Jerry."

2   I don't know Mr. Falwell but in my associations with men of the cloth I have never overcome the awe and respect for their calling that Uncle Irvey taught me as a child. Accordingly, I felt duty bound to warn Mr. Falwell that a machine was writing letters over his name and trying to cadge money from strangers.

3   I knew Uncle Irvey would have wanted to hear about it if the machine had surreptitiously written to a perfect stranger, asked for $5, $10 or $25 immediately, and signed itself "Irv." In my childhood Uncle Irvey was the superintendent at the Shinar Lutheran Church and, as such, became my model of sound churchly behavior.

4   Machines, for example, had no place in churchly doings. Though he owned an automobile, Uncle Irvey preferred the horse and buggy when he went to church, at least until age, infirmity and the decline of the horseshoe overtook him. He chose to approach the Lord's house in a peace undefiled by the clattering of soulless machinery.

5   He would have considered it indecent to ask anyone to put a $5 bill in the plate, and obscene to press for $10 or $25. Any plutocrats hoping to pass through the eye of the needle by dropping a princely $1 bill were expected to conceal their shameful wealth in sealed envelopes.

6   A machine putting the muscle on people for sums of $5, $10 or $25 would have been an abomination of Satan, in Uncle Irvey's view. If the preacher was hard pressed for money or the church needed repairs, he was not above putting the muscle on certain well-to-do farmers during pious chats by the corncrib, but if a machine calling itself "Irv" had gone public all across the county, he would have wanted to know about it.

7   I assumed Mr. Falwell would want to know about it too. I had just started to write a letter to him when the telephone interrupted. A woman's voice said a machine wanted to speak to me. Would I talk to it?

8   "Does it call itself 'Jerry'?" I asked.

9   No, the woman said, it was the voice of one of Elvis Presley's closest friends. The machine came on the line. It spoke in a gooey cornpone voice. It had heard I was a devoted Elvis fan. Would I like to hear a message from Elvis?

10   "Look here," I said, "I am not that much of an Elvis fan and I am busy writing to the Rev. Jerry Falwell about a machine that's sending out letters over his name, and I don't have time to . . ."

11   "Before he died," said the machine, "Elvis told me he wanted every one of his fans to enjoy the greatest bargain in recorded music . . ."

12   I hung up and returned to my letter. "Dear Mr. Falwell: I am sure

you will be as outraged as I to learn that a certain machine, calling itself 'Jerry,' is trying to cadge sums of $5, $10 or $25 . . ."

The phone rang again. A machine spoke. It had the affidavit voice of an F.B.I. agent. 13

"Are you the person who just hung up on the machine bringing you a message from one of Elvis Presley's best friends?" 14

"Is your name Jerry?" I replied. 15

"I'll ask the questions," the machine said. "How long do you want to live?" 16

"Are you threatening my life?" I asked. 17

"Are you aware that a new physical fitness program designed by foremost physiological scientists can add years of glowing health to your life? This life-enhancing miracle is now available exclusively for only $39.95 . . ." 18

I hung up and waited for the next ring. This time it was a machine under the misapprehension that I had received some mail-order aspidistra plants and refused to pay the bill after four warning notices. I hung up before it threatened to haul me into machine court. 19

"Dear Mr. Falwell," I began again. "You probably never heard of my Uncle Irvey, but . . ." 20

Telephone. "I am one of Uncle Irvey's longtime associates," said a machine. "Before his death Uncle Irvey spoke to me down by the corncrib. He had just put the muscle on me for $5, $10 or $25 to buy shoes for the preacher's little children, and he said, 'Wouldn't it be nice if there was a wonderful machine somewhere that could just reach out to all the wonderful people in this good old world of ours and tell folks to send in $5, $10 or $25 immediately?'" 21

I was too stunned to argue. "This is Jerry, isn't it?" I whispered. 22

"Send me $5, $10 or $25 immediately," it said. "Yes, sir," I said. I meant it at the time, but next day I saw things more clearly and sent Mr. Falwell a note. 23

"If you and the missus are pinched for food money," I said, "let me know and I will bake you an apple pie and send it along." 24

I'm pretty certain that would have been Uncle Irvey's way. 25

TYPES OF WRITING:
comparison, example/illustration, humour, narration

Topics for Discussion

1. Baker does not specify ways of limiting the use of machines for telephone solicitation, nor in fact does he advocate direct controls at all. How might his essay have an effect on this nuisance nonetheless?

2. Given the wide variety of examples available, why do you think Baker chose those he did?

3. What are the common characteristics of the persona through which Baker writes in this essay and in "Beastly Manhattan"? How does this persona contribute to the humour of his essays and to their influential effect?

Topics for Writing

1. Using specific examples, write an essay intended to raise consciousness about the waste and bother of junk mail, advertising promotions that lead people to believe they have won prizes, door-to-door selling of home renovations, or some other contemporary aggravation aimed at making money.
2. The effectiveness of Baker's essay depends on his success in capturing convincingly the tone of recorded telephone solicitations. Paying particular attention to Baker's use of descriptive words and phrases and the phrasing he attributes to callers, write an essay evaluating and explaining his success in depicting these messages.

Beastly Manhattan

Russell Baker

After moving to Manhattan I bought a camel. I did not want a camel, but 1
in Manhattan it was absolutely vital to own an animal of some sort, and
of all the animal kingdom a camel seemed to me the most sensible sort
to own.

It is peaceable, requires infrequent feeding, affords basic transporta- 2
tion and makes very little noise. If one must have an animal in a place
like Manhattan, and it seemed that one must, a camel seemed the least
troublesome choice. So I bought a camel.

This did not sit well with New Yorkers. New Yorkers are partial to 3
dogs, which they harbor in all sizes and shapes, keeping them imprisoned
most of the day in tiny apartments and bringing them out morning and
evening to evacuate on sidewalks and streets.

The dogs vary from mammoth beasts capable of consuming a po- 4
liceman in three bites to creatures no larger than mice, and come in a
startling variety of forms. There is one breed that resembles a woman's
wig. The first time I saw one at the curb on Second Avenue, I undertook
to retrieve it for its owner, mistaking it for an escaped wig, before I
discovered that it had four legs and was being walked.

At that time I had no animal at all, and New Yorkers viewed me 5
with that distaste which the animal lover cannot conceal for the beastless
man. When the camel was delivered, I looked forward with satisfaction
to the approving smiles they would shed upon us both — me and my
camel — at the spectacle of man and beast in harmonious communion.

This approval was never granted. To the contrary. There was 6
undisguised hostility toward the camel. The landlord, who kept a pair of
boxers big enough to kick a camel to death, protested the camel's size.

The neighbors complained that the camel, which at first I kept at the 7
curb, took up a precious parking space, and I soon had to bring him into
the apartment, which depressed both of us — the camel because he
couldn't get comfortable on the couch, me because the camel kept wandering into the dining room at the dinner hour and wolfing the salad.

Walking the camel put strains on neighborly relations. In Manhattan, 8
the custom is to walk your animal around the corner or into the next
block and pretend to be studying a distant horizon while he surreptitiously fouls someone else's turf.

New Yorkers understand this about dogs and make no protest. They 9
live by the dog owner's code. You foul my shoes; I foul yours. But the
sight of a poor camel ambling around the corner to do as the dogs do
incensed them. The owners of the neighborhood's fiercer man-eating
mastiffs would threaten to unleash their pets on the camel if he persisted
in using the asphalt sacred to canines.

I saw that I was not winning New Yorkers with my love of animals 10
and that they thought me eccentric for not preferring a dog that looked

like a wig, a giant hound that could tear the mailman to shreds or even a cat that would claw the upholstery to ribbons.

11   Determined to gain their respect, I tried to teach the camel tricks of the sort that captivate dog lovers. I attempted to teach the camel to howl in the night, but that was useless.

12   I did succeed, however, in teaching him to leap enthusiastically against visitors and slobber over their neckties. I even trained him to issue something that sounded vaguely like a menacing growl, suggesting that he was preparing to sink his teeth into the thigh of any guest heartless enough not to be a totally devoted camel lover.

13   I taught him to wag his tail and, with one bound across the room, pounce happily into the lap of anyone who was elegantly dressed. And when he had mastered all these endearing tricks, I invited neighbors to visit.

14   The camel performed faithfully, although he was clearly bored and thought that humans must be an asinine bunch to require such arch displays from beasts. The neighbors were not warmed.

15   The man on whose necktie the camel slobbered lost his temper, the woman at whom the camel growled menacingly left, threatening to have me before the magistrates for harboring an unleashed camel.

16   The man in whose lap the camel triumphantly pounced with wagging tail has filed a suit claiming mental pain and suffering.

17   The camel, whose sensitivity was at least as great as the average dog's, was crestfallen at our failure to win the neighbors' affection and respect. I was quite touched by his despondency, so much so, in fact, that I hesitated to get rid of him after the fiasco.

18   Accordingly, I made him an offer. With surgical removal of the identifying hump, I suggested, he could easily pass for a dog in the bizarre pound that was New York, and immediately win the heart of all Manhattan. The camel had nothing to lose except his hump, and shortly afterwards New Yorkers were delightedly letting him nuzzle their neckties, and void thunderously on their doorsteps.

19   I sold him to a dog lover for a very good price, never having believed that a city is a fit place to keep a dog.

TYPES OF WRITING:
description, humour, narration

Topics for Discussion

1. This essay is mainly concerned with dogs in Manhattan. Why would Baker lead into his complaint about city dog owners with a deliberately ridiculous account of his fictional camel?

2. Although this piece will have the ready support of readers who share Baker's feeling that a very crowded city is no place to keep a dog, it

will accomplish more if it can encourage dog owners to become more considerate, or if it can discourage big-city dwellers from acquiring dogs in the first place. What aspects of Baker's approach might allow him to hold the interest and influence the behaviour and opinions of the dog owners in his audience?

3. Baker frequently uses exaggeration for humorous effect in this essay. Is this exaggeration likely to offend urban dog owners? Why or why not?

4. What is the effect of Baker's short concluding paragraph?

Topics for Writing

1. Compare the naive, apparently humourless persona adopted by the author to that of Bil Gilbert in "Fast As an Elephant, Strong As an Ant." Would these adopted poses have roughly the same effect on those who share the writers' views as on those who find their position attacked, or would the effect be different?

2. Write a humorous essay criticizing a group such as rowdy teenagers at a mall, elderly people who wear garish clothes, or noisy couples who take their seats after a concert or movie has begun. Keep the humour light, and make your points indirectly.

To Lie, or Not to Lie? —
I: The Doctors' Dilemma

Sissela Bok

Note: The following three essays by Sissela Bok originally appeared on April 18, 19, and 20, 1978, in the New York Times *as a three-part series entitled "To Lie, or Not to Lie?" The original order of publication is retained in this text.*

1   Should doctors ever lie to benefit their patients — to speed recovery or to conceal the approach of death? In medicine as in law, government, and other lines of work, the requirements of honesty often seem dwarfed by greater needs: the need to shelter from brutal news or to uphold a promise of secrecy; to expose corruption or to promote the public interest.

2   What should doctors say, for example, to a 46-year-old man coming in for a routine physical checkup just before going on vacation with his family who, though he feels in perfect health, is found to have a form of cancer that will cause him to die within six months? Is it best to tell him the truth? If he asks, should the doctors deny that he is ill, or minimize the gravity of the prognosis? Should they at least conceal the truth until after the family vacation?

3   Doctors confront such choices often and urgently. At times, they see important reasons to lie for the patient's own sake; in their eyes, such lies differ sharply from self-serving ones.

4   Studies show that most doctors sincerely believe that the seriously ill do not want to know the truth about their condition, and that informing them risks destroying their hope, so that they may recover more slowly, or deteriorate faster, perhaps even commit suicide. As one physician wrote: "Ours is a profession which traditionally has been guided by a precept that transcends the virtue of uttering the truth for truth's sake, and that is 'as far as possible do no harm.'"

5   Armed with such a precept, a number of doctors may slip into deceptive practices that they assume will "do no harm" and may well help their patients. They may prescribe innumerable placebos, sound more encouraging than the facts warrant, and distort grave news, especially to the incurably ill and the dying.

6   But the illusory nature of the benefits such deception is meant to bestow is now coming to be documented. Studies show that, contrary to the belief of many physicians, an overwhelming majority of patients do want to be told the truth, even about grave illness, and feel betrayed when they learn that they have been misled. We are also learning that truthful information, humanely conveyed, helps patients cope with illness: helps them tolerate pain better, need less medication, and even recover faster after surgery.

Not only do lies not provide the "help" hoped for by advocates of 7
benevolent deception; they invade the autonomy of patients and render
them unable to make informed choices concerning their own health,
including the choice of whether to *be* a patient in the first place. We are
becoming increasingly aware of all that can befall patients in the course
of their illness when information is denied or distorted.

Dying patients especially — who are easiest to mislead and most 8
often kept in the dark — can then not make decisions about the end of
life: about whether or not to enter a hospital, or to have surgery; about
where and with whom to spend their remaining time; about how to
bring their affairs to a close and take leave.

Lies also do harm to those who tell them: harm to their integrity and, 9
in the long run, to their credibility. Lies hurt their colleagues as well. The
suspicion of deceit undercuts the work of the many doctors who are
scrupulously honest with their patients; it contributes to the spiral of
litigation and of "defensive medicine," and thus it injures, in turn, the
entire medical profession.

Sharp conflicts are now arising. Patients are learning to press for 10
answers. Patients' bills of rights require that they be informed about
their condition and about alternatives for treatment. Many doctors go to
great lengths to provide such information. Yet even in hospitals with the
most eloquent bill of rights, believers in benevolent deception continue
their age-old practices. Colleagues may disapprove but refrain from re-
monstrating. Nurses may bitterly resent having to take part, day after
day, in deceiving patients, but feel powerless to take a stand.

There is urgent need to debate this issue openly. Not only in medicine, 11
but in other professions as well, practitioners may find themselves repeatedly in straits where serious consequences seem avoidable only
through deception. Yet the public has every reason to be wary of professional deception, for such practices are peculiarly likely to become ingrained, to spread, and to erode trust. Neither in medicine, nor in law,
government, or the social sciences can there be comfort in the old saw,
"What you don't know can't hurt you."

TYPES OF WRITING:
direct argument, example/illustration

Topics for Discussion

1. What is the effect of the relatively pejorative term "lie" in the title and
   opening sentences of this essay? What would be the effect of substituting the word "tell" for "lie" in the title? How might avoiding references to lying, substituting instead phrases such as "withholding details" and "shielding patients," change this essay's effect on various
   concerned audiences?

2. What does the fairly abrupt introduction to the essay suggest about Bok's intended audience? Do you think she is trying mainly to influence doctors in this piece?

3. Apart from unifying the essay to some extent, what is the effect of Bok's tactic of linking the dilemma of doctors, as she perceives it, to similar conflicts in other professions?

4. Consider the support Bok provides after the transitional statement: "But the illusory nature of the benefits such deception is meant to bestow is now coming to be documented." Consider the progression toward certainty from "studies show," to "we are also learning" and "we are becoming increasingly aware," to direct, unqualified statements about the benefit of truth. Is the effect of Bok's argument weakened because she asks the reader to accept so much on faith, referring as she does to the authority of unspecified and unexamined studies?

5. How could "The Doctors' Dilemma" be modified to generate more interest in the remaining two essays in the series?

Topics for Writing

1. Write an essay presenting the other side of this argument.

2. Write an essay arguing for or against complete honesty in one of the other areas mentioned by Bok — "law, government, or the social sciences."

To Lie, or Not to Lie?—II: Here a Pseudo—, There a Pseudo—

Sissela Bok

In fairy tales, princes dressed as shepherds go out among their people to   1
learn what they won't be told at court — how the sick and the poor live;
how the courtiers and the counselors do their work; how power is
wielded. A curious analogue to these quests has sprung up in the last
15 years with the help of social scientists: the pseudo-patient study.

Investigators pretending to suffer from depressions, delusions, aches   2
and pains go into clinics and hospitals to seek "help." In fact, they hope
to learn first-hand about the care of the sick and the needy, and about
the use and misuse of public funds.

These studies have now become so common that doctors are advised   3
to be on the lookout for a new kind of "patient": the pseudo-patient.
They have responded with shock and hostility to the deviousness of the
research techniques and to the invasion of the privacy of their dealings
with patients. They ask why such knowledge could not be acquired
quite openly: Surely there are few secrets left about the abuses that the
pseudo-patient studies document.

Social scientists admit that such studies break no new ground. But   4
they defend their duplicity in two ways. In the first place, they argue,
deceptive research flourishes in sociology and social psychology generally. Many deceptive tactics of research are now commonplace: tests that
say they measure perception while in reality measuring bias or suggest-
ibility; questionnaires falsely claiming anonymity for respondents; infiltration of groups such as Alcoholics Anonymous or religious sects; and
the staging of fake accidents complete with victim, blood and debris to
measure "helping behavior" among passers-by. These techniques are
taught to countless students, and recounted in journals and textbooks
the world over. Why, the investigators ask, should pseudo-patient studies
be differently judged?

Unfortunately, this question does not help to justify such studies. On   5
the contrary, it only underscores the growing uneasiness over all forms
of deceptive research in the social sciences.

Investigators argue, in the second place, that although it is not news   6
that those most in need of help may be abused, given medication and operations they do not need, and ignored in institutional care, the pseudo-patient
studies may *dramatize* these facts, and thus help to bring about reform.

As for the argument that such studies invade the privacy of the   7
doctor-patient relationship, social scientists reply that professional relationships differ from, for example, private sexual or religious practices
precisely in that they ought to be open to public scrutiny, and that our
laws permit publicity at the expense of privacy in matters where the
public has a legitimate interest.

8   In weighing these claims, it helps to place pseudo-patient studies in the larger context of surreptitious monitoring in many other lines of work — in the use of unmarked police cars, in television repair, in restaurants and banking — and to compare the role of the students and social scientists sent to act as pseudo-patients with that of private investigators, journalists, local police and Federal agents in uncovering other kinds of abuses.

9   To being with, all can agree that those who may be subjected to surreptitious monitoring ought at least to be alerted to such a possibility. They would then be less shocked at having been duped in any one instance. We can agree, also, that whenever there are nondeceptive alternatives for learning about abuse and waste, they should be preferred.

10   Next, we must ask how much surveillance and infiltration our society needs and how much it can tolerate. The necessity that is claimed for these practices should be weighed against the toll they take.

11   We must ask, also, how free people should be to infiltrate: whether all who want to do so, out of curiosity or in pursuit of some worthy cause, should have the right to go ahead. Do we really want pseudo-students in classrooms, pseudo-converts to religious creeds, pseudo-party-members and pseudo-legal clients? How far, finally, do we want to use taxpayer and scholarship funds to train some to spy on their fellows?

12   These should be matters for public choice. It will then be possible to set standards for what communities regard as tolerable forms of monitoring. Until such standards are set, health professionals and others would do well to assume that they may become the subjects of deceptive studies. The wisest course may yet be to treat all strangers well. Who knows — they may be princes in disguise.

TYPES OF WRITING:
analysis, direct argument, example/illustration

Topics for Discussion

1. How is the title relevant to this essay?
2. After you have finished reading this essay, re-read the introductory paragraph. Do you believe that the "fairy tale" opening is effective?
3. Does the final sentence help to unify the essay? If so, how? If not, why not?
4. Does Bok's assertion in the last half of her essay that pseudo-patient studies should be viewed in the context of other surreptitious monitoring clarify or cloud her particular issue of concern?
5. Bok concludes that limits on all sorts of surreptitious monitoring — including pseudo-patient studies, journalistic investigation, and the use of unmarked police cars — should be determined by public standards. She does not, however, explain in any detail how or by whom

these standards will be established or enforced. To what extent might greater detail strengthen or weaken the general point she is making?

Topics for Writing

1. "We must ask how much surveillance and infiltration our society needs and how much it can tolerate," says Bok. What is your reply to this question?
2. Bok comments that it may "be possible to set standards for what communities regard as tolerable forms of monitoring." In the community you come from, what might these standards be? Your essay on this problem should carefully examine the moral and social standards of your home town; you should then draw tentative conclusions about where your neighbours would set limits to monitoring.

To Lie, or Not to Lie?—III:
Bricks and Mortar and Deceit

Sissela Bok

1   No misconception is so dangerous, wrote the Marquis de Condercet, the 18th-century social philosopher and revolutionist, as the view that Government lies can sometimes serve the public interest: no error gives rise to so many other delusions.

2   We have had a vivid demonstration of how lies undermine a political system. The webs of deceit from Vietnam and Watergate were of an intricacy and a scope that may not soon be surpassed. But most observers would agree that deception is also part and parcel of many everyday Government decisions. Government officials may sometimes look at lies as the only way to cope with what they take to be an unmanageable bureaucracy, a needlessly suspicious press, or an uncomprehending public.

3   In this way false rumors may be leaked by subordinates who believe that unwise administrative action is about to be taken. Statistics may be presented in such a way as to diminish the gravity of embarrassing problems. Government officials may hotly deny rumors of policy changes one day only to implement the changes the next. And they may misrepresent altogether some policies — preparations for war, for example — that they take to be beyond the comprehension of citizens.

4   Public obtuseness is also involved by candidates who make promises they know they cannot keep, or take stands they plan to reverse if elected. And members of Congress may deny having made deals that led them to vote for measures they would otherwise have opposed.

5   The incentives to deceit are often strong. Consider the Administration official who has worked long in the hope that Congress will enact new anti-poverty legislation. Should he lie to a Congressman he believes unable to understand the importance and urgency of the proposed bill, yet powerful enough to block its passage? Should he warn — contrary to fact — that the Administration will press for a far more extensive measure unless the present bill is enacted?

6   He may regard such a lie as a trifling concession for a pressing goal, and have full confidence in his disinterested motives and in his ability to distinguish such lies from more harmful ones.

7   Such thinking is shortsighted. The most fundamental error that people make when weighing lies is to evaluate the costs and benefits of a particular lie in an isolated case, and then to favor the lie if the benefits seem to outweigh the costs. In doing so, they overlook two factors. Bias, first of all, skews all judgment, but never more than in the search for good reasons to deceive. Liars tend to overestimate their own good will, high motives, and chances to escape detection, to underrate the intelligence of the deceived and to ignore their rights.

Second, in focusing on the isolated lie it is easy to ignore the most   8
significant costs of lying: to ignore what lying — even in a good cause —
does to the standards of those who tell the lies, as well as to their credibility: to overlook the effects of lies on the co-workers who witness
them, and who may imitate them, or on others who learn about them
and who may deceive in retaliation or merely to stay even. Above all,
such a narrow focus ignores the cumulative effects of lies — many told
for what seemed at the time "good reasons" as they build up into vast
institutional practices. The long-range effects of the narrow and biased
calculations that underlie each isolated lie are severe.

Lying by public officials is now so widely suspected that voters are   9
at a loss to know when they can and cannot believe what a Government
spokesman reports, or what a candidate says in campaigning. The damage
to trust has been immense. Two years ago, 69 percent of the respondents
to a national poll agreed that this country's leaders have consistently lied
to the people over the last 10 years. And over 40 percent agreed that
most politicians are so similar that it does not really matter who is elected.

Many refuse to vote under such circumstances. Others look to ap-   10
pearance or to personality factors for clues as to which candidate might
be more trustworthy than the rest. Once trust has eroded to this extent, it
is hard to regain. Even the most honest public officials then meet with
suspicion. And in times of national stress when problems require joint
efforts — problems, for example, of preparing for energy shortages or
for inflation — the cynicism and apathy that greet Government calls to
common sacrifice are crippling. Citizens and governments alike are the
true losers when a political system has reached such a low level of trust.

TYPES OF WRITING:
cause and effect, direct argument

Topics for Discussion

1. What recent examples do you recall of deceit by public officials? Can
   you identify any of the persuasive strategies they used?
2. Because Bok's audience is extremely wide (this essay first appeared in
   the *New York Times*), she makes general rather than specific references
   — "government officials," for instance. Do you, nevertheless, find that
   her examples are persuasive?
3. In paragraph 3 Bok uses the expression "false rumors." In your opinion is there such a thing as a true rumour? Or does the word "rumour"
   connote, for you, a falsehood?
4. What persuasive advantage does Bok gain from devoting much of the
   first half of her essay to reviewing reasons for dishonesty by government
   officials? Why does she position this section of her essay where she
   does?

5. Compare the conclusion of this essay to the conclusions of the preceding two in the series. Does the conclusion to this final essay also function as a conclusion to the series? If so, how?

Topic for Writing

1. Have you ever told a lie because you thought that the benefits would outweigh the costs? Discuss the circumstances in detail, and then draw conclusions from your experience. The last part of your essay should reflect on this type of problem and what you have learned from it, or why you have learned nothing of much value.

SISSELA BOK/TO LIE, OR NOT TO LIE?
Series of Three Essays

Topics for Discussion

1. What influential advantage does Bok derive from presenting her case against lying in three short essays rather than one long essay?
2. Why do you think Bok arranged these three essays as she did? Would dealing in a different order with these three areas of dishonesty have worked as well?
3. What difficulties would integrating Bok's three essays pose?

Topic for Writing

1. Write an essay considering how the cumulative effect of Bok's three essays would exceed that of any one alone. Put yourself in the place of a *New York Times* reader encountering these essays on April 18, 19, and 20, 1978, and approach the question imaginatively as well as logically.

The Creationism Controversy:
The Religious Issues

Anne Brennan

The Institute for Creation Research and the Creation Research Society, with the support of the Moral Majority and similar religio-political groups, have been waging a nationwide campaign to require the teaching of creationism alongside evolution in public school biology classes. Last year, Florida's Hillsborough County School Board voted in favor of such a requirement. This was a regrettable decision, one that will cost a lot in time, energy, and taxpayers' dollars, not to mention student confusion, before it is inevitably reversed. It does reveal how prevalent are popular misconceptions about religion and science. But it obscures the real concerns at the heart of the fundamentalist attack on contemporary culture, and so delays any rational attempts to resolve the deeper issues. 1

Evolution is not a religious issue any more than creation is a proper object of scientific investigation. Evolution is a scientific theory. This doesn't mean that it's a guess which will become a fact when we're absolutely sure of it. A fact is merely a description of something we have observed. A theory is a tentative explanation of how a lot of facts are related. After repeated observations and debates, scientists may accept a theory as a reasonably sound and useful explanation of the available facts, knowing that the theory may have to be revised in light of future discoveries. The scientific academy is currently debating the mechanism of evolution, but it is unanimous in its acceptance of the theory of evolution, on the basis of an overwhelming body of confirming evidence. 2

Creation names a divine activity which is certainly beyond our powers of observation. Religious belief in creation is rooted in an awareness of our dependence on mysterious powers that shape our origin and destiny. This sense of radical dependence has found expression in myth and ritual, belief systems, and moral codes. Myth is the language proper to religious experience. It expresses in drama and imagery the otherwise inexpressible awareness of a transcendent Other just beyond the reach of our imagination. 3

The Judeo/Christian belief in our absolute dependence on the God of Abraham and Jesus is beautifully expressed in the ancient Hebrew creation myths. The discovery in the past century of languages and texts from the biblical cultures gave scholars the tools they needed to unlock, at last, the meanings intended by the authors of Genesis. Their profound religious insights and literary genius had been obscured by centuries of mistaking superb poetic drama for something akin to the Congressional Record. 4

Faith in the biblical Creator is not based on such misinterpretation of Genesis. Nor is it based on scientific evidence, but on the religious experience of our contingency. The faith in creation expressed in Genesis 5 does not answer our scientific questions about how things in the universe work, but our deeper questions about why there is anything at all, and why we assume it makes sense and is worth mastering.

6   It follows that a term like "scientific creationism" is self-contradictory, and about as meaningful as "mathematical love-making." Its widespread use is yet one more indication of what we might boldly call the scientific and religious illiteracy of the products of our nation's educational system. Equally revealing are debates entitled "Evolution vs. Creationism," which promise as much enlightenment as might debates entitled "Statistical Probability vs. Divine Providence," or "Penicillin vs. Prayer," or "Love vs. Vitamins."

7   Creationists and evolutionists often argue their cases like opponents in a lawsuit. Each claims to have an authentic photo of, say, an accident, while charging that the other's contradictory picture has been fraudulently touched up. The crucial insight that is missing is that science and religion are different but complementary ways of knowing, each with its own language and rules. They function not so much like contradictory pictures of the world, but more like different kinds of lenses through which we can view the world from different angles or in different lights. The discovery and growing ability to use both kinds of lenses is the story of civilization.

8   Primitive peoples saw their world through the single lens of their tribal myth. It was an all-encompassing view which fused the practical knowledge of common sense with a religious awareness of transcendent mystery. It provided an integrated system of answers to two basic kinds of questions: how do things in our world work relative to our survival; and why are so many things beyond our control? The tribal myth, fundamentally religious, indeed religious fundamentalism in its origins, was the certain and secure basis for tribal culture. It dictated the rituals and customs, the values and lifestyle, that insured tribal uniformity and survival.

9   The needs of critical thought eventually broke through the hard ground of tribal conformity, raising doubts about the adequacy of the myths to explain recurring natural events. As thinking developed and people began asking how things work in themselves, apart from practical or religious concerns, science was born. Centuries of theoretical questioning produced the various branches of science we have today. The twentieth-century mind is the product of a long, irreversible process of development of what we might call its multiple-lens approach to reality. It is a regression for us to be arguing religion vs. science, creation vs. evolution at this stage of our civilization, as though we could only see through a single lens.

10   Evolution has been made to appear a religious issue by two opposing groups of religious fundamentalists, each proposing a single-lens view of reality. The biblical fundamentalists, interpreting the creation narratives in Genesis as historical and scientific records dictated by God, are compelled to reject any scientific theory which, like evolution, appears to

contradict what God said. Never mind that their biblicism flies in the face of a century of biblical scholarship and is rejected by the majority of religious denominations whose traditions stem from the same biblical witness. This only reinforces their conviction that they are the righteous few who will be saved. Never mind that, like the churchmen who refused to look through Galileo's telescope, they must deny an enormous body of scientific evidence for evolution. This only proves that scientists are the tools of Satan, using the theory of evolution to spread vice and corruption everywhere. Never mind that many scientists see an evolving universe as an even more magnificent tribute to a Creator than a static one. They are lying, for only atheists "believe in" evolution. Salvation for us all lies in conversion to, or legal enforcement of, the biblical fundamentalists' tribal myth, with its unquestionable morals and mores.

The opposite extreme of religious fundamentalism is represented by 11 the "secular humanists." Their creed is the Humanist Manifesto, I and II. Since they are neither secular nor humanistic, in the traditional sense, and their basic premise seems to be that science has displaced religion as the only valid way of acquiring knowledge of the real world, a better name for them might be "scientistic fundamentalists." This group does not seem bent on proselytizing, perhaps because it assumes that those who can leave behind the religious myths (read "fantasies") of mankind's childhood will be limited to the enlightened few. Their biases appear as gratuitous snipes at religion, such as sometimes mar the otherwise lucid writings of Isaac Asimov.

A perfect metaphor for scientistic fundamentalism is the TV program, 12 *Cosmos*. Carl Sagan has managed to take good scientific material and present it as a religious trip through the heavens, in a cathedral-like ship, enveloped in ethereal lighting and filled with hushed, tremulous tones, interspersed with sophistic sneers at those religious myths of our ancestors which science has displaced. Here is the reverse image of biblical fundamentalism. In place of the biblical myth, the scientistic fundamentalists propose the "science-is-all" myth. Instead of denying the evidence for evolution, they would deny the evidence for the validity of religious experience and knowledge. They would reject the deepest realm of human inquiry. But the religious quest can no more be extinguished by their sneers than can the scientific quest by religious dogmatism.

Religious Fundamentalism, whether biblical, scientistic, or any other va- 13 riety, will be ever with us. It is rooted in the fundamentally religious nature of human persons. Our most primitive religious impulse is to get some measure of control over the mystery that surrounds our existence. We are frightened by our vulnerability. We want to be sure about our ultimate well-being, however we imagine our salvation. By contrast, the message of the Bible is that we are called to go beyond our fear-ridden religious impulses and surrender in faith to the God who made us. That God promises light and life at the end of our quest.

14   Religious leaders of the Judeo/Christian tradition would do the public a service by speaking out clearly against these false prophets, who offer certitudes and guarantees of salvation in place of that relationship with God, full of risk and uncertainty, that is biblical faith. They also might remind everyone that fidelity to the biblical Creator inspires an enthusiastic pursuit of scientific enquiry, not suspicion and condemnation.

15   Scientists, in turn, would be doing everyone a service if they would find ways to help the public understand just what it is they are doing and not doing when they are doing science. They need to make very clear which kinds of questions they can hope to answer and which they cannot, and why. They should refrain from giving the impression that scientific theories can prove religious beliefs, theistic or atheistic. And, they might caution those who would suggest that religious belief is necessarily opposed to science or is an outmoded approach which science has supplanted.

16   Religious fundamentalism is flourishing in our land, as elsewhere, because of the insecurity we are feeling in the wake of profound cultural changes. The information explosion of this century and rapid technological advances have made us unsure of things we once thought were unquestionable — and this at a time when we are challenged with increasingly complex kinds of ethical decisions. At the edge of our religious faith are some anxious doubts awakened by the new knowledge and by traumatic experience of evil on a global scale. And, beneath the excitement of our new conquests in science, there are some disquieting questions about whether our pursuits of meaning and happiness are absurd flounderings in a meaningless world, or whether there might, after all, be some ultimate source of meaning and value outside ourselves.

17   The fundamentalist grasp for absolutes is an understandable regression to the mythological security of the primitive tribe. It is a little like the ten-year-old, the first night in the new house, who clutches the old teddy bear to assuage his reawakened fears of the dark. We are all afraid of the dark. We need to stop whistling dissonant tunes at each other and turn on some lights!

18   Religious leaders, humanists, scientists, educators — all have a responsibility to help create a more intelligent and better informed American society. We cannot afford to lose our own or future generations to ignorance and bigotry. The challenge facing us in this age is to integrate a vast amount of new knowledge with authentic religious and moral values. We need to develop a new, rich self-image, one that can permeate the "brave new world" of our technology with human intelligence, freedom, and compassion. One powerful model for such an endeavor is the late French paleontologist theologian, Pierre Teilhard de Chardin, who presented cosmic evolution as an illuminating framework for science, humanism, and Christianity. "Scientific creationism," however, is a facile attempt at the needed integration. It will inevitably fail, because it is true neither to the new knowledge nor to the biblical faith it is trying to

preserve. But, it will have a far longer day in court because our schools have not produced citizens who can understand and think critically about the issues involved.

Rather than mandate the teaching of religion in science classes, school 19 boards would better serve our society by adopting more fruitful policies, such as: (1) making comparative religion a required subject rather than an elective; (2) insuring that scientific method be clearly explained in all science courses from the earliest grades; (3) incorporating into the curriculum at every level exercises in critical thinking and problem-solving. What is at stake is our survival and growth as a free, pluralistic society, dedicated to the cause of advancing humanity on this planet and beyond, without fear, in the presence of the living God.

TYPES OF WRITING:
analysis, comparison, definition, direct argument

Topics for Discussion

1. Why does Brennan begin her essay by reporting a recent incident? What effect might her opening paragraph have on the average reader?
2. "Evolution is not a religious issue any more than creation is a proper object of scientific investigation." Discuss this sentence as the key statement in the entire essay. Can any other sentence be chosen as the most important in Brennan's argument?
3. Consider Brennan's final sentence in the light of these questions: How does it serve as an adequate conclusion? Does it seem exaggerated, or is it very much appropriate? Has it persuaded you?
4. In paragraph 1 Brennan mentions the "popular misconceptions about religion and science." Which misconceptions has she clarified for you?
5. In paragraph 7 Brennan states this: "The crucial insight that is missing is that science and religion are different but complementary ways of knowing, each with its own language and rules." How important a part of her overall argument do you find this statement?
6. In dealing with this difficult problem, does Brennan present both sides fairly? Or is it clear that she is on one side or the other? Substantiate your answer by specific references.

Topics for Writing

1. Brennan has taken on a daunting task: in just a few pages she is trying to persuade the two sides in a widespread controversy that they must think far more clearly and precisely about their respective positions. Has she persuaded you? Your reply to this question should deal specifically with those points in her argument which you find most, or least, persuasive, and why.

2. Putting yourself in the place of a member of one of the two "fundamentalist" groups identified by Brennan, defend your position on creation versus evolution. Design your argument to reinforce the commitment of a sympathetic audience that has read Brennan's essay.

Suit, Ties Give Way to Polo Shirts, Loafers

Harry Bruce

Like the bartender's jacket, the mechanic's coveralls and the surgeon's 1
smock, the three-piece suit has long been a workingman's uniform, but a
rebellion against both it and the necktie has begun to sweep across North
America. More and more executives are showing up at the office dressed
for golf, nature trails, trout streams, chopping wood or mowing lawns.

The change has been sudden. As recently as 1990, Professor Arthur 2
Asa Berger, an American student of the hidden significance of underwear,
socks, shirts and ties, declared that the striped, vested three-piece suit
was still "the signifier of solemnity, status, reserve . . . the standard
costume of professional people who want to be taken seriously."

I took this as an insult. I had one grey suit, with no vest, and I wore 3
it about as often as the Toronto Maple Leafs made the playoffs. For
decades, my working costume as a writer and editor had been cotton
trousers and sweatshirts, and by what right did Berger exclude me from
the professionals who wanted to be taken seriously?

Nobody can write well dressed like a bank president. That superb 4
American fiction writer John Cheever, a professional who wanted to be
taken very seriously indeed, not only doffed his business suit when he
sat down at his typewriter, but stripped right down to his boxer shorts.

I also resented Berger's insisting the necktie served to "connect a 5
person with society, and to demonstrate that the person recognizes a
social order." If this were true, I was both a hermit and an anarchist.
While wearing a tie, I couldn't write a laundry list, much less a magazine
article. My policy on ties, which I violated only while making a speech to
chartered accountants, was to restrict my wearing of nooses to weddings
and funerals. I never went to funerals.

At last, I am respectable. Other professionals who want to be taken 6
seriously are scrambling to ape my sartorial style.

Consider what recently happened at L & F Products of Montvale, 7
N.J., manufacturer of Lysol, home permanents and other household goods.
When the air conditioning broke down, the company president, Michael
R. Gallagher, mercifully ruled that everyone could come to work in cotton
twill and polo shirts, and guess what?

"People's attitudes seemed to improve," Gallagher told the *New* 8
York Times. "There was more give-and-take, and our productivity
increased."

Even with the air conditioning fixed, L & F managers refused to go 9
back to their boring traditional uniforms. They went right on reporting
for work in their khakis, twills, and chambray shirts. They now boast a
look that the fashion industry has already dubbed "business casual." It
has led to a happier, more democratic atmosphere at L & F.

10   As Dominick Pisciotta, a senior product manager, put it, "People tend to forget about who's the boss and who's the employee when everyone is wearing loafers and polo shirts."

11   But L & F isn't the only outfit encouraging managers to wear "business casual." The marketing department of Citibank is experimenting with "casual days," and the executive offices of the aluminum giant Alcoa now have "the look."

12   Bruno Bich, the 45-year-old chairman of the BIC Corporation, maker of disposable pens, lighters, and shavers, says, "There's something strange about putting a tie around your windpipe." He and his engineers and salespeople now go to work as happily tieless as schoolboys.

13   The trend is so strong that sales of traditional suits are slumping badly, and many suit manufacturers have had to cut production. While profits of Brook Brothers dropped 50 percent in 1991, Levi Strauss & Company sold more casual twill trousers than ever before: $850 million worth.

14   One reason why suit sales are down is that, thanks to the recession, scads of lawyers, bankers and stockbrokers who once wore suits to signify their "solemnity, status, reserve" no longer have jobs. Another is that a pair of Levi's dockers pants, for example, sells for less than a 10th the price of the cheapest business suit. Moreover, Florida, Southern California and other steamy parts of the U.S. are gaining economic importance, and wearing a three-piece woollen suit in the Sun Belt is a sign not of solemnity but of madness.

15   If "business casual" leads to the rout of the traditional executive's uniform for men, they will owe much to the rise of women managers. With dresses, trousers and suits of their own — in all manner of light fabrics, breezy styles and splashy colors — women looked both more comfortable and more lively than the guys sweating out their days while swathed in hot, boring-looking suits, with ties knotted at their throats. The women led by example, and some men finally got wise.

16   Dressing in the style of "business casual" and at last free of the silken noose, many businessmen say they're more creative and productive than ever before. If they'd only strip down to their underwear at work, as Cheever did, their creative juices would flow so furiously that North America might soon dominate the entire world economy.

TYPES OF WRITING:
cause and effect, example/illustration, humour

Topics for Discussion

1. Why does Bruce introduce the business suit as a "uniform"?
2. How does Bruce diminish Professor Berger's authority as an expert?

3. John Cheever, we may safely assume, indulged in his habit of writing in his underwear mainly in the privacy of his home. Is Bruce's extension of his argument for informality in his final paragraph likely to strengthen or weaken the influential force of his article? Why?
4. Bruce is writing for a newspaper and, in the style of the medium, his paragraphs are short. Does this lack of development in paragraphs result in inadequately developed ideas?
5. Bruce supports his argument in favour of informal working clothes by reporting examples of the change. How might this approach, together with the news medium (a daily newspaper) in which the piece appears, assist him in influencing readers?

Topics for Writing

1. Write an essay arguing for the benefits of retaining traditional suits and ties in the workplace. One of your persuasive strategies should be to show how one-sided Bruce's views are.
2. Should students be allowed to dress as they please in the classroom? Your essay on this topic might consider the whole range of clothing, and it should deal with both sexes.

A Few Kind Words for Superstition

Robertson Davies

1   In grave discussions of "the renaissance of the irrational" in our time, superstition does not figure largely as a serious challenge to reason or science. Parapsychology, UFO's, miracle cures, transcendental meditation and all the paths to instant enlightenment are condemned, but superstition is merely deplored. Is it because it has an unacknowledged hold on so many of us?

2   Few people will admit to being superstitious; it implies naïveté or ignorance. But I live in the middle of a large university, and I see superstition in its four manifestations, alive and flourishing among people who are indisputably rational and learned.

3   You did not know that superstition takes four forms? Theologians assure us that it does. First is what they call Vain Observances, such as not walking under a ladder, and that kind of thing. Yet I saw a deeply learned professor of anthropology, who had spilled some salt, throwing a pinch of it over his left shoulder; when I asked him why, he replied, with a wink, that it was "to hit the Devil in the eye." I did not question him further about his belief in the Devil: but I noticed that he did not smile until I asked him what he was doing.

CONSULTING ORACLES

4   The second form is Divination, or consulting oracles. Another learned professor I know, who would scorn to settle a problem by tossing a coin (which is a humble appeal to Fate to declare itself), told me quite seriously that he had resolved a matter related to university affairs by consulting the *I Ching*. And why not? There are thousands of people on this continent who appeal to the *I Ching*, and their general level of education seems to absolve them of superstition. Almost, but not quite. The *I Ching*, to the embarrassment of rationalists, often gives excellent advice.

5   The third form is Idolatry, and universities can show plenty of that. If you have ever supervised a large examination room, you know how many jujus, lucky coins and other bringers of luck are placed on the desks of the candidates. Modest idolatry, but what else can you call it?

6   The fourth form is Improper Worship of the True God. A while ago, I learned that every day, for several days, a $2 bill (in Canada we have $2 bills, regarded by some people as unlucky) had been tucked under a candlestick on the altar of a college chapel. Investigation revealed that an engineering student, worried about a girl, thought that bribery of the Deity might help. When I talked with him, he did not think he was pricing God cheap, because he could afford no more. A reasonable argument, but perhaps God was proud that week, for the scientific oracle went against him.

48

TERROR OF THE DEITY

Superstition seems to run, a submerged river of crude religion, below   7
the surface of human consciousness. It has done so for as long as we
have any chronicle of human behavior, and although I cannot prove it, I
doubt if it is more prevalent today than it has always been. Superstition,
the theologians tell us, comes from the Latin *supersisto*, meaning to stand
in terror of the Deity. Most people keep their terror within bounds, but
they cannot root it out, nor do they seem to want to do so.

The more the teaching of formal religion declines, or takes a socio-   8
logical form, the less God appears to great numbers of people as a God
of Love, resuming his older form of a watchful, minatory power, to be
placated and cajoled. Superstition makes its appearance, apparently
unbidden, very early in life, when children fear that stepping on cracks
in the sidewalk will bring ill fortune. It may persist even among the
greatly learned and devout, as in the case of Dr. Samuel Johnson, who
felt it necessary to touch posts that he passed in the street. The psycho-
analysts have their explanation, but calling a superstition a compulsion
neurosis does not banish it.

Many superstitions are so widespread and so old that they must   9
have risen from a depth of the human mind that is indifferent to race or
creed. Orthodox Jews place a charm on their doorposts; so do (or did)
the Chinese. Some peoples of Middle Europe believe that when a man
sneezes, his soul, for that moment, is absent from his body, and they
hasten to bless him, lest the soul be seized by the Devil. How did the
Melanesians come by the same idea? Superstition seems to have a link
with some body of belief that far antedates the religions we know —
religions which have no place for such comforting little ceremonies and
charities.

People who like disagreeable historical comparisons recall that when   10
Rome was in decline, superstition proliferated wildly, and that something
of the same sort is happening in our Western world today. They point to
the popularity of astrology, and it is true that sober newspapers that
would scorn to deal in love philters carry astrology columns and the
fashion magazines count them among their most popular features. But
when has astrology not been popular? No use saying science discredits
it. When has the heart of man given a damn for science?

Superstition in general is linked to man's yearning to know his fate,   11
and to have some hand in deciding it. When my mother was a child, she
innocently joined her Roman Catholic friends in killing spiders on July
11, until she learned that this was done to ensure heavy rain the day
following, the anniversary of the Battle of the Boyne, when the Orangemen
would hold their parade. I knew an Italian, a good scientist, who watched
every morning before leaving his house, so that the first person he met
would not be a priest or a nun, as this would certainly bring bad luck.

THE LUCKY BABY

12 I am not one to stand aloof from the rest of humanity in this matter, for when I was a university student, a gypsy woman with a child in her arms used to appear every year at examination time, and ask a shilling of anyone who touched the Lucky Baby; that swarthy infant cost me four shillings altogether, and I never failed an examination. Of course, I did it merely for the joke — or so I thought then. Now, I am humbler.

TYPES OF WRITING:
classification, definition, example/illustration, humour

Topics for Discussion

1. Is Davies especially interested in reaching conventionally religious readers in this essay? Why or why not? If not, why would Davies draw on theologians in his explanation of what superstition is?
2. With the help of a good dictionary, consider Davies's use of the words "condemned" and "deplored" in his opening paragraph. How is this distinction appropriate to the concluding sentence of the paragraph?
3. Davies makes a convincing case that the "comforting little ceremonies and charities" of superstition serve a human need. Is his related view, that conventional religions fail to serve this need, equally convincing? Why or why not?
4. In the middle of his essay, Davies muses, "The more the teaching of formal religion declines, or takes a sociological form, the less God appears to great numbers of people as a God of Love, resuming his older form of a watchful, minatory power, to be placated and cajoled." How does Davies relate this idea to the rest of his essay in support of his premise that superstition is an ingrained, even necessary, aspect of human nature?

Topics for Writing

1. To strengthen his claim that astrology is immune to scientific discredit, Davies asks a rhetorical question: "When has the heart of man given a damn for science?" Write an essay arguing that "the heart of man," or woman, can care just as much about science as about superstition.
2. Write an essay arguing that scientific understanding, either of the physical world or of human society, need not undermine religious faith.

The Hurled Ashtray

Nora Ephron

I once heard a swell story about Gary Cooper. The person I heard the   1
story from did this terrific Gary Cooper imitation, and it may be that
when I tell you the story (which I am about to), it will lose something in
print. It may lose everything, in fact. But enough. The story was that
Gary Cooper was in a London restaurant at a large table of friends. He
was sitting in a low chair, with his back to the rest of the room, so no one
in the restaurant even knew that he was tall, much less that he was Gary
Cooper. Across the way was a group of Teddy boys (this episode took
place long long ago, you see), and they were all misbehaving and making nasty remarks about a woman at Cooper's table. Cooper turned
around to give them his best mean-and-threatening stare, but they went
right on. Finally he got up, very very slowly, so slowly that it took
almost a minute for him to go from this short person in a low chair to a
ten-foot-tall man with Gary Cooper's head on top of his shoulders. He
loped over to the table of Teddy boys, looked down at them, and said,
"Wouldja mind sayin' that agin?" The men were utterly cowed and left
the restaurant shortly thereafter.

Well, you had to be there.   2

I thought of Gary Cooper and his way with words the other day.   3
Longingly. Because in the mail, from an editor of *New York* magazine,
came an excerpt from a book by Michael Korda called *Male Chauvinism:
How It Works* (Random House). I have no idea whether Korda's book is
any good at all, but the excerpt was fascinating, a sort of reverse-twist
update on Francis Macomber, as well as a pathetic contrast to the Gary
Cooper story. It seems that Korda, his wife, and another woman were
having dinner in a London restaurant recently. Across the way was a
table of drunks doing sensitive things like sniggering and leering and
throwing bread balls at Mrs. Korda, who is a looker. Her back was
to them, and she refused to acknowledge their presence, instead apparently choosing to let the flying bread balls bounce off her back onto the
floor. Then, one of the men sent over a waiter with a silver tray. On it
was a printed card, the kind you can buy in novelty shops, which read:
"I want to sleep with you! Tick off your favorite love position from the
list below, and return this card with your telephone number . . . ." Korda
tore up the card before his wife could even see it, and then, consumed
with rage, he picked up an ashtray and threw it at the man who had sent
the card. A fracas ensued, and before long, Korda, his wife, and their
woman friend were out on the street. Mrs. Korda was furious.

"If you ever do that again," she screamed, "I'll leave you! Do you   4
think I couldn't have handled that, or ignored it? Did I ask you to come
to my defense against some poor stupid drunk? You didn't even think,
you just reacted like a male chauvinist. You leapt up to defend *your*
woman, *your* honor, you made me seem cheap and foolish and power-

51

less. . . . God Almighty, can't you see it was none of your business! Can't you understand how it makes me feel? I don't mind being hassled by some drunk, I can take that, but to be treated like a chattel, to be robbed of any right to decide for myself whether I'd been insulted, or how badly, to have you react for me because I'm *your* woman . . . that's really sickening, it's like being a slave." Korda repeats the story (his wife's diatribe is even longer in the original version) and then, in a *mea culpa* that is only too reminiscent of the sort that used to appear in 1960s books by white liberals about blacks, he concludes that his wife is doubtless right, that men do tend to treat women merely as appendages of themselves.

5   Before printing the article, *New York* asked several couples — including my husband and me — what our reaction was to what happened, and what we would have done under the circumstances. My initial reaction to the entire business was that no one ever sends me notes like that in restaurants. I sent that off to the editor, but a few days later I got to thinking about the story, and it began to seem to me that the episode just might be a distillation of everything that has happened to men and women as a result of the women's movement, and if not that, at least a way to write about etiquette after the revolution, and if not that, nothing at all. Pulled as I was by these three possibilities, I told the story over dinner to four friends and asked for their reaction. The first, a man, said that he thought Mrs. Korda was completely right. The second, a woman, said she thought Korda's behavior was totally understandable. The third, a man, said that both parties had behaved badly. The fourth, my friend Martha, said it was the second most boring thing she had ever heard, the most boring being a story I had just told her about a fight my college roommate had with a cabdriver at Kennedy Airport.

6   In any case, before any serious discussion of the incident of the hurled ashtray, I would like to raise some questions for which I have no answers. I raise them simply because if that story were fed into a computer, the only possible response it could make is We Do Not Have Sufficient Information To Make An Evaluation. For example:

7   Do the Kordas have a good marriage?

8   Was the heat working in their London hotel room the night of the fracas?

9   Was it raining out?

10   What did the second woman at the table look like? Was she as pretty as Mrs. Korda? Was she ugly? Was part of Michael Korda's reaction — and his desire to assert possession of his wife — the result of the possibility that he suspected the drunks thought he was with someone funny-looking?

11   What kind of a tacky restaurant is it where a waiter delivers a dirty message on a silver tray?

12   What about a woman who ignores flying bread balls? Wasn't her husband justified in thinking she would be no more interested in novelty cards?

Did Michael Korda pay the check before or after throwing the ash- 13
tray? Did he tip the standard 15 percent?

Since the incident occurs in London, a city notorious for its rampant 14
homoerotic behavior, and since the table of drunks was all male, isn't it
possible that the printed card was in fact intended not for Mrs. Korda but
for Michael? In which case how should we now view his response, if at all?

There might be those who would raise questions about the ashtray 15
itself: was it a big, heavy ashtray, these people might ask, or a dinky little
round one? Was it glass or was it plastic? These questions are irrelevant.

In the absence of answers to any of the above, I would nonetheless 16
like to offer some random musings. First, I think it is absurd for Mrs.
Korda to think that she and she alone was involved in the incident. Yes,
it might have been nice had her husband consulted her; and yes, it
would have been even nicer had he turned out to be Gary Cooper, or failing
that, Dave Debusschere, or even Howard Cosell — anyone but this suave
flinger of ashtrays he turned out to be. But the fact remains that the men
at the table *were* insulting Korda, and disturbing his dinner, as well as
hers. Their insult was childish and Korda's reaction was ludicrous, but
Mrs. Korda matched them all by reducing a complicated and rather
interesting emotional situation to a tedious set of movement platitudes.

Beyond that — and the Kordas quite aside, because God Almighty 17
(as Mrs. Korda might put it) knows what it is they are into — I wonder
whether there is any response a man could make in that situation which
would not disappoint a feminist. Yes, I want to be treated as an equal
and not as an appendage or possession or spare rib, but I also want to be
taken care of. Isn't any man sitting at a table with someone like me
damned whatever he does? If the drunks in question are simply fools,
conventioneers with funny paper hats, I suppose that a possible reaction
would be utter cool. But if they were truly insulting and disturbing,
some response does seem called for. Some wild and permanent gesture
of size. But on whose part? And what should it consist of? And how tall
do you have to be to bring it off? And where is the point that a mild
show of strength becomes crude macho vulgarity; where does reserve
veer off into passivity?

Like almost every other question in this column, I have no positive 18
answer. But I think that if I ever found myself in a similar situation, and
if it was truly demeaning, I would prefer that my husband handle it. My
husband informs me, after some consideration, that the Gary Cooper
approach would not work. But he could, for example, call over the captain
and complain discreetly, perhaps even ask that our table be moved. He
could hire a band of aging Teddy boys to find out where the drunks
were staying and short-sheet all their beds. Or — and I think I prefer this
— he could produce, from his jacket pocket, a printed card from a novelty shop reading: "I'm terribly sorry, but as you can see by looking at
our dinner companion, my wife and I have other plans."

I'm going out to have those cards made up right now. 19

TYPES OF WRITING:
analysis, humour, narration, personal experience

Topics for Discussion

1. What audience might Ephron have hoped to influence with this essay when it was written in 1973?
2. Where in "The Hurled Ashtray" does Ephron most plainly reveal her reaction to Mr. and Mrs. Korda's understanding of correct behaviour in the incident around which the essay is built? Why does she not make her feelings plain at the start of the essay?
3. How does Ephron prepare the reader for her critical reaction to the Kordas' views of appropriate roles?
4. Look carefully at paragraph 18, especially the first line, and at the final one-sentence paragraph. What do they reveal about Ephron's attitude towards her subject?
5. What is the main point that Ephron is trying to make to her readers? To what extent, if at all, has she persuaded you?

Topic for Writing

1. Assuming either the male or the female role in the kind of embarrassing situation in which the Kordas found themselves (or any other similarly awkward situation), how would you react? Your essay should describe the situation itself, how you would behave, and, especially, the reasons for your approach.

Revision and Life

Nora Ephron

I have been asked to write something for a textbook that is meant to teach college students something about writing and revision. I am happy to do this because I believe in revision. I have also been asked to save the early drafts of whatever I write, presumably to show these students the actual process of revision. This too I am happy to do. On the other hand, I suspect that there is just so much you can teach college students about revision; a gift for revision may be a developmental stage — like a 2-year-old's sudden ability to place one block on top of another — that comes along somewhat later, in one's mid-20's, say; most people may not be particularly good at it, or even interested in it, until then.

When I was in college, I revised nothing. I wrote out my papers in longhand, typed them up and turned them in. It would never have crossed my mind that what I had produced was only a first draft and that I had more work to do; the idea was to get to the end, and once you had got to the end you were finished. The same thinking, I might add, applied in life: I went pell-mell through my four years in college without a thought about whether I ought to do anything differently; the idea was to get to the end— to get out of school and become a journalist.

Which I became, in fairly short order. I learned as a journalist to revise on deadline. I learned to write an article a paragraph at a time — and to turn it in a paragraph at a time — and I arrived at the kind of writing and revising I do, which is basically a kind of typing and retyping. I am a great believer in this technique for the simple reason that I type faster than the wind. What I generally do is to start an article and get as far as I can — sometimes no farther in than a sentence or two — before running out of steam, ripping the piece of paper from the typewriter and starting all over again. I type over and over until I have got the beginning of the piece to the point where I am happy with it. I then am ready to plunge into the body of the article itself. This plunge usually requires something known as a transition. I approach a transition by completely retyping the opening of the article leading up to it in the hope that the ferocious speed of my typing will somehow catapult me into the next section of the piece. This does not work — what in fact catapults me into the next section is a concrete thought about what the next section ought to be about — but until I have the thought the typing keeps me busy, and keeps me from feeling something known as blocked.

Typing and retyping as if you know where you're going is a version of what therapists tell you to do when they suggest that you try changing from the outside in — that if you can't master the total commitment to whatever change you want to make, you can at least do all the extraneous things connected with it, which make it that much easier to get there. I was 25 years old the first time a therapist suggested that I try changing from the outside in. In those days, I used to spend quite a lot of time lying awake at night wondering what I should have said earlier in the evening and revising my lines. I mention this not just because it's a way of illustrating that a gift for revision is practically instinctive, but also (once again) because it's possible that a genuine ability at it doesn't really come into play until one is older — or at least older than 25, when it seemed to me that all that was required in my life and my work was the chance to change a few lines.

5   In my 30's, I began to write essays, one a month for *Esquire* magazine, and I am not exaggerating when I say that in the course of writing a short essay — 1,500 words, that's only six double-spaced typewritten pages — I often used 300 or 400 pieces of typing paper, so often did I type and retype and catapult and recatapult myself, sometimes on each retyping moving not even a sentence farther from the spot I had reached the last time through. At the same time, though, I was polishing what I had already written: as I struggled with the middle of the article, I kept putting the beginning through the typewriter; as I approached the ending, the middle got its turn. (This is a kind of polishing that the word processor all but eliminates, which is why I don't use one. Word processors make it possible for a writer to change the sentences that clearly need changing without having to retype the rest, but I believe that you can't always tell whether a sentence needs work until it rises up in revolt against your fingers as you retype it.) By the time I had produced what you might call a first draft — an entire article with a beginning, middle and end — the beginning was in more like 45th draft, the middle in 20th, and the end was almost newborn. For this reason, the beginnings of my essays are considerably better written than the ends, although I like to think no one ever notices this but me.

6   As I learned the essay form, writing became harder for me. I was finding a personal style, a voice if you will, a way of writing that looked chatty and informal. That wasn't the hard part — the hard part was that having found a voice, I had to work hard month to month not to seem as if I were repeating myself. At this point in this essay it will not surprise you to learn that the same sort of thing was operating in my life. I don't mean that my life had become harder — but that it was becoming clear that I had many more choices than had occurred to me when I was marching through my 20's. I no longer lost sleep over what I should have said. Not that I didn't care — it was just that I had moved to a new plane of late-night anxiety: I now wondered what I should have done. Whole areas of possible revision opened before me. What should I have done instead? What could I have done? What if I hadn't done it the way I did? What if I had a chance to do it over? What if I had a chance to do it over as a different person? These were the sorts of questions that kept me awake and led me into fiction, which at the very least (the level at which I practice it) is a chance to rework the events of your life so that you give the illusion of being the intelligence at the center of

it, simultaneously managing to slip in all the lines that occurred to you later. Fiction, I suppose, is the ultimate shot at revision.

Now I am in my 40's and I write screenplays. Screenplays — if they 7 are made into movies — are essentially collaborations, and movies are not a writer's medium, we all know this, and I don't want to dwell on the craft of screenwriting except insofar as it relates to revision. Because the moment you stop work on a script seems to be determined not by whether you think the draft is good but simply by whether shooting is about to begin: if it is, you get to call your script a final draft; and if it's not, you can always write another revision. This might seem to be a hateful way to live, but the odd thing is that it's somehow comforting; as long as you're revising, the project isn't dead. And by the same token, neither are you.

It was, as it happens, while thinking about all this one recent sleep- 8 less night that I figured out how to write this particular essay. I say "recent" in order to give a sense of immediacy and energy to the preceding sentence, but the truth is that I am finishing this article four months after the sleepless night in question, and the letter asking me to write it, from George Miller of the University of Delaware, arrived almost two years ago, so for all I know Mr. Miller has managed to assemble his textbook on revision without me.

Oh, well. That's how it goes when you start thinking about revision. 9 That's the danger of it, in fact. You can spend so much time thinking about how to switch things around that the main event has passed you by. But it doesn't matter. Because by the time you reach middle age, you want more than anything for things not to come to an end; and as long as you're still revising, they don't.

I'm sorry to end so morbidly — dancing as I am around the subject 10 of death — but there are advantages to it. For one thing, I have managed to move fairly effortlessly and logically from the beginning of this piece through the middle and to the end. And for another, I am able to close with an exhortation, something I rarely manage, which is this: Revise now, before it's too late.

TYPES OF WRITING
example/illustration, personal experience

Topics for Discussion

1. In her opening sentence Ephron says she has been asked to write "something" to teach students "something" by an unspecified party. Why does Ephron provide so little detail? How does this note of vagueness and ambiguity prepare the reader for what follows?

2. Ephron's account of her own methods of revision, which require "typ-

ing like the wind" and, in the case of this essay, two years to revise, seems calculated to show that revision can be highly idiosyncratic, a reflection of an individual's personality as much as a technique to be recorded in a textbook for imitation. What practical points does she make about revision, notwithstanding her personal approach?

3. In the course of her essay, Ephron refers to revision as "a developmental stage" and a gift that is "practically instinctive." Do such speculations suggest that Ephron believes that the ability to revise efficiently cannot be learned by the average young writer?

4. Throughout her essay, Ephron associates revision with maturity. How might this association affect the audience of college students for whom her essay is, ostensibly at least, intended?

Topics for Writing

1. In discussing the stages in her progression as a writer, Ephron mentions some psychological parallels to revision, such as revision and maturity, and revision and therapy. Discuss these parallels in your own development as a writer.

2. Write an essay about the effects of Ephron's recurring practice of volunteering unflattering information about herself. Do you see this as a rhetorical tactic or a habit of mind? Support your views with specific references to her two essays in this textbook.

The Motive for Metaphor

Northrop Frye

For the past twenty-five years I have been teaching and studying English 1
literature in a university. As in any other job, certain questions stick in
one's mind, not because people keep asking them, but because they're
the questions inspired by the very fact of being in such a place. What
good is the study of literature? Does it help us to think more clearly, or
feel more sensitively, or live a better life than we could without it? What
is the function of the teacher and scholar, or of the person who calls
himself, as I do, a literary critic? What difference does the study of literature make in our social or political or religious attitude? In my early
days I thought very little about such questions, not because I had any of
the answers, but because I assumed that anybody who asked them was
naïve. I think now that the simplest questions are not only the hardest to
answer, but the most important to ask, so I'm going to raise them and try
to suggest what my present answers are. I say try to suggest, because
there are only more or less inadequate answers to such questions —
there aren't any right answers. The kind of problem that literature raises
is not the kind that you ever 'solve'. Whether my answers are any good
or not, they represent a fair amount of thinking about the questions. As I
can't see my audience, I have to choose my rhetorical style in the dark,
and I'm taking the classroom style, because an audience of students is
the one I feel easiest with.

There are two things in particular that I want to discuss with you. In 2
school, and in university, there's a subject called 'English' in English-
speaking countries. English means, in the first place, the mother tongue.
As that, it's the most practical subject in the world: you can't understand
anything or take any part in your society without it. Wherever illiteracy
is a problem, it's as fundamental a problem as getting enough to eat or a
place to sleep. The native language takes precedence over every other
subject of study: nothing else can compare with it in usefulness. But then
you find that every mother tongue, in any developed or civilized society,
turns into something called literature. If you keep on studying 'English',
you find yourself trying to read Shakespeare and Milton. Literature,
we're told, is one of the arts, along with painting and music, and, after
you've looked up all the hard words and the Classical allusions and
learned what words like imagery and diction are supposed to mean,
what you use in understanding it, or so you're told, is your imagination.
Here you don't seem to be in quite the same practical and useful area:
Shakespeare and Milton, whatever their merits, are not the kind of thing
you must know to hold any place in society at all. A person who knows
nothing about literature may be an ignoramus, but many people don't
mind being that. Every child realizes that literature is taking him in a
different direction from the immediately useful, and a good many children complain loudly about this. Two questions I want to deal with,

then, are, first: what is the relation of English as the mother tongue to English as a literature? Second: what is the social value of the study of literature, and what is the place of the imagination that literature addresses itself to, in the learning process?

3   Let's start with the different ways there are of dealing with the world we're living in. Suppose you're shipwrecked on an uninhabited island in the South Seas. The first thing you do is to take a long look at the world around you, a world of sky and sea and earth and stars and trees and hills. You see this world as objective, as something set over against you and not yourself or related to you in any way. And you notice two things about this objective world. In the first place, it doesn't have any conversation. It's full of animals and plants and insects going on with their own business, but there's nothing that responds to you: it has no morals and no intelligence, or at least none that you can grasp. It may have a shape and a meaning, but it doesn't seem to be a human shape or a human meaning. Even if there's enough to eat and no dangerous animals, you feel lonely and frightened and unwanted in such a world.

4   In the second place, you find that looking at the world, as something set over against you, splits your mind in two. You have an intellect that feels curious about it and wants to study it, and you have feelings or emotions that see it as beautiful or austere or terrible. You know that both these attitudes have some reality, at least for you. If the ship you were wrecked in was a Western ship, you'd probably feel that your intellect tells you more about what's really there in the outer world, and that your emotions tell you more about what's going on inside you. If your background were Oriental, you'd be more likely to reverse this and say that the beauty or terror was what was really there, and that your instinct to count and classify and measure and pull to pieces was what was inside your mind. But whether your point of view is Western or Eastern, intellect and emotion never get together in your mind as long as you're simply looking at the world. They alternate, and keep you divided between them.

5   The language you use on this level of the mind is the language of consciousness or awareness. It's largely a language of nouns and adjectives. You have to have names for things, and you need qualities like 'wet' or 'green' or 'beautiful' to describe how things seem to you. This is the speculative or contemplative position of the mind, the position in which the arts and sciences begin, although they don't stay there very long. The sciences begin by accepting the facts and the evidence about an outside world without trying to alter them. Science proceeds by accurate measurement and description, and follows the demands of the reason rather than the emotions. What it deals with is there, whether we like it or not. The emotions are unreasonable: for them it's what they like and don't like that comes first. We'd be naturally inclined to think that the arts follow the path of emotion, in contrast to the sciences. Up to a point they do, but there's a complicating factor.

That complicating factor is the contrast between 'I like this' and 'I   6
don't like this'. In this Robinson Crusoe life I've assigned you, you may
have moods of complete peacefulness and joy, moods when you accept
your island and everything around you. You wouldn't have such moods
very often, and when you had them, they'd be moods of identification,
when you felt that the island was a part of you and you a part of it. That
is not the feeling of consciousness or awareness, where you feel split off
from everything that's not your perceiving self. Your habitual state of
mind is the feeling of separation which goes with being conscious, and
the feeling 'this is not a part of me' soon becomes 'this is not what I
want'. Notice the word 'want': we'll be coming back to it.

  So you soon realize that there's a difference between the world you're   7
living in and the world you want to live in. The world you want to live
in is a human world, not an objective one: it's not an environment but a
home; it's not the world you see but the world you build out of what
you see. You go to work to build a shelter or plant a garden, and as soon
as you start to work you've moved into a different level of human life.
You're not separating only yourself from nature now, but constructing a
human world and separating it from the rest of the world. Your intellect
and emotions are now both engaged in the same activity, so there's no
longer any real distinction between them. As soon as you plant a garden
or a crop, you develop the conception of a 'weed', the plant you don't
want in there. But you can't say that 'weed' is either an intellectual or an
emotional conception, because it's both at once. Further, you go to work
because you feel you have to, and because you want something at the
end of the work. That means that the important categories of your life
are no longer the subject and the object, the watcher and the things being
watched: the important categories are what you have to do and what
you want to do — in other words, necessity and freedom.

  One person by himself is not a complete human being, so I'll provide   8
you with another shipwrecked refugee of the opposite sex and an eventual
family. Now you're a member of a human society. This human society
after a while will transform the island into something with a human
shape. What that human shape is, is revealed in the shape of the work
you do: the buildings, such as they are, the paths through the woods, the
planted crops fenced off against whatever animals want to eat them.
These things, these rudiments of city, highway, garden and farm, are the
human form of nature, or the form of human nature, whichever you like.
This is the area of the applied arts and sciences, and it appears in our
society as engineering and agriculture and medicine and architecture. In
this area we can never say clearly where the art stops and the science
begins, or vice versa.

  The language you use on this level is the language of practical sense,   9
a language of verbs or words of action and movement. The practical
world, however, is a world where actions speak louder than words. In
some ways it's a higher level of existence than the speculative level,

because it's doing something about the world instead of just looking at it, but in itself it's a much more primitive level. It's the process of adapting to the environment, or rather of transforming the environment in the interests of one species, that goes on among animals and plants as well as human beings. The animals have a good many of our practical skills: some insects make pretty fair architects, and beavers know quite a lot about engineering. In this island, probably, and certainly if you were alone, you'd have about the ranking of a second-rate animal. What makes our practical life really human is a third level of the mind, a level where consciousness and practical skill come together.

10   This third level is a vision or model in your mind of what you want to construct. There's that word 'want' again. The actions of man are prompted by desire, and some of these desires are needs, like food and warmth and shelter. One of these needs is sexual, the desire to reproduce and bring more human beings into existence. But there's also a desire to bring a social human form into existence: the form of cities and gardens and farms that we call civilization. Many animals and insects have this social form too, but man knows that he has it: he can compare what he does with what he can imagine being done. So we begin to see where the imagination belongs in the scheme of human affairs. It's the power of constructing possible models of human experience. In the world of the imagination, anything goes that's imaginatively possible, but nothing really happens. If it did happen, it would move out of the world of imagination into the world of action.

11   We have three levels of the mind now, and a language for each of them, which in English-speaking societies means an English for each of them. There's the level of consciousness and awareness, where the most important thing is the difference between me and everything else. The English of this level is the English of ordinary conversation, which is mostly monologue, as you'll soon realize if you do a bit of eavesdropping, or listening to yourself. We can call it the language of self-expression. Then there's the level of social participation, the working or technological language of teachers and preachers and politicians and advertisers and lawyers and journalists and scientists. We've already called this the language of practical sense. Then there's the level of imagination, which produces the literary language of poems and plays and novels. They're not really different languages, of course, but three different reasons for using words.

12   On this basis, perhaps, we can distinguish the arts from the sciences. Science begins with the world we have to live in, accepting its data and trying to explain its laws. From there, it moves towards the imagination: it becomes a mental construct, a model of a possible way of interpreting experience. The further it goes in this direction, the more it tends to speak the language of mathematics, which is really one of the languages of the imagination, along with literature and music. Art, on the other hand, begins with the world we construct, not with the world we see. It

starts with the imagination, and then works towards ordinary experience: that is, it tries to make itself as convincing and recognizable as it can. You can see why we tend to think of the sciences as intellectual and the arts as emotional: one starts with the world as it is, the other with the world we want to have. Up to a point it is true that science gives an intellectual view of reality, and that the arts try to make the emotions as precise and disciplined as sciences do the intellect. But of course it's nonsense to think of the scientist as a cold unemotional reasoner and the artist as somebody who's in a perpetual emotional tizzy. You can't distinguish the arts from the sciences by the mental processes the people in them use: they both operate on a mixture of hunch and common sense. A highly developed science and a highly developed art are very close together, psychologically and otherwise.

Still, the fact that they start from opposite ends, even if they do meet   13 in the middle, makes for one important difference between them. Science learns more and more about the world as it goes on: it evolves and improves. A physicist today knows more physics than Newton did, even if he's not as great a scientist. But literature begins with the possible model of experience, and what it produces is the literary model we call the classic. Literature doesn't evolve or improve or progress. We may have dramatists in the future who will write plays as good as *King Lear*, though they'll be very different ones, but drama as a whole will never get better than *King Lear*. *King Lear* is it, as far as drama is concerned; so is *Oedipus Rex*, written two thousand years earlier than that, and both will be models of dramatic writing as long as the human race endures. Social conditions may improve: most of us would rather live in nineteenth-century United States than in thirteenth-century Italy, and for most of us Whitman's celebration of democracy makes a lot more sense than Dante's Inferno. But it doesn't follow that Whitman is a better poet than Dante: literature won't line up with that kind of improvement.

So we find that everything that does improve, including science,   14 leaves the literary artist out in the cold. Writers don't seem to benefit much by the advance of science, although they thrive on superstitions of all kinds. And you certainly wouldn't turn to contemporary poets for guidance or leadership in the twentieth-century world. You'd hardly go to Ezra Pound, with his fascism and social credit and Confucianism and anti-semitism. Or to Yeats, with his spiritualism and fairies and astrology. Or to D. H. Lawrence, who'll tell you that it's a good thing for servants to be flogged because that restores the precious current of blood-reciprocity between servant and master. Or to T. S. Eliot, who'll tell you that to have a flourishing culture we should educate an élite, keep most people living in the same spot, and never disestablish the Church of England. The novelists seem to be a little closer to the world they're living in, but not much. When Communists talk about the decadence of bourgeois culture, this is the kind of thing they always bring up. Their own writers don't seem to be any better, though; just duller. So the real question is a bigger one. Is it possible that literature, especially poetry, is something that a scientific civilization like ours will eventually outgrow? Man has always wanted to fly, and thousands of years ago he was making sculptures of winged bulls and telling stories about people who flew so high on artificial wings that the sun melted them off. In an Indian play fifteen hundred years old, *Sakuntala*, there's a god who flies around in a chariot that to a modern reader sounds very much like a private aeroplane. Interesting that the writer had so much imagination, but do we need such stories now that we have private aeroplanes?

15   This is not a new question: it was raised a hundred and fifty years ago by Thomas Love Peacock, who was a poet and novelist himself, and a very brilliant one. He wrote an essay called *Four Ages of Poetry*, with his tongue of course in his cheek, in which he said that poetry was the mental rattle that awakened the imagination of mankind in its infancy, but that now, in an age of science and technology, the poet has outlived his social function. 'A poet in our times,' said Peacock, 'is a semi-barbarian in a civilized community. He lives in the days that are past. His ideas, thoughts, feelings, associations, are all with barbarous manners, obsolete customs, and exploded superstitions. The march of his intellect is like that of a crab, backwards.' Peacock's essay annoyed his friend Shelley, who wrote another essay called *A Defence of Poetry* to refute it. Shelley's essay is a wonderful piece of writing, but it's not likely to convince anyone who needs convincing. I shall be spending a good deal of my time on this question of the relevance of literature in the world of today, and I can only indicate the general lines my answer will take. There are two points I can make now, one simple, the other more difficult.

16   The simple point is that literature belongs to the world man constructs, not to the world he sees; to his home, not his environment. Literature's world is a concrete human world of immediate experience. The poet uses images and objects and sensations much more than he uses abstract ideas; the novelist is concerned with telling stories, not with working out arguments. The world of literature is human in shape, a world where the sun rises in the east and sets in the west over the edge of a flat earth in three dimensions, where the primary realities are not atoms or electrons but bodies, and the primary forces not energy or gravitation but love and death and passion and joy. It's not surprising if writers are often rather simple people, not always what we think of as intellectuals, and certainly not always any freer of silliness or perversity than anyone else. What concerns us is what they produce, not what they are, and poetry, according to Milton, who ought to have known, is 'more simple, sensuous and passionate' than philosophy or science.

17   The more difficult point takes us back to what we said when we were on that South Sea island. Our emotional reaction to the world varies from 'I like this' to 'I don't like this'. The first, we said, was a state of identity, a feeling that everything around us was part of us, and the second is the ordinary state of consciousness, or separation, where art

and science begin. Art begins as soon as 'I don't like this' turns into 'this is not the way I could imagine it'. We notice in passing that the creative and the neurotic minds have a lot in common. They're both dissatisfied with what they see; they both believe that something else ought to be there, and they try to pretend it is there or to make it be there. The differences are more important, but we're not ready for them yet.

At the level of ordinary consciousness the individual man is the 18 centre of everything, surrounded on all sides by what he isn't. At the level of practical sense, or civilization, there's a human circumference, a little cultivated world with a human shape, fenced off from the jungle and inside the sea and the sky. But in the imagination anything goes that can be imagined, and the limit of the imagination is a totally human world. Here we recapture, in full consciousness, that original lost sense of identity with our surroundings, where there is nothing outside the mind of man, or something identical with the mind of man. Religions present us with visions of eternal and infinite heavens or paradises which have the form of the cities and gardens of human civilization, like the Jerusalem and Eden of the Bible, completely separated from the state of frustration and misery that bulks so large in ordinary life. We're not concerned with these visions as religion, but they indicate what the limits of the imagination are. They indicate too that in the human world the imagination has no limits, if you follow me. We said that the desire to fly produced the aeroplane. But people don't get into planes because they want to fly; they get into planes because they want to get somewhere else faster. What's produced the aeroplane is not so much a desire to fly as a rebellion against the tyranny of time and space. And that's a process that can never stop, no matter how high our Titovs and Glenns may go.

For each of these six talks I've taken a title from some work of 19 literature, and my title for this one is 'The Motive for Metaphor', from a poem of Wallace Stevens. Here's the poem:

You like it under the trees in autumn,
Because everything is half dead.
The wind moves like a cripple among the leaves
And repeats words without meaning.

In the same way, you were happy in spring,
With the half colors of quarter-things,
The slightly brighter sky, the melting clouds,
The single bird, the obscure moon —

The obscure moon lighting an obscure world
Of things that would never be quite expressed,
Where you yourself were never quite yourself
And did not want nor have to be,

> Desiring the exhilarations of changes:
> The motive for metaphor, shrinking from
> The weight of primary noon,
> The A B C of being,
>
> The ruddy temper, the hammer
> Of red and blue, the hard sound —
> Steel against intimation — the sharp flash,
> The vital, arrogant, fatal, dominant X.

What Stevens calls the weight of primary noon, the A B C of being, and the dominant X is the objective world, the world set over against us. Outside literature, the main motive for writing is to describe this world. But literature itself uses language in a way which associates our minds with it. As soon as you use associative language, you begin using figures of speech. If you say this talk is dry and dull, you're using figures associating it with bread and breadknives. There are two main kinds of association, analogy and identity, two things that are like each other and two things that are each other. You can say with Burns, 'My love's like a red, red rose', or you can say with Shakespeare:

> Thou that art now the world's fresh ornament
> And only herald to the gaudy spring.

One produces the figure of speech called the simile; the other produces the figure called metaphor.

20   In descriptive writing you have to be careful of associative language. You'll find that analogy, or likeness to something else, is very tricky to handle in description, because the differences are as important as the resemblances. As for metaphor, where you're really saying 'this *is* that', you're turning your back on logic and reason completely, because logically two things can never be the same thing and still remain two things. The poet, however, uses these two crude, primitive, archaic forms of thought in the most uninhibited way, because his job is not to describe nature, but to show you a world completely absorbed and possessed by the human mind. So he produces what Baudelaire called a 'suggestive magic including at the same time object and subject, the world outside the artist and the artist himself'. The motive for metaphor, according to Wallace Stevens, is a desire to associate, and finally to identify, the human mind with what goes on outside it, because the only genuine joy you can have is in those rare moments when you feel that although we may know in part, as Paul says, we are also a part of what we know.

TYPES OF WRITING:
analogy, analysis, classification, comparison, example/illustration

Topics for Discussion

1. How appropriate is the title to the text of Frye's essay? Why does he wait nearly until the end to bring in the Stevens poem from which he takes his title?
2. Frye adopts, as he announces, the style of the classroom. Does this approach assist him in influencing his audience?
3. In paragraph 2 Frye makes an extraordinary statement: "Wherever illiteracy is a problem, it's as fundamental a problem as getting enough to eat or a place to sleep." Does the rest of his discussion persuade you that this is true?
4. This essay was originally read on CBC radio, and Frye would therefore have known that his audience would vary considerably in intellectual ability and knowledge of his subject. How does his opening paragraph prepare this diverse audience for his chosen method of delivery?
5. Locate, if possible, the topic sentences in a selection of Frye's paragraphs. Do the topic sentences appear in a typical position within paragraphs? Are there paragraphs that you could make more accessible by moving or adding topic sentences?

Topics for Writing

1. Compare Frye's classifications of "levels of the mind" with King's use of classification in "Where Do We Go from Here?" Could either writer be accused of oversimplifying his subject in the interest of clarifying a particular perspective?
2. At the beginning of his essay Frye asks four questions. Choose any one of these questions and discuss the extent to which Frye has succeeded in answering it.
3. "A highly developed science and a highly developed art are very close together, psychologically and otherwise." Frye is more concerned with art than science in his essay. Write an essay expanding on the idea that a highly developed science is much like an art.

By the Book

Robert Fulford

1   When he wrote his textbook *Canada: A Political and Social History* (Holt, Rinehart, and Winston) in 1947, Edgar McInnis made some remarkable comments about the natives of Canada. "The aborigines," he wrote, "made no major contribution to the culture that developed in the settled communities of Canada." Later he spoke of the difficult life of a Catholic missionary who was assigned to preach to the Indians: "He shared their rude and often repulsive life around the campfires or in crowded communal shelters filled with smoke and filth and the stench of unwashed humanity."

2   McInnis's book was used as an introductory text in universities, and also in some high schools. It sold more than 200,000 copies, and went into new editions in 1959 and 1969. The 1969 edition, from which I've quoted, was in use at least as recently as 1981 in a course at the University of Toronto.

3   The people who have been trying to reform the textbooks of Canada would say, with justice, that McInnis's comments on the Indians symbolize all that was wrong with our textbooks for a century or more. His comments are racist, beyond question. They are degrading to the people they describe, they fortify stereotypes, and they are factually questionable. Far from making no contribution to the culture of Canadian settlements, the Indian (it could as well be argued) made many settlements possible by the part he played in the fur trade. McInnis's reference to the stench of unwashed humanity is surely a prejudiced selection of fact: in the eighteenth century most people, Indian and white, were unwashed most of the time, as indeed they had been through history. McInnis was a white Canadian setting forth views that could be comfortably accepted only by other white Canadians who happened to share his prejudices.

4   But he was just one among hundreds of textbook authors writing from that point of view. The texts with which most of us grew up contained — and some still contain — many similar forms of narrowness. Our textbooks largely ignored not only the values of the Indians but the histories of everyone in Canada except the British and the French. They tended also to ignore women who were other than wives, mothers, or nuns. In primary and secondary schools, textbooks — in subjects ranging from social studies to arithmetic — presented a world populated mainly by white males. All the executives, politicians, policemen, and athletes were men; women occasionally appeared as secretaries or teachers. In an office-practice textbook, a sample letter would always be written by one male businessman to another; a young woman using the book would be expected to identify with their secretaries.

5   This was largely unconscious. I doubt whether any author set out intentionally to alienate Indians or girls or Ukrainians who might use his book. And the effect was also partly unconscious. Like the American

situation comedies on TV a generation ago, the textbooks presented a world in which anyone outside the majority was made to feel slightly odd.

All this is changing, and nowhere more than in the treatment 6 of Indians. A recent text for senior high-school grades, *Heartland and Hinterland: A Geography of Canada* (Prentice-Hall, 1982), edited by L. D. McCann, presents a view McInnis would have found astonishing. The stench of unwashed humanity has been replaced by the "rich culture" of B.C. Indians and the "distinctive culture" which is the "greatest source of spiritual strength" of Alberta Indians. In discussing the natives of the North, *Heartland and Hinterland* sees intrusive Christianity and British law as negative forces. Every reference to Indians is an attempt to see their point of view.

In books intended for elementary schools, the contrast is even more 7 striking. *The Scottish Canadians* (Van Nostrand Reinhold, 1981), by Allen Andrews, part of a multicultural series for grades six to nine, depicts the Indians as the friends and eager helpers of white settlers. In a typical passage, Andrews discusses the work of a nineteenth-century Hudson's Bay Company apprentice named Angus: "Although their appearance was wild and strange to him, Angus soon found that the Métis and Indian employees of the Company were very kind and helpful. They showed the new arrivals how to prepare for the journey to Fort Garry. . . ." Each reference to Indians praises them. One section speaks of the Métis and Indian guides teaching the Scots "shooting, horseback riding, canoe handling, and trapping." The actual lives of Indians in Canada may not have been noticeably bettered during the last generation; but their status in the textbooks of the nation has improved enormously.

Changes of this sort have not come about by accident. They are the result 8 of a carefully organized movement to create textbooks — and therefore, perhaps, teaching — free of racial and sexual bias. Unlike most movements, this one can be dated with precision. It was set in motion in the Ontario legislature on June 2, 1965, when William Davis, then the minister of education, said: "In cooperation with the Ontario Human Rights Commission . . . we are about to make a thorough examination of all school textbooks, not just for the purpose of removing material which may be offensive to any of the groups which make up our multinational family, but more important, to make sure that our textbooks do contain the type of material which does full justice to the contribution of many people to the development of our province and nation."

In textbooks, as in so many other things, Ontario sets the standard 9 for English-speaking Canada. Ontario is the largest part of the market, and the first goal of every publishing company is to place its products on Circular 14, the document that lists all books authorized for use in Ontario schools. If a book appears on Circular 14 it has at least a chance of being widely adopted and therefore of turning a profit; if it doesn't make

Circular 14 it will probably lose money for the publisher. The Ontario ministry of education therefore makes the rules for English-speaking Canada; only a very few texts, such as regional social-studies books, are designed primarily for other provinces.

10   The rules made in Ontario have turned out, over nineteen years, to be complex and demanding. The ministry of education officials have consulted with, and been pressured by, various ethnic and feminist groups, and their current standards are largely a result of those pressures. In 1980 the ministry produced a booklet, *Race, Religion, and Culture in Ontario School Materials*, which sets forth their demands in detail. Like Davis's original statement, their prescriptions for school books have two aspects, negative and positive.

11   On the one hand, the booklet bans all bias in race, religion, and culture and singles out certain specific problems, such as material "demeaning to the image of Islam." It warns against such phrases as "inscrutable Orientals" and — rather curiously — "darkest Africa," a cliché which the authors of the booklet appear to see as a slur but which I've always thought referred to the fact that Africa is impenetrable to outsiders. The booklet says minority groups should never be described by derogatory adjectives, such as "warlike" or "uncivilized." It says that the Third World should not be consistently presented as "underdeveloped." It says the phrase "Blacks were given freedom" is wrong because it may suggest that blacks played a passive role in historical change. "Instead, the information should be conveyed in a way that suggests the active role Blacks took in their liberation."

12   What if the writer thinks that blacks in some area under discussion did *not* play a role in their liberation? What if the writer believes that the Third World *is* largely underdeveloped? Presumably the writer should write something other than texts for approval in Ontario.

13   When it deals with positive prescriptions for textbooks, the ministry becomes even more demanding. It is not enough to be free of bias against minorities; authors and publishers must be careful to draw those minorities into their books, always in a positive way. "Adequate representation should be provided of as many racial groups as possible," the booklet says, which conjures up a picture of publishers searching frantically for photographs of ever more obscure ethnic groups. In discussing illustrations, the booklet says: "Minorities must sometimes be featured as the focus of a picture and be shown as initiating actions and participating in them with members of other groups. They should not be pictured only in the background helping out." The booklet also says minorities should be shown living in suburbs and well-to-do districts as well as inner-city and rural areas.

14   This advice is given, of course, to those who are planning to write books. After the books are written and published, the ministry evaluates them before adding their titles to Circular 14. They are read by freelance evaluators, who judge according to a set of specific guidelines. The

evaluators, the guidelines say, are to ask themselves, among other things: "Do the text and illustrations show men and women, girls and boys in non-stereotyped roles?... Are women portrayed positively in a variety of roles whether they work inside or outside the home and whether or not they have children? Are men and boys, women and girls shown in household and nurturing tasks? Is there a variety of family patterns shown in a positive way (extended, nuclear, two-parent, one parent)?" The ministry of education clearly has in mind a certain kind of ideal world, and it wants that world depicted with sympathy.

The people who edit and publish textbooks have responded to all 15 this with an almost pathetic eagerness. If the government wants multiculturalism and liberated women, the publishers will provide multiculturalism and liberated women. The pages of new textbooks in every subject are dotted with Oriental and black faces, and women and girls have as large a place in the scheme of things as men and boys.

The cover of *Focus on Science* (D. C. Heath Canada, 1983), for grades 16 four to six, shows a black child and two white children examining a moth; inside, along with other approvable material, there are pictures of a little boy happily at work in a kitchen. And no longer do Mr. Smith and Mr. Jones work out problems in mathematics to the exclusion of people with non-English names. *Mathbase: Practical Skills and Applications* (Copp Clark Pitman, 1981), prepared by three Ontario high-school teachers for grade ten, works almost every conceivable ethnic group into its mathematical problems — the first ten names mentioned in questions are Bob May, Sue Wang, Eric Wanner, Kate Flynn, Marie Lalonde, Bill Black, Lisa Meti, Lars Anderson, Sharon Singh, and Martin Vito. ("Sue Wang's car holds 50 L of gas. Find the cost of ....") One can imagine the authors carefully doling out the names according to some formula of ethnicity at least as complicated as the questions they put to students. In fact, the book has no real need for last names at all — the problems would be just as clear to the students if the imaginary characters were named Sue or Lisa. The last names are there to beef up the ethnic content and make the book more palatable to the bureaucrats in the ministry of education.

Long ago, in Hollywood movies, all Indians were bad; then, sometime in 17 the 1950s, Hollywood changed its mind and from that point all Indians were honest and brave. In the same way, textbooks are moving from an atmosphere of unthinking prejudice to an atmosphere of sanitized, dreamlike unreality. Ontario schools — and thus the schools of the whole country — will soon be depicting a Canada in which no Indian ever did anything ignoble, Asians live in Rosedale and Westmount, all little boys are good cooks, and at least fifty per cent of airline pilots are women. No doubt this is an improvement. But it is also a rather melancholy demonstration of the fact that it is not possible to codify tolerance without going to slightly ridiculous extremes.

TYPES OF WRITING:
analysis, direct argument, example/illustration

Topics for Discussion

1. Why does Fulford open his essay by examining a particularly biased textbook, one that would serve well to justify the regulations he eventually questions? What does this opening suggest about Fulford's perception of his audience?
2. Fulford sees early bias as "largely unconscious" in contrast to later efforts to eliminate bias, which he characterizes as "a carefully organized movement," the result of "pressures" from feminist and ethnic groups. How is this distinction likely to affect the way readers receive his message?
3. Fulford never uses the word "censorship," although his comments on the effects of decisions by Ontario's Ministry of Education on English Canadian textbooks make it clear that a very effective form of censorship is taking place. Also, his conclusion concentrates on "ridiculous extremes" and stops short of suggesting that any official action should be taken. What does Fulford gain by this restraint?

Topics for Writing

1. Write an essay explaining why you believe that a positive depiction of minority groups is necessary in Canadian textbooks.
2. Using the information provided in Fulford's essay, restate his position for an audience you know to be highly critical of efforts to reform thinking through textbooks.
3. Fulford summarizes his main point in his final words: "it is not possible to codify tolerance without going to slightly ridiculous extremes." Apply these words to a different issue, such as the legalizing of marijuana for use by the general public, censorship of whatever kind, or speed limits.

Fast As an Elephant, Strong As an Ant

Bil Gilbert

One day recently I was reading a story about the San Diego Chargers   1
when I came across the following sentence describing Mr. Ernie Ladd, a
tackle who is said to be 6 feet 9 inches tall and to weigh 300 pounds.
Ladd, the report stated, has "a body that a grizzly bear could be proud
of." Now, this is an example of the falsely anthropomorphic and the
factually inaccurate natural-history metaphor, a literary device widely
used by sportswriters and one that I have long thought should be reported to authorities and stamped out.

The description of Ernie Ladd is objectionable on two counts. First,   2
there is no evidence that bears take pride in their personal appearance,
physical prowess or muscular development. Among animals, only men
seem susceptible to narcissism. And even if grizzlies did have the emotions of a beach boy and sat about the woods admiring their physiques,
no bear would be proud of having a body like that of Mr. Ladd.

According to my copy of *Mammals of the World* (Ernest P. Walker,   3
The Johns Hopkins Press, 1964, page 1173), "Grizzlies 2.5 meters [about 8
feet] in length and 360 kg. [800 pounds] in weight have been recorded. . . ."
In brief, Mr. Ladd is simply too puny to impress a grizzly even if grizzlies were impressionable in these matters.

I have never been one to criticize without offering constructive alter-   4
natives. Additional reading of *Mammals of the World* has uncovered some
statistics that may prove useful in the future. Should the need arise, one
might accurately (though still anthropomorphically) write that Mr. Ernie
Ladd has a body that female gray seal (150 kg., 2 meters) or a pygmy
hippopotamus (160 kg., 1.9 meters, counting tail) might be proud of.

It is not my purpose to embarrass or harass the man who wrote the   5
story. Rather, it is to point out that he is the inheritor, the victim, of a bad
journalistic tradition. Sportswriters have been comparing such and such
an athlete to this or that animal since the dawn of sports. Many of these
long-standing figures, metaphors, similes and tropes are even more wildly
inaccurate and ridiculous than the comparison of Mr. Ladd to a grizzly
bear.

An example that comes quickly to mind is the expression "wild as a   6
hawk," used to describe either erratic performance (a baseball pitcher
who cannot throw the ball across the plate) or untamable behavior (a
fractious horse). In both senses the phrase is misleading. As far as control
goes, the birds of prey are the antithesis of wildness (in the baseball use
of the word). A duck hawk, for example, flying a mile high in the sky,
can suddenly turn, dive earthward at 175 mph and strike a tiny sandpiper
flying just a few feet above the ground. Sandy Koufax should be so
accurate. As to being untamable, I, as a falconer, have often captured a
feral adult hawk and in a month had the bird flying free, returning to my
hand in response to a whistled command.

7   My own suggestion is that "wild as a heron" would better suggest the kind of behavior that wild as a hawk is supposed to describe. In many situations herons appear uncoordinated, almost spastic. Seeing a long-legged, gangly heron trying to land or take off from the ground is an experience. Furthermore, herons are far wilder (in the ferocious sense) than hawks. The most painful injury I ever received from an animal was given me by an American bittern (a heron type), who gouged a large hole in my wrist as I was attempting to free him from a fish trap.

8   "Loose as a goose" is an avian simile, supposedly suggesting extreme suppleness. Actually, geese have rigid pinions and are more or less bound like weight lifters by a heavy layer of pectoral muscle. Straight as a goose, stiff as a goose, pompous as a goose would be all right. But loose as a goose? Never. A better expression of the notion would be: "Though Slats Slattern has been a stellar NBA performer for 12 seasons, he remains young in spirit and loose as a mink." The slim-bodied minks, as well as weasels, ferrets and otters, are designed along the lines of a wet noodle. They look, and in fact are, far looser than a goose can possibly be.

9   Turning to mammals, an agility simile is "quick as a cat," often used in connection with such athletes as shortstops and goalies. It is true that cats are quicker than some things — turtles, mice, goldfish in bowls for example — but they are much less quick than many other creatures. Any wheezing old dog worth its salt can catch a cat. I once had a crow so quick that it could fly down and deliver three pecks between the eyes of a cat (which the crow despised) before the feline could raise a paw in self-defense. Not long ago I was watching a tame baboon which had the run of a yard in which was caged an ocelot. The baboon, even though working through bars, would reach into the cage and, while the ocelot was trying to get her reflexes in order, grab the cat by both her handsome tail and pointed ears. Baboon-quick is accurate and has a nice exotic ring to it.

10   Cats may not be the quickest animals, but at least one of the family, the cheetah, is the swiftest mammal as far as straight-ahead sprinting goes. It would seem that "run like a cheetah" would be a natural simile for sportswriters, but what do we have? "Ziggy Zagowski, slashing left half for the Keokuk Kidneys, ran like a rabbit through the defending Sioux City Spleens." Now, for a few jumps a rabbit can move at a rate of 30 or 35 miles an hour, but 20 mph is its pace for a distance as great as 100 yards. This rate is about the same as — or a bit slower than — that of a journeyman human sprinter over the same course. The chances are that if old Zig could not outleg a bunny he would not have even made his high school team. If, however, he could run like a cheetah, it would be a different matter, since those cats can do the 440 at 71 mph.

11   Since an elephant can skip along as fast as 25 mph (a bit faster than Bob Hayes or the average cottontail), it would be highly complimentary to say of an athlete that he runs like an elephant. However, the expression "elephantine" is actually used in sports as a term of derision, to twit a

ponderous, slow-moving, clumsy performer. Actually, elephants are not only swift beasts but graceful ones. Despite their size they are almost as quick as a baboon or as loose as a mink. They can slip quietly through the jungle, stand on a barrel or a ballerina at the behest of a ringmaster. "Horsine" would be a better term to designate a stumblebum. Horses are forever falling over small pebbles, ropes and their own feet. When a horse and rider start down even a gradual incline or up a path slightly narrower than the Pennsylvania Turnpike, the rider must dismount, and it is he who must lead, guide and, in general, prop up the horse.

Great strength has its place in sports, and it is traditional to describe   12
the athlete who possesses it as being "strong as an ox." As in the case of quick cats and fast rabbits, the simile is not completely false, only inadequate. In proportion to their bulk, oxen are relatively strong but not overpoweringly so. A team of oxen weighing 3,400 pounds can move a dead weight, say a block of granite, equal to about three times its own weight. This is a fair feat when compared to a 150-pound weight lifter who can dead-lift 300 pounds. However, it is a feeble effort when one considers the ant, which can pick up a load 50 times heavier than itself. To speak of a fullback as being strong as an ant would be high praise indeed, since it would signify that the player could, without undue strain, carry the entire opposing team not only across the goal line, but right up into Row E.

Held in high regard by coaches, reporters and fans is the athlete who   13
works incessantly at mastering the fundamentals of his game. Often such persevering types are admired as "beavers." This, of course, is a contraction of the folksy expressions "to work like a beaver" or "to be as busy as a beaver," both of which are based upon a misunderstanding of the beaver's nature and misobservation of the animal's customary behavior. Unlike some animals that must travel many miles a day just to rustle up a square meal, beavers seldom forage more than a hundred yards from their home. Beavers construct their well-publicized dams and lodges only when it is absolutely impossible to find a suitable natural waterscape. The lowly mole, on the other hand, may dig several hundred yards of tunnel in a day in an incessant effort to keep body and soul together. "I like that boy, all spring long he's been moling away," would be an apt way for a coach to describe and praise industriousness.

Canines have a strong attraction for scribes looking for a vivid, if   14
fallacious, phrase. There is, for example, the veteran who is a "sly foxy" competitor. (If foxes are so sly, how come they never run down the hounds? Who ever heard of a hunt catching a skunk?) Then there is the prizefighter about to addle the brains of his opponent or the fast-ball pitcher poised to stick one in a batter's ear. These violent men, we are often told, have a "wolfish grin" on their faces.

One of the few naturalists who have been close enough long enough   15
to *au naturel* wolves to observe their facial expressions is Farley Mowat, who spent a summer camped virtually on the den step of a family of

Arctic wolves. Mowat in his delightful book, *Never Cry Wolf*, claims that *his* wolves were kindly, affectionate, tolerant animals who looked and acted more like diplomats than thugs. This stands to reason. Many creatures besides man are predatory, but hardly any species except man tries to do real violence to its own kind in play while contemplating the prospect with a grin. If such a premayhem facial expression as a "wolfish grin" actually exists, it is probably unique to man. If this peculiar look of violence must be compared to that of some other animal, I recommend the short-tailed shrew.

16   The short-tailed shrew is one of the commonest animals of North America and one of the most perpetually predatory. Ounce for ounce (which is what a large shrew weighs), there is no busier killer in the world. Awake, the shrew is almost always preparing to kill, is killing or has just killed, and its victims include rodents, reptiles, birds and mammals several times its own size. The shrew, like almost all other mammals, does not kill out of capriciousness or playfulness, but rather because it has an extraordinarily high metabolic rate. It must daily consume the equivalent of its own body weight in order to keep the inner fires burning. (Eat like a shrew, rather than eat like a horse, would better describe the habits of a first baseman who is such a formidable trencherman that he can no longer bend down to scoop up low throws.) When a shrew closes in to kill something, say a white-footed mouse, it wears a really dreadful expression. A shrew is chinless, and its long mouth slashes across the underpart of its muzzle in a cruel, sharklike line. As the tiny killer closes in, its eyes glitter with excitement and two long brown fangs (which, incidentally, drip with a venomous saliva) are exposed. If Sonny Liston looked only half as wicked as a short-tailed shrew he might still be heavyweight champion of the world.

17   I fully realize that many of the criticisms and suggestions offered here do violence to some of the most cherished traditions of sports journalism, but there is no holding back literary and scientific progress. Consider, for example, the manner in which the style I advocate, high-fidelity zoological metaphor, injects color as well as accuracy into the following interview with Sig Schock of the Pardy Pumas:

18   "Sig Schock, a big horsine man, grizzled as a Norway rat, leaned back against the plywood bench, taking up a position so that the hot sun beat down on his ant-like shoulders. The eyes, old but still sharp as a barn owl's, flicked over the practice field, where the young Pumas cavorted as quick as so many baboons. 'I'll tell you,' Sig confided in his disconcertingly high, spring-peeperlike voice. 'These kids has got it. The most of them can run like elephants, a couple like cheetahs. And size. We finally got some. We got six boys with builds like a female gray seal's. Course, they're still young, some of them are wild as herons — that's O.K., they got the old desire. Every one of them is a snapping turtle or a raccoon. And I'll tell you something,' the sly, skunky veteran

added, lowering his squeaky voice. 'We'll chew 'em up and lay 'em out this season.' A shrewish grin spread across the battered old face."

Leaving you with that, I remain pretty as a peacock, sassy as a jaybird, 19 happy as a clam.

TYPES OF WRITING:
example/illustration, humour

Topics for Discussion

1. Why does Gilbert, himself a writer about sports, go out of his way to make himself seem pedantic, overly concerned with propriety and fairness, and short-sighted about the implications of metaphors — in short, quite humourless?
2. What groups might Gilbert hope to reach and influence with this piece?
3. What devices serve Gilbert best to make this essay amusing?

Topics for Writing

1. Write an essay, either humorous or not, exploring some specialized field of interest or knowledge, and concentrating on its characteristic jargon and mode of expression.
2. If you were to write an article about a local sports team, would you use the kinds of metaphors that Gilbert advocates? As you deal with this question in detail, you should lead up to the main point: whether or not Gilbert has managed to convince you — and why.

Loosening the Ties That Bind

Linda Goyette

1   Ron Hayter woke up one morning last week to find that his universe had changed overnight. It would have been wonderful to pay a penny for his thoughts as he straightened his necktie, and trudged off to city hall.

2   The transformation had nothing to do with the Edmonton alderman's worried musings about whether to enter provincial politics. That's a subject for another day. No, the sudden shift in Hayter's world view was related to that narrow strip of cloth that decorates the male chest. The necktie, I'm happy to report, is in mortal danger.

3   You will remember the alderman's impassioned defence of the necktie in his feud with open-collared colleagues at city council last fall. He made it sound as if the very future of parliamentary democracy depended on a politician's willingness to tie one on — a necktie, that is — and aldermen who refused to follow the Rigid Ron Hayter Dress Code were creatures from the blue lagoon.

4   So it must have come as a shock last Thursday when the *Report on Business*, that repository of narrow, navy-blue neckties, carried a picture of William Etherington, the president of IBM Canada, wearing a tie-less, plaid shirt, *in public*. The accompanying story was even more surprising. Etherington has just ordered his senior executives to abandon IBM's traditional corporate costume of blue suits, white shirts and bland ties to "accelerate the transformation to a more free-thinking and open-to-change culture."

5   Don't take this too hard, Ron. The news was unsettling for most people. If IBM workers abandon their trademark neckties for plaid shirts, what's next in the revolutionary scheme of things? Will lawyers go to the bar in Lycra jogging shorts? Will Royal Bank managers pull on Hawaiian shirts? Hawaiian skirts, even? It could be the end of civilization as we know it.

6   Now, there's an intriguing possibility. That IBM man could be on to something. It might be a good idea to think about our uniforms, and anti-uniforms, because most of us wear them like a second skin without any prompting. Why?

7   Etherington points out that IBM never had a formal dress code even though the public and employees had that distinct impression. The company didn't need a rule because unspoken, tenacious peer pressure worked even better.

8   In the old days, IBM wanted to convey the impression of professionalism and high technical standards. Hence, the ties that bind. In 1993, Etherington is just as calculating when he encourages his employees to experiment with corporate fashion. In the most superficial sense, he wants his staid, establishment company to compete with the innovative up-starts on the block. The employee's personal image — as much as the

real person under the clothing, as much as the ideas in the head under the haircut — becomes the marketing commodity.

You can't help wondering whether Etherington is creating a new, 9 equally tyrannical uniform. If the IBM president wears a plaid shirt to work, you can bet his corporate boardroom will look like a lumberjacks' camp in a week. For that matter, he could wear underwater goggles and his senior vice-presidents would soon be begoggled with snorkels. And guess what a few rebels down in the payroll department will soon be wearing around their skinny throats? Neckties, of course: an anti-uniform that might be more an expression of resentment at a boss's interference than true distinctiveness.

This pattern isn't limited to corporate culture. Try to encourage a 10 kindergarten kid to wear slip-on runners when friends are wearing lace-ups. Tell a high school student to buy generic jeans in the bargain-basement store. Unwritten rules about clothing serve the function of social control. Is it only a coincidence that women in the baby-factory 1950s padded their bosoms while women in the career-crazy 1980s padded their shoulders? The structural work was bulky and uncomfortable in both places but most sufferers accepted it. It was the uniform. The universal goal: to be relentlessly, rigidly, the same.

Could we break the habit? Wouldn't it be great to peel off our con- 11 formity like a pair of smelly socks at the end of the day and dress in comfortable, colorful clothing that expressed just the tiniest bit of individuality? Don't give up hope. If the president of IBM can toss out his necktie, even for crass reasons, the world is really changing.

TYPES OF WRITING:
direct argument, humour

Topics for Discussion

1. Goyette introduces her assault on conformity in dress with a reference to a local public figure with which most readers of her newspaper would be at least superficially familiar. Is Goyette's irreverent treatment of Mr. Hayter's conservative views on dress likely to elicit sympathy for him, thereby weakening the influential effect of her editorial? Why or why not?

2. What is the tone of the last sentence of the first three paragraphs? What does this tone reveal about Goyette's attitude toward her topic?

3. In paragraph 8, Goyette uses the expression "the ties that bind." What two meanings does this expression have?

4. Despite Goyette's humorous, almost playful, attitude toward her subject, does she also have a serious persuasive intent? If so, who do you think she is trying to persuade: the general public? her co-workers at the *Edmonton Journal*? professionals? some other group?

Topics for Writing

1. In paragraph 10 Goyette makes this statement: "Unwritten rules about clothing serve the function of social control." Discuss to what extent this is the main point of Goyette's argument and to what extent it is also the main point being argued in the essays by Carolyn Leitch and Harry Bruce.

2. School uniforms are still quite common today in private schools. After considering the arguments for and against school uniforms, write a letter to the editor of your hometown newspaper arguing in favour of uniforms — or at least in favour of regulations requiring that all students dress in more or less the same type of clothing — in public high schools. Mention the disadvantages of uniform dress briefly, and refute them by emphasizing how they are outweighed by the advantages.

3. Compare and contrast Goyette's humorous style, tone, and diction with Bil Gilbert's in "Fast As an Elephant, Strong As an Ant." How do the personalities projected by these writers enhance humorous effect?

In Praise of the Humble Comma

Pico Iyer

The gods, they say, give breath, and they take it away. But the same   1
could be said — could it not? — of the humble comma. Add it to the
present clause, and, of a sudden, the mind is, quite literally, given pause
to think; take it out if you wish or forget it and the mind is deprived of a
resting place. Yet still the comma gets no respect. It seems just a slip of a
thing, a pedant's tick, a blip on the edge of our consciousness, a kind of
printer's smudge almost. Small, we claim, is beautiful (especially in the
age of the microchip). Yet what is so often used, and so rarely recalled,
as the comma — unless it be breath itself?

Punctuation, one is taught, has a point: to keep up law and order.   2
Punctuation marks are the road signs placed along the highway of our
communication — to control speeds, provide directions and prevent head-
on collisions. A period has the unblinking finality of a red light; the
comma is a flashing yellow light that asks us only to slow down; and the
semicolon is a stop sign that tells us to ease gradually to a halt, before
gradually starting up again. By establishing the relations between words,
punctuation establishes the relations between the people using words.
That may be one reason why schoolteachers exalt it and lovers defy it
("We love each other and belong to each other let's don't ever hurt each
other Nicole let's don't ever hurt each other," wrote Gary Gilmore to his
girlfriend). A comma, he must have known, "separates inseparables," in
the clinching words of H. W. Fowler, King of English Usage.

Punctuation, then, is a civic prop, a pillar that holds society upright.   3
(A run-on sentence, its phrases piling up without division, is as unsightly
as a sink piled high with dirty dishes.) Small wonder, then, that punctuation was one of the first proprieties of the Victorian age, the age of the
corset, that the modernists threw off: the sexual revolution might be said
to have begun when Joyce's Molly Bloom spilled out all her private thoughts in 36 pages of unbridled, almost unperioded and officially
censored prose; and another rebellion was surely marked when
E. E. Cummings first felt free to commit "God" to the lower case.

Punctuation thus becomes the signature of cultures. The hot-blooded   4
Spaniard seems to be revealed in the passion and urgency of his doubled
exclamation points and question marks ("¡Caramba! ¿ Quien sabe?"), while
the impassive Chinese traditionally added to his so-called inscrutability
by omitting directions from his ideograms. The anarchy and commotion
of the '60s were given voice in the exploding exclamation marks, riotous
capital letters and Day-Glo italics of Tom Wolfe's spray-paint prose; and
in Communist societies, where the State is absolute, the dignity — and
divinity — of capital letters is reserved for Ministries, Sub-Committees
and Secretariats.

Yet punctuation is something more than a culture's birthmark: it   5
scores the music in our minds, gets our thoughts moving to the rhythm

81

of our hearts. Punctuation is the notation in the sheet music of our words, telling us when to rest, or when to raise our voices; it acknowledges that the meaning of our discourse, as of any symphonic composition, lies not in the units but in the pauses, the pacing and the phrasing. Punctuation is the way one bats one's eyes, lowers one's voice or blushes demurely. Punctuation adjusts the tone and color and volume till the feeling comes into perfect focus: not disgust exactly, but distaste; not lust, or like, but love.

6   Punctuation, in short, gives us the human voice, and all the meanings that lie between the words. "You aren't young, are you?" loses its innocence when it loses the question mark. Every child knows the menace of a dropped apostrophe (the parent's "Don't do that" shifting into the more slowly enunciated "Do not do that"), and every believer, the ignominy of having his faith reduced to "faith." Add an exclamation point to "To be or not to be . . ." and the gloomy Dane has all the resolve he needs; add a comma, and the noble sobriety of "God save the Queen" becomes a cry of desperation bordering on double sacrilege.

7   Sometimes, of course, our markings may be simply a matter of aesthetics. Popping in a comma can be like slipping on the necklace that gives an outfit quiet elegance, or like catching the sound of running water that complements, as it completes, the silence of a Japanese landscape. When V. S. Naipaul, in his latest novel, writes, "He was a middle-aged man, with glasses," the first comma can seem a little precious. Yet it gives the description a spin, as well as a subtlety, that it otherwise lacks, and it shows that the glasses are not part of the middle-agedness, but something else.

8   Thus all these tiny scratches give us breadth and heft and depth. A world that has only periods is a world without inflections. It is a world without shade. It has a music without sharps and flats. It is a martial music. It has a jackboot rhythm. Words cannot bend and curve. A comma, by comparison, catches the gentle drift of the mind in thought, turning in on itself and back on itself, reversing, redoubling and returning along the course of its own sweet river music; while the semicolon brings clauses and thoughts together with all the silent discretion of a hostess arranging guests around her dinner table.

9   Punctuation, then, is a matter of care. Care for words, yes, but also, and more important, for what the words imply. Only a lover notices the small things: the way the afternoon light catches the nape of a neck, or how a strand of hair slips out from behind an ear, or the way a finger curls around a cup. And no one scans a letter so closely as a lover, searching for its small print, straining to hear its nuances, its gasps, its sighs and hesitations, poring over the secret messages that lie in every cadence. The difference between "Jane (whom I adore)" and "Jane, whom I adore," and the difference between them both and "Jane — whom I adore —" marks all the distance between ecstasy and heartache. "No iron can pierce the heart with such force as a period put at just the right

place," in Isaac Babel's lovely words: a comma can let us hear a voice break, or a heart. Punctuation, in fact, is a labor of love. Which brings us back, in a way, to gods.

TYPES OF WRITING:
allusion, example/illustration, humour

Topics for Discussion

1. How does Iyer's use of commas in this essay reinforce the effect of what he is saying? Consider a separate sentence in each of three paragraphs.
2. Consider the various things with which the comma, explicitly and implicitly, is compared or associated in this essay. What are the influential implications of these links?
3. Consider the organization of Iyer's paragraphs. How many have topic sentences announcing their subject at or near the beginning? Are paragraphs characteristically unified in their treatment of the subjects so announced? How does Iyer provide transitions between paragraphs while linking each paragraph with its neighbours?
4. In an essay like this one, which deals with a wide variety of sometimes quite fanciful representations of a common subject, what influential advantage is gained from structuring paragraphs carefully?

Topics for Writing

1. In his second-last sentence, Iyer states, "Punctuation, in fact, is a labor of love." This is not, however, likely to be the case for the majority of university students. What does punctuation mean to you? Your essay should deal with questions such as the following: Which punctuation marks do you use with confidence? How did you learn to use them? What strategies did your best teachers use? Which marks do you still have trouble with, and why? What, specifically, do you intend to do about these problems?
2. Write an essay revealing how apparently mundane, insignificant things — traffic signs, garbage cans, lawns, for example — function symbolically in our society.

Born Free? The Poetry Beast in the Classroom

Paulette Jiles

POETRY AS A BLUNT INSTRUMENT

1   It is unfortunate, but true, that through the hands of English teachers most of us pass and then emerge with either a love of poetry or a stolid resistance to it. It is no longer sung in bardic halls of meat-gnawing barons, or read in the gentlemanly circles of the court, or recited by travelling troubadors in country inns. Most people meet the beast called Poetry in our school system.

2   When we were going through *Don Quijote* in a university class, I was amazed that most of the peasants were represented as knowing many long ballads and romanceros by heart, fragments of "El Cid" and "El Conde de Lara" and so on. No doubt they knew a lot of slush as well, which is what the *Quijote* is about, in part, but the truth is that not very many people went to school and took literature classes, and therefore didn't know any better than to quote "El Cid" on the road.

3   Poetry today, on the other hand, seems only an excuse for scholastic criticism, with questions at the end of each period asking what the poet meant by

> Who ever comes to shroud me, do not harme nor question much
> That subtile wreath of haire, which crowns my arme.

4   Not that I am against scholastic criticism, far from it. But the teaching of poetry to school kids is something else; it is the transmission of a cultural heritage that belongs to everybody, not a way of developing a few literary critics.

5   Unfortunately this doesn't happen very often in our schools. Instead kids are ruined on literature in general and on poetry specifically by the time they get through high school. They learn that it is too difficult, or dealing with very esoteric subjects, or not for the likes of them. This is particularly true for that mass of children from working-class backgrounds. These kids think that a poet, writing about going somewhere:

> No, no go not to Lethe, neither twist
> Wolf's bane, tight-rooted, for it's poisonous wine

may have something important to say, but not to Betty Ann Cochrane and Jimmy O'Brien from the public housing; that the poet may be telling someone a terrific truth but doesn't want too many people to understand anything about it.

6   A teacher often doesn't know how to reach the average student and engage them with the poetry; they remain unengageable, like mismatched

84

gears. Instead there is a tendency to concentrate on making professionals out of a handful of bright, competitive kids. The avenues of expression become very narrow under these circumstances. The competitive system of teaching poetry appoints some students to be critics, some writers, and some philistines. The poems that are produced are manufactured ones, not organic. They are contaminated with pesticides and artificial fertilizers; do not go near them if you value your teeth. Poets pop up anyway, like weeds, they can rarely be mowed down if they are determined to write poetry, or write anything at all, and the kid who is bent on being a writer probably has ceased to listen to the English teacher's drone long ago. What teacher who ever loved poetry could bear to see one student "win" over another, scrambling like alley cats over historical references and allusions? In a system like that, if you don't win you don't even finish; loser lose all, to quote Michael Caine.

What schools tend to produce is a small group of people who can   7 deal with poetry and a mob who cannot. Nevertheless there are teachers who manage to generate some interest in poetry among their students. I was fortunate to have two of them.

TWO WAYS OF GETTING AT STUDENTS: MR. HARRISON AND MS. ROLLER

In my secondary school there were two kinds of English classes and two   8 very different kinds of people teaching them. I had just come out of a tiny rural high school into an urban one, and was ready to learn all about city ways and the wonders of poetry. I used to write it in the little high school out in the country; things about Christmas bells for Christmas and things about rainbows for Easter. I was ready to continue with this kind of success.

The first English class was called "advanced" — for serious students   9 only — taught by a twenty-four year old fireball with a wit like a scalpel and no tolerance for philistines. His name was Harrison, and he was an entertaining and terrifying man. He was afire with a love for modern literature and was determined to put it across, despite texts and the administration.

My first mistake in this class was to fall for Harrison's jargon that we   10 were there to express ourselves. He asked us all to write something about life or time or the state of the world; to see if this "advanced English class" was going to get off the ground.

All my training before, in public school had been to accept the myth   11 of how wonderful and promising life was if only we would hold our end up, there being no such thing as poverty or social classes, and how happy we all were. Being clever with words, I had written that kind of mucus for several years. I proceeded to do it now; several pages about how promising life was, what with the trees and flowers and all. I was sixteen and had not read anything more sophisticated than Kipling, whom I then quoted:

> Life is so full of a number of things
> I am sure we should all be as happy as kings.

12   The reaction of the urbane and acerbic Harrison was not even scorn; he proceeded to forget I existed and concentrated on those members of the class whom he considered sane. Harrison was in love with literature in the most refined way; he approved of expressions of alienation and did not care for the sentimental. He taught our special group of ten (I was there because he couldn't get me out) who were bent on writing Great Literature, that we should regard anyone who didn't appreciate poetry as humanoids. Harrison was no coward. He was open in his contempt for the principal, he attacked organized religion in any form, which for high school students can be quite frightening. He sneered at the teacher of the required English class, a Ms. Roller, whom he openly called Steam Roller. Any student in his class whom he considered a corpse past saving, he would refer to by the clothes they wore. "You there!" he once bellowed at an unfortunate athletic hero; "You there, Red-Boats-On-White-Shirt; read!" I think he once referred to me as Howdy Doody. Harrison was developing an elite.

13   Ms. Roller was a different type altogether, and so were the people in her class. We were there because we had to be. She knew this and was determined to spoon a little bit of poetry down our throats in any way she could, democratically, indiscriminately. She was a large woman, breasty, with rigid corsets and long, flowing green and/or magenta scarves. The way she taught poetry was to grind through it flamboyantly. If this sounds impossible, I assure you that it was a fact. What she did was to try and make us imagine, while pumping up and down the green and/or purple scarves, the beauty of the spring day when they all rode off to Canterbury. In one of these transports a button shot off her suit and ricocheted across the room. We appreciated this very much, as a distraction and respected Roller because of it, and hoped that other buttons would soon follow their predecessor; none did. If the students in that class wanted to know what it was like to be out in a spring day, they would rather have been out in one themselves. Those of us who were also Harrison's students wanted to develop some alienation, despair, loneliness and the condition of man.

14   Then Roller, after trying to get us involved in Chaucer emotionally, would turn around and test us on it. What sort of character was the Reeve? What was reeving? Who Reeved? Who cared?

15   But we learned the Canterbury Tales, if nothing else. I think it was partly the button, and also that she herself was delighted with them, and even seemed to know the people:

> Her wimpled veil, and on her head a hat
> as broad as a buckler or a targe
> a foot-mantle about her hippes large . . .

I could have bullshitted Roller with any sort of tripe and often did;   16
she was too intimidated by the discipline of modern criticism to help the
students with their poetry, and liked everything, hoping to encourage
us.

Harrison wrote things in the margins of our poems I shudder to   17
think of, even today.

I endured Harrison's remarks, and as time went on I ceased to think   18
of the world as very wonderful, after all, and wrote alienated things full
of suffering and definite articles, about walking in the rain alone:

> He walked in the soft and voiceless rain
> Where the haunting, tearful ambience
> was as exquisite as pain . . .

which Harrison said was "promising". I was not a he but a she, and had
sense enough to come in out of the rain. But I was learning to compete.

Harrison taught only the "modern" poets (starting with Eliot) and   19
Henry James for prose, and encouraged us to write. I began to buy Ezra
Pound and Rimbaud, and write things in the margins. You may wonder
what this man did to get such a creative response from his students. It
was because he loved poetry — he read it to us, made parodies of the
heavy stuff and we laughed with him. Once he confided to us that the
night before he had awoken with a line of poetry in his head that had
said all he ever felt, and had quickly written it down. We leaned forward
to hear what it had been.

"Oh god, I could never tell you."   20

He made us feel that we would carry on the torch flung from his   21
utter conviction that literature *mattered*, since the world was awash with
crew-cut chimpanzees who could no more appreciate poetry than they
could a *blanquette d'agneau*. There were a few, he decided, who knew in
the depths of the night that Mankind was Absurd. (This was in 1961
when Sartre was very much in fashion. Mind you, I don't blame Sartre
for all this.) These students could generally be recognized by their ur-
banity, accent, paleness, the way they referred to obscure works and
otherwise differentiated themselves from the mass. Poets starved,
Rimbaud ran off to Abyssinia, things happened to them; the middle-
class suburbia where Harrison took place made all this seem infinitely
preferable; to think and feel and write.

Harrison bullied the administration until he got a creative writing   22
class. After a year we came up with four real poems. We pooled our
money and bought a page in the high school year book, and printed
them, alongside the cheerleaders and *Cercle Français*. He made us laugh
at ourselves as well as the cheerleaders, and was smart enough to realize
that it was not only he — the foreman with grimly serious little workers
under him — who had created this surprising burst of poetry, but that
we had encouraged each other as well.

Harrison derived his passion for literature from his own insights   23
and an amount of determination that overcame some gross mistakes on

his part as a teacher — among those I would include faddishness, a worship of the alienated individual, class snobbery and a real dislike of his girl students. If Harrison could manage to motivate students as he did with those kind of serious errors, think what you could do.

24   The kids that Harrison turned off got something from Roller. Roller had no instinct for the trendy. She would indulge herself and us with poets that were considered beyond the pale, without even realizing how backward she was.

25   Take Robert Burns. If I can't think of a cornier or more passé poet then it's just that I'm not up on what is considered corny these days. The person who taught him to us was the school busdriver; an embarrassed Scot whom we had talked into lecturing to us in Roller's class about Scotland's National Poet. We had done this because we had heard him quoting Burns on our journeys to and from school; and because he was good-looking and the girls had a crush on him, and he was a nice guy. Ms. Roller was delighted with the idea.

26   She told us about the crofters' huts, and the sheep, and the battle of Bannockburn with blood running down the claymores, pipers and their tragic, Celtic *pibrochs*. By the time he had been convinced to come we were all hoping that there was Scottish somewhere in our ancestry.

27   (When Harrison found out what Roller had permitted to happen in her class he slapped his forehead and groaned, "Robert *Burns!*")

28   McFee had red cheeks and a stringy body and an unbrushable clot of red hair. He shuffled his grubby notebooks and his Bible-like collection of Burns around on the desk and confided that he hadn't had much farrmal eddication. He stood struck like a mule for five minutes before being able to speak. A blush rose up on his neck like a candy thermometer. Finally he stared at the far wall and, bright red, we assumed, all over, spoke about Robert Burns.

29   Ms. Roller said "Ah!" and "How wonderful! In your own home!" She managed to convey to McFee that, even with her Master's degree she felt far more unlettered than he; as Robert Burns was his own, his true, his heroic poet. McFee loosened up and began to rip off Burns at a great rate: he read "MacPherson's Farewell" with a voice that threatened to become awesome:

> Sae rantingly sae wantonly
> Sae dauntingly gaed he
> He play'd a spring and danced it round
> Below the gallows-tree.
>
> Oh! What is death but parting breath
> On mony a bloody plain
> I've dared his face and in this place
> I scorn him once again!
>
> Untie these bands from off my hands
> and bring to me my sword!
> And there's no man in all Scotland
> But I'll brave him at a word.

"If you haven't been raised up with a poet, then you can hardly 30 understand what it is to know his lines." He smiled. "My father knew him much better than meself, of course." He looked down at his enormous leather bound collection. "In Scotland, everybody knows Robert Burns. I was taught him when I was wee."

I'll never forget McFee. Every time I get an anthology of poetry in 31 my hands I turn to Robert Burns to read him over again and find out why I liked him so much and thought he was so great. I never have figured out why.

In that session, we were being taught a love of poetry, and not 32 criticism of poetry. We were read to by someone who really liked the poet's work, and that was the lesson. And don't think the supposedly ludicrous Ms. Roller didn't know it!

Harrison and Roller remained true to form to the end. At graduation 33 Harrison handed us over one last mimeographed sheet from J. B. Priestly's *Literature and Western Man*:

> Even if we believe that the time of our civilization is running out fast,
> like sugar from a torn bag, we must wait. But while we are waiting we
> can try to think and feel and behave, to some extent . . . as if we were
> certain that Man cannot even remain Man unless he looks beyond him-
> self, as if we were finding our way home again in the Universe . . . and
> if we openly declare what is wrong with us, what is our deepest need,
> then perhaps the despair and death will by degrees disappear from our
> modern arts.

During graduation exercises Steam Roller came around to all of us, 34 dressed in primrose and turquoise scarves for the occasion and con-gratulated us all. Harrison went off, I heard (O scandal! O envy!) and got drunk.

SOME SUGGESTIONS FROM A SURVIVOR

I graduated from secondary school with a zealous interest in poetry, and 35 even began to write it, and am therefore a survivor. As for teaching it I have some suggestions for those English teachers who have not given up on trying to get it across to their students.

Bring Your Own Selection

Harrison mimeographed a good deal of poetry which was not in the 36 anthologies and brought it to class; we ended up with a sort of textbook of our own. Bring your own poems to class, your favourites, the ones you really like. Critical evaluation can come later. Your first job is merely to get these students to realize that poetry is not going to hit them in the back of the head, or insult them, or laugh at them. So teach only your own, personal favourites and do not grind through a required anthology. Here are some of my favourite poems. I offer them because their content spoke to me, and their technique taught me:

Nocturnal Upon St. Lucie's Day — Donne
House Guest — Purdy
There Is Only One of Everything — Atwood
Elm — Plath
London — Blake
The Tyger — Blake
I Have Tasted My Blood — Acorn
Crow Song — Atwood
We Live in a Rickety House — Alexander McLaughlin
The Lotos Eaters — Tennyson
The Hand — Keats
Ode on a Grecian Urn — Keats
Union Dead — Tom Wayman
Calamus Poems — Whitman
When Lilacs Last in the Dooryard Bloom'd — Whitman
Parody on the Wreck of the Hesperus — Mark Twain
Death of Beatle Paul — Satu Repo
Easy Street — Alexa DeWiel
various Catullus and Lesbia and Eliot

37   I offer these as things I would teach because they have to do with my taste, and I could therefore teach *about* them. I think there is enough technique in these poems that they could serve as examples of meter, rhyme, scansion, allusion, everything but a Petrarchan Sonnet. I think they would be all I needed. All you have to hook a student with is *one poem*, not a book full of them.

38   So there you are, Harrison or Roller or maybe McFee. You are afraid you are going to end up teaching something sentimental or mediocre. Pay no attention to the critics, to the text, nor shy away from content. Critical opinions vary with the writers, and the years, and the economic situation. You may feel that, who are you, a grubby English teacher with chalk on your sleeves fumbling about in bookstores to find anthologies to teach your students what is or is not good. Many times teachers and students alike see it as a kind of shootout between the critics and the poets — with the alleged poets hiding out in rundown houses while outside large blue critics with loaded adjectives and megaphones beg the poets to give themselves up without a struggle. This may not be too far from the truth. What *you* do with this situation is ignore it, Montreal-style. Look the other way and pretend you never saw a thing.

Don't Test Them

39 Students will invariably feel that they must understand the content. Many teachers will search for poems that seem to have understandable content. This brings grave problems with Purdy's fuck poems and Whitman's

Calamus poems and Robert Frost. Frost, for some reason, is often re-printed in high school anthologies. But his simple, homely subjects often lead to vast conclusions, and they tend to be a bit too understated for adolescents. Especially where the picking of apples leads up to:

One can see what will trouble
This sleep of mine, whatever sleep it is.
Were he not gone
the woodchuck could say whether it is like his
long sleep, as I describe its coming on,
or just some human sleep.

The content of the poems you choose to begin your students on 40 should be fairly direct. Then you won't have to ask the question "What does this poem mean?" to a vast silence.

So you will probably have to give up testing or grading on poetry, 41 or even asking the kids a direct question about poetry, until you get them to realize that it is not a blunt instrument; until you can get them to like it.

Reconciliation-in-old-age-with-father Content

Poems about parents also tend to attract teachers. The problem with this 42 is that most of the poems written about parents are reconciliation-in-old-age-with-father poems, and she-was-beautiful-when-she-was-young poems. Students are at the age when they are not in any way reconciled with their parents, and do not stop to reflect on how beautiful their mother is while contemplating a quick get-a-way. The adult poets who write these poems have reached an age where they can afford to look back with calmness and reconciliation. Most of your students have not reached that stage. The anthology *I Am A Sensation* (McClelland & Stewart, Toronto) is crammed full of these poems. The anthology is meant for students and the editors must have thought this would be attractive to them. I would assume, and know from my own experience, the exact opposite. Parental *conflict* poems are rare, at least in such direct terms that adolescents would understand any of them.

Love Poetry Content

Some of the best poems in the world are fuck poems, but to get the 43 student to understand them is another thing. When I was first taught Donne's "The Sunne Rising", it was couched in such archaic terms that I didn't even know he was talking about screwing. I thought they were sitting politely on the bed talking to each other; and Ms. Roller certainly did not clear this point up for us. Your students will most likely be in a very experimental stage as sex goes; they think that screwing is the property of adults, and for them to admit they have, are about to, or would like to indulge in it would be tantamount to madness. The sexual revolution has not gone as far as you think, and it certainly has not got as far as your school administration. The second problem here is that, aside from sexuality *per se*, a lot of the fuck poems are written by males, so you have just lost all the girls in the class. Many of them speak of the bitter war between the sexes, which is something that develops in an adult context, in sexual terms — in marriages, affairs and other liaisons which teenagers do not have. Here you find that most students may reject the poetry outright because of the inappropriateness of the emotions contained in it. The teacher may have to do the relating for them, experience the emotions, take the risk. Try teaching Milton Acorn's "I Shout Love" — in its directness it may speak to teenagers not yet caught up in the sexual games of cheat and win:

> For my heart's a furry sharp-toothed thing
> that charges out whimpering . . .

and it is a very long poem, giving these younger people a chance to relate Love (that dangerous subject) not only to

> You my love in springtime instant
> when I wince half pain half joy to notes from
> an oriole

but also to:

> The herring with his sperm makes milk of the
> wide wrinkling wriggling ocean
> where snowy whales jump rolling among
>   whitecaps.

I think students could relate to many parts of this poem without being made to writhe in embarrassment: or feel that it is a matter of adults, who are free to fuck. Another from *You Are Happy* (Margaret Atwood, Oxford University Press, Toronto) would also take some of the grim seriousness out of the sexual battle for your students; (they will learn all that later, when they read Mike Hammer novels and poems where women's thighs are like milk and their breasts like globes of cheese, or some other sort of sexual dairy product). In the meantime, tenderness can mix with sexuality without putting the finger on them to understand bedroom techniques:

> But the way you dance by yourself
> on the tile floor to a worn song, flat and
>   mournful
> so delighted, spoon waved in one hand, wisps of
>   roughened hair
>
> sticking up from your head, it's your surprised
> body, pleasure I like. I can even say it,
> though only this once and it won't
>
> last: I want this. I want
> this.

Teenagers cannot take their sexuality unmixed. This leads to another question, which is: can any of us? But we'll leave that for later. This article is threatening to ramble off in all sorts of directions. The only other suggestion I have would be Catullus and Lesbia, who wrote some of the sexiest and yet most innocent poems I know. They do not have in them the same bitter war which often occurs in modern poetry, and are not utterly male-oriented.

Poems about the Poor

If poets write about the working-class or the poor, they often use terms 44 more suited to the nineteenth century, where the "poor" "squat" in "rags". A student will read this and know he has chairs to sit in, so the poem is not talking to anyone he knows. The food may be running out and dad hasn't got a job, but they do not squat, therefore they are not poor.

> . . . the holes of Cartier
> where the poor squat, numb with winter
> and my poverty is their rags . . .

This is out of "Cold Colloquy" by Patrick Anderson, from *Blasted Pine* "an anthology of disrespectful verse" (MacMillan of Canada). Is this guy being satirical when he talks about the poor? A working class kid would not be able to figure it out. Most poetry about the working class or the poor would arouse our pity for them; and pity is the precise emotion which a young arc-welder welding arcs at Castle Frank would not like to have applied to him. These young people who are trying to move into the working world would rather laugh at it, at first. Try reading Zieroth's "Queen Street Trolley":

> There are nearly fifty people here, all
> uncomfortable, non familiar or recognized.
> The driver continues to insist there is plenty
> of room somewhere in the back . . .

ending up with:

> . . . each day
> is the same and brings us one day closer to the
> angry ideology of random targets and stones.

And I would not teach the poem, often reprinted, "Indian Reservation: 45 Caughnawaga" by A. M. Klein to *any* adolescent — white, red or purple.

> Beneath their alimentary shawls
> sit like black tents their squaws: while
>   for the tourists'
> brown pennies scattered at the old church door,
> the ragged papooses jump, and bite the dust . . .

is less likely to arouse compassion in an adolescent than contempt. Compare it to a native poet, Simon Frogg:

> Log cabin, sod and moss piled on top,
> no mansion, true,
> but still a home.
>
> Candles, oil lamp to light
> wood-burning stove to heat
> and still a comfort.
>
> Just the necessities
> Ranged and hung on walls and rafters.
> Work tools.

If you want new poetry by native people you can get it by subscribing to Wawatay News, General Delivery, Sioux Lookout, Ontario. They have a poet's page and come up with something new every two weeks. Costs four dollars.

46   The problem with teaching poetry to working-class kids is that the poet is generally speaking from a different life experience. References to yachts and crystal and even picnics will often leave them gaping. You might start them out on song-lyrics. From the anthology *Listen: Songs and Poems of Canada* (Methuen, Toronto), you can find "Bus Rider" by the Guess Who; there's also Roger Miller:

> Trailer for sale or rent,
> room to let, fifty cents . . .
> ain't got no cigarettes . . .

47   One poem I would definitely recommend in this context is Whitman's thoughts in section 32 of "Song of Myself", about animals:

> They do not sweat and whine about their
>   condition
> they do not lay awake in the dark and weep
>   for their sins,
> they do not make me sick discussing their
>   duty to god
> Not one is dissatisfied, not one is demented with
>   the mania of owning things
> not one kneels to another, nor to this kind
>   that lived thousands of years ago . . .

Takeoffs and Parodies

48   So far I have been concentrating on content, because poems first of all say things. If you are concerned that your students develop some critical acumen, you will find that takeoffs and parodies will help. I used to swallow everything Dylan Thomas ever wrote until Harrison once read him —

49   "And I *rolled*, I simply *wallowed* in my *chains* like the sea!" he exclaimed, throwing his well-dressed arms around. "And I was *honoured*, don't you know, by foxes and unicorns and Adam and the kids were

green and golden and I don't know *what*-all . . ." We didn't stop liking Thomas but we got the point.

Mad Magazine did an excellent takeoff on "The Wreck Of The   50 Hesperus", so did Mark Twain; *National Lampoon* has done similar things with Shakespeare and Eliot. *Northern Blights* does the same with most Canadian poets.

When Students Bring Their Own

When your students write poems and hand them to you with trembling   51 fingers, they have just given to you their deepest emotions. Other poets may barb themselves about the allusions and metaphor, but generally students write from the heart, and if you criticize their poetry, you are criticizing their hearts. It is not for the teacher to say who will or who will not go out of this class and continue on to write great poetry. There are students who pick up things fast, and can turn out a finished product and then go on to major in forestry and never write another poem. Generally it is to them that the majority of the praise and encouragement will go. Others write awful things that rhyme, with end-stopped lines, about The Little Shirt My Mother Made For Me, because they heard it in a country-western song; and then go on to become genuine poets. Too often the teacher judges students' products by their academic facilities; a cleverly turned metaphor, done by a student who has adjusted to an academic way of writing, can be quite taking. But I would again recommend that teachers pay attention to the content of the poem, and help the student to become clearer about it, even with the worst ones. It is, at a certain level, not for the teacher to judge. He is there to teach — he has not been hired to teach or encourage certain brilliant succeeders, but every student in the class. And remember that any poem handed in is a great compliment to you as a teacher. You might end up sounding like a shrink: "Is this how you really feel about the shirt?"; but after you have assured the student that you are not going to dump on his poem and mark it up with red things and hand it back with a failing grade, then you might be able to teach them something: like they don't *have* to write end-stopped lines, or make it rhyme *all* the way through.

Older Poets

As for teaching the older poetry, I have a few very oddball suggestions.   52 The tarot pack, for one. If high school kids can learn the complicated symbolism of the Tarot Pack they sure can do it with the Canterbury Tales. You can try to match up the different cards with the characters; they will fall quite nicely into shape. And use the cards to teach them. The cards are brightly coloured, and can be used to get across the medieval notions of hierarchy, interlocking symbolism and so on.

You can use these cards for poems like "The Pearl", and "Sir Gawain   53 and The Green Knight". Don't be afraid to range through the older literature to teach the kids. "Sir Gawain and The Green Knight" must be the first totally green man in literature outside of science-fiction. He rides right into the king's hall, where said king is dining on roast serf or something, in a beautifully splashy way:

> He came there all green, both the clothes and
> the man . . .
> bright with a trimming of blaunner and a hood
> to match
> at his ankles hung gleaming spurs
> on gold-embroidered bangles richly barred
> their guard-leather under his legs where the man
> rode
> and everything on him was entirely green . . .

If your students learn to enjoy this poetry, later, in another class somewhere, if they make it to the university, they will learn that it is a strange, anonymous poem from northwestern England, with remnants of Anglo-Saxon alliteration and the bob-and-wheel verse endings — but never mind. In the meantime he makes Clint Eastwood look like a midnight cowboy. Teach it as a feast not to be missed.

54   For good, spare descriptions, look for things in the older Gaelic (Irish) Literature.

> And after the space of a day they left the woods and came to an open plain; and there were meadows on one side of them and mowers mowing the meadows. And they came to a river before them and the horses bent their heads and drank the water. So they went up out of the water and onto a steep bank . . .

55   Especially if they have read *Lord Of The Rings*, the stories contained in the Gaelic poems can be related to Tolkien's complex arrangement of genealogies and battles, heroes and villains. It's amazing how much literature young people can absorb when they want to, and *Lord Of The Rings* is a good example. Meanwhile you can try to drum Tennyson into their heads for months and a year later they will ask "Alfred Who?"

Anthologies

56 As for anthologies designed for students, I would highly recommend *Listen!* and turn thumbs-down on *I Am A Sensation*. The latter book is designed with a very flashy layout; lots of comic-strip illustrations with creatures like Galactus, a tower of roaring steel, crying: "I seek no wealth, no personal gain, no petty, paltry treasure which Zenn-La may possess, instead I crave the total energy of your hapless world!!" The purpose of this, I assume is to illustrate E. J. Pratt's poem, "The Truant", which contains ideas that high school students may find difficult to grasp, to say the least. There are groovy, overexposed photographs and many more imitation comic-strip characters. But the choice of poetry I find

appalling. It offers an enormous amount of modern poetry with no guide whatsoever to the student who, poetryless, may have stumbled upon it. The comic-strip illustrations are patently imitation and do not connect the world of real comic strips to poetry at all. It is modish to the extent that the reader would have to know what modish *is*, in poetry, before he or she could begin to enjoy any of the poems. At one point poems are printed upside down and sideways, which I suppose the layout artist thought was groovy but which makes it really hard to read in bed, or in the bathtub. There are quotes from Laing, from Bishop Berkeley and Ken Kesey, scattered in amongst the *I Ching* and William Blake. It would be hard for anyone without a more general experience of poetry and social criticism to put this together in their heads. It is not a book that kids could be turned loose with and be expected to enjoy on their own; and if you are out for an anthology, you could just as well put something together by yourself that makes more sense rather than have all this thrown together in one book and then printed upside down.

In contrast, an anthology called *Listen!* is not only easy to read in the bathtub, but contains song lyrics (Canadian), poetry (Canadian), and Canadian students' high school poetry. A student could look through this book and find poems by other high school students from across Canada to compare with his or her own, a really valuable experience when you are beginning to write poetry. They can compare the techniques of song-writing with those of poetry. I find the selection is excellent, the photographs good and the content understandable for a high school student. It even includes traditional native songs.   57

P.S. The best thing about writing this article, other than having it come back three times from the editor in shreds, was going through anthologies and collections looking for poems. I was once again led astray by Whitman and Wayman and other long-winded subversives, found a tattered copy of Catullus somewhere, "Sir Gawain and The Green Knight" which should have gone back to the library long ago, discovered *Blasted Pine* and read "The Truant" for the first time, read *Listen!* again from cover to cover and generally wasted time re-reading poetry that I already knew and could have quoted by heart. Try it, you'll like it.   58

TYPES OF WRITING:
allusion, analysis, comparison, description, example/ illustration, humour, narration, personal experience

Topics for Discussion

1. Does the primary audience Jiles is seeking to influence consist of English teachers? Would her comical, sometimes unflattering, albeit sympathetic, depiction of Mr. Harrison and Ms. Roller be likely to

offend teachers? Why or why not? What other groups might Jiles hope to influence with her essay?

2. Why would Jiles, who appears to have a good deal of experience teaching poetry from which to draw examples, lead into her ideas about teaching with an example drawn from her days as a student?

3. In dealing with approaches to teaching poetry, Jiles concentrates on describing examples of teachers: Mr. Harrison and Ms. Roller, not to mention Mr. McFee, the poetry-reciting bus driver. What advantages does this approach offer over a more expository review of the qualities these characters represent? Are there disadvantages to Jiles's approach?

4. How does Jiles treat herself in this essay? How does her attitude toward herself help her to reach, hold, and influence her readers?

5. Is Jiles too ambitious in the last half of her essay? Do the accumulating fragments of advice lessen the effect of the general lessons for which they provide practical support?

6. What do you see as the primary goal of Jiles's essay? Are there secondary goals?

Topics for Writing

1. Write an essay disagreeing with one of the sections of advice Jiles includes in the last half of her essay. Even though you will be disagreeing with Jiles on this point, follow her example of supporting conclusions with lively illustrations.

2. Write an essay explaining how either a good or a bad method of teaching math, science, or history — some subject other than poetry — influences students. Illustrate your ideas by describing a teacher or teachers you have known and explaining your own reactions to the method.

3. What has been your experience with poetry? Your discussion might consider such points as parental influence for or against poetry, the good or bad influence of your peers, good and bad teachers, poems that you liked or detested, memorable poems you encountered outside of any school context, and excellent readers you have heard in public or on the radio.

Legally Bombed

George Jonas

My great-uncle in Vienna used cocaine. The family thought him a fool, 1
but that didn't prevent them from fobbing off nephews and nieces on
him for holidays. In addition to being a cocaine user and a bit of a rake,
great-uncle Erwin was a shrewd businessman and a kindly soul. He
made his money, then gave a lot of it away to people who asked for it.
He never abused his wife, ran no-one over with his Packard (mind you,
he always kept a chauffeur), and when he eventually committed suicide
it had nothing to do with his drug habit. He killed himself because Hitler
marched into Austria in 1938.

I'm not telling this story to make a point about cocaine use, which I 2
consider moronic. I'm telling the story a) because it happened, b) because
it happened half a century ago (indicating that there's nothing very new
about cocaine), and c) because my great-uncle, whatever his failings, was
an ordinary middle-class citizen. He was neither a criminal nor a menace
and he certainly required no social support. On the contrary, he supported
other people. He had good reasons to fear Hitler (he was a Jew), but I
dare say he'd have been surprised to hear a president of the United
States declaring war on him.

President George Bush's celebrated declaration of war on drugs per- 3
mits us to look at the question in military terms. In a war it's useful to
have an answer to the following question: who is the enemy and what
are we fighting for? In this case the answer seems to be that the enemy is
us, or at least many of us. What we are fighting for is to be different from
what we are.

As human beings, we're drug users. Few societies, ancient or modern, 4
have been without mind-altering substances. Their earliest use, as the
Toronto psychiatrist Dr. A. I. Malcolm pointed out in his 1971 book, *The
Pursuit of Intoxication*, was probably ritual. Chewing or sniffing certain
leaves and roots seemed to put us in touch with the great beyond.

Soon we started chewing or sniffing them for conviviality and fun. 5
The recreational use of many drugs became intertwined with their me-
dicinal, religious, or ceremonial use — as it still is, to a vestigial extent, in
our society. We toast the queen with a glass of wine (we'd consider it
unseemly to do so with a can of 7-Up), and some of us firmly believe
that a hot toddy is an excellent cure for the common cold.

A "drug problem" exists because many of us take drugs. A few of us 6
become dependent on drugs and permit them to rule and ruin our lives.
Also, at times, the lives of our families or neighbours.

While taking drugs is universal, the drugs that are dearest to our 7
minds and hearts — or stomachs, lungs, and veins — vary with the
culture in which we live. Even within the same culture they vary among
social classes or historical periods. Different drugs have different
pharmacologies. This means that their use is likely to have different

social consequences. Smoking a few cigarettes and knocking back a few glasses of port are both enjoyable (and unhealthy) to the user, but they have vastly different effects on his ability to make reasoned decisions, touch his own nose, or walk a straight line.

8   Even the same drug may differ in its influence on different individuals and, perhaps, on different groups. Societies develop different ways of coping or failing to cope with drugs. All these variables are liable to create confusion in the minds of U.S. presidents, to say nothing of legislators, talk-show hosts, drug users, and drug-enforcement officials. In recent years it has become difficult to comment on the subject without sorting out a few things first.

9   When we say "drugs" we're obviously not talking about aspirin. Aspirin reduces physical pain; the drugs we're talking about reduce the pain of everyday perception. They're mood-altering or psychoactive substances such as alcohol, marijuana, cocaine, nicotine, or caffeine — in other words, stimulants or depressants people take primarily for pleasure. Why is it a pleasure to take them?

10   The chief reasons are that 1) many of these drugs create a feeling of wellbeing or euphoria, and 2) they tend to reduce tension and existential anxiety in human beings.

11   All recreational drugs are addictive. Though addictiveness varies with the chemical properties of specific drugs, anything that's strong enough to give you a high (or even to take away your pain) is likely to be strong enough to hook you. Still, it's common knowledge that some individuals become dependent on the same drug in worse ways than others. Seventy-eight per cent of the population of Canada drinks alcohol, but only about ten per cent of the drinkers end up as alcoholics. Why?

12   Here the answers are more complex. One harsh view is that abusers are losers. Their ambitions outstrip their abilities, so they turn to the bottle. Alternatively — or maybe in addition — they suffer from an unusual degree of existential anxiety, which needs continual relief.

13   Some are craven in their yearning for acceptance and can be swayed by fashions of drug use and abuse that crop up in some cultures or subcultures from time to time. In certain settings — corporate, social, or artistic — a drug may become a symbol of reliability: gin and tonic for the country-club set, marijuana for peaceniks, vodka for members of the Politburo. If you fail to imbibe or shoot up with the boys, you're just not one of them.

14   A drug taken in such circumstances may become part of a person's cultural identity. Any attempt to dissuade him may be resented as a rejection of his entire system of values. Conversely, a stubborn individualist may resist social pressure to give up his habit as an attack on his sovereignty. Of course, people also become addicted simply because many drugs create a physical dependency. If a person stops taking them, he feels sick.

15   While culture and personality seem to define the addict, recent studies

tend to confirm some age-old suspicions, namely that biological and genetic dispositions for dependency also vary, perhaps not just among individuals but among sexual, ethnic, and racial groups. One study suggests that females have about thirty per cent fewer enzymes for breaking down alcohol in their systems than males. In some Oriental groups a percentage of people "produce" their own Antabuse, as it were, by a different enzyme reaction. They soon feel sick when they drink, so they learn not to drink too much. Anyone can become an alcoholic, but your chances may be less if you're Chinese or Jewish and greater if you're an Irishman or a native American.

Not all of these facts are undisputed. However, even the facts we know 16 beyond a doubt fail to lead us to a consensus. We still try to control the social use of drugs with strategies that fly in the face of what we know.

If all drugs that are currently illicit were to be legalized tomorrow, 17 there's little doubt (none in my mind) that two things would happen.

The number of users would double; maybe even triple. That's the 18 bad news. Since it's estimated that about 30-million people use illicit drugs in the U.S. (compared with about 140-million users of alcohol and about 50-million users of nicotine), legalizing substances like marijuana, heroin, and cocaine would probably result in 30- to 60-million additional users. This is just a guess, but it's a reasonable one: it's extrapolated from the 350-per-cent increase in the use of alcohol that reportedly followed Prohibition. (Canada's figures are similar when expressed in percentages. According to a 1987 Gallup Poll, seventy-eight per cent of adult Canadians use alcohol [in the U.S. it's eighty per cent], thirty-four per cent use tobacco [U.S. thirty per cent], and about fifteen per cent use all other drugs combined [U.S. sixteen per cent] — though the last number may include legal prescription drugs here, according to Manuella Adrian of the Addiction Research Foundation of Ontario.)

If about ten to fifteen per cent of users become abusers this should 19 result in an increase of 3- to 9-million abusers in the U.S. Translate this dry figure into an additional 3- to 9-million sick human beings who would suffer like dogs and die before their time. Even worse, translate it into 3- to 9-million unpredictable zombies who would not only require social support but might annoy and assault the rest of us, shunt our trains on the wrong track, or run us down in their cars.

Now for the good news. With legalization, the criminal activities 20 associated with illegal drug traffic would drastically diminish. Fewer citizens would be mugged, burgled, or murdered in their beds by addicts seeking to support their habit. Dealers would no longer shoot it out on street corners to protect their turf. In fact, dealers and drug barons would be out of business. The public expense of fighting drug traffickers would be replaced by a public revenue from the controlled sale of drugs.

Taxpayers, instead of wasting money on other people's cocaine habit, 21 would be *making* money on it. Professor Ethan A. Nadelmann, of Princeton University, estimates that the net upside, after combining the savings on

law enforcement with the expected tax revenues, would amount to some
$10-billion annually in the U.S.

22   Less tangibly but just as importantly, the private conduct of peaceable
citizens would no longer be criminalized by the authorities. Those who
commit crimes under the influence of drugs would still be penalized, but
only for their actual breach of the queen's peace. People who endanger
no-one with their temperate, civilized enjoyment of drugs would no
longer be hounded and punished.

23   Measures that are distasteful to a liberal society but that any "war"
on drugs inevitably entails — drug-testing employees, say, or body-search-
ing high-school students — could be happily shelved. Wiretaps and other
police-state methods, now used against activities no more inherently
criminal than selling or buying a case of beer, could be reserved for
genuine threats like terrorism or espionage. Our civil liberties would not
be devalued by a false sense of emergency.

24   To me, the increase in drug abuse and the decrease in criminal activity are both predictable consequences of legalization — but many serious
and thoughtful people disagree. Those who detest the idea of legalized
drugs tend to dispute the good news, i.e. that, if drug prohibition ended,
fewer citizens would be hurt by crimes engendered solely by our desire
to keep certain drugs illegal. Those who'd like to see drugs legalized
dispute the first consequence, i.e. that drugs, if legally available, would
hurt many more people.

25   Princeton's Nadelmann, whose 1988 essay in the U.S. quarterly *Foreign
Policy* did much to spark the current debate, points to the fact that cocaine,
opium, and cannabis were more or less legal in North America throughout the late nineteenth and early twentieth centuries. The earliest U.S.
federal legislation to restrict the sale of cocaine and the opiates was the
1914 Harrison Act. Canada's first narcotics-control act is a little older: it
received royal assent in 1908. According to Nadelmann, before the passage
of the Harrison Act, the U.S. "had a drug abuse problem of roughly
similar magnitude to today's problem."

26   So, to paraphrase Nadelmann's argument — and the arguments of
those who, like the Berkeley criminologist Rosann Greenspan, agree with
him — the rate of addiction is more or less constant in a given society, no
matter what the society's laws or enforcement policies may be. The main
variables are cultural and personal. "There is good reason to assume,"
Nadelmann writes, "that even if all the illegal drugs were made legally
available, the same cultural restraints that now keep most Americans
from becoming drug abusers would persist and perhaps even
strengthen . . . . In this respect, most Americans differ from monkeys,
who have demonstrated in tests that they will starve themselves to
death if provided with unlimited cocaine." In support of this view,
Nadelmann cites the experience of the Netherlands, *inter alia*, where
marijuana abuse stayed level or even diminished after the relaxation of
legal controls.

The Princeton professor also takes the view that forbidden drugs are 27
no more inherently harmful or addictive than legal drugs. In other words,
cocaine, heroin, the hallucinogens, and marijuana are capable of being
enjoyed as moderately and harmlessly as wine or Scotch are at present
by most social drinkers. And more harmlessly than tobacco in terms of
the user's health.

Nadelmann relies on a 1986 study by the National Institute on Drug 28
Abuse to show that cocaine put only three per cent of the people who
tried it at risk of becoming abusers. Even among those who used it
monthly, only ten per cent were at risk — much the same as the figure for
alcohol. As for heroin, it *is* very addictive, though no more so than nicotine. Since Nadelmann sees the dangers as roughly equivalent, he concludes: "The 'moral' condemnation of some substances and not others is
revealed as little more than a prejudice in favor of some drugs and
against others."

Utter rubbish, opponents say. For one thing, the population at risk 29
is simply a percentage of the population exposed. If in a given culture
30-million people experiment with drugs that are illegal, significantly
more can be expected to experiment with them when they're legal. And
if users increase, so will abusers. In Dr. Malcolm's words, "The number
of people injured by a drug will, in general, vary directly with the overall
consumption of that drug."

The U.S. criminologist James Q. Wilson, appointed in 1972 as chair- 30
man of the National Advisory Council on Drug Abuse Prevention, and
today one of the most eloquent opponents of legalization, feels that Professor Nadelmann's argument is based on "a logical fallacy and a factual
error." Writing in the February, 1990, issue of *Commentary* magazine,
Wilson points out the fallacy: "The percentage of occasional cocaine
users who become binge users *when the drug is illegal* (and thus expensive
and hard to find) tells us nothing about the percentage who will become
dependent when the drug is legal (and thus cheap and abundant)." As
for Nadelmann's factual error, Wilson says that his conclusions are based
on a 1985 study done "before crack had become common. Thus the
probability of becoming dependent on cocaine was derived from the
responses of users who snorted the drug. The speed and potency of
cocaine's action increases dramatically when it is smoked."

Dr. Malcolm has a similar view. He feels that there's "no justification 31
for cocaine whatsoever. It can be taken in ever more dramatic fashions.
It's vicious. It has no utility, has not been acculturated, and can still be
controlled."

This is at the core of the disagreement: bad as legal drugs are, say 32
prohibitionists, the drugs that are now illegal are worse. As Dr. Malcolm
points out, crack, hash, LSD, ice (the new smokable form of speed), or
heroin are almost invariably used to get stoned, bombed out of one's
mind, while alcohol is being used by most people not to get roaring
drunk but as a pleasant accompaniment to a meal or a genial get-together.

33   It's nonsense to talk about only 3,562 people dying in the U.S. in a given year (1985) from all illegal drugs combined, as opposed to nearly 500,000 dying as the direct or indirect result of alcohol and tobacco use. There's no evidence that this has been due to the benign properties of illicit drugs and all sorts of evidence that it has been due to their illegality. If they were legalized, cocaine, heroin, marijuana, or hallucinogens would also kill at least 500,000 people. "Suppose that in the 1920s we had made heroin and cocaine legal and alcohol illegal," says Wilson. "Can anyone doubt that Nadelmann would now be writing that it is folly to continue our ban on alcohol because cocaine and heroin are so much more harmful?"

34   As for legalization putting drug barons out of business, prohibitionists dismiss the idea. They say that racketeers will simply find another racket, and burglars another reason to burgle. Nor are prohibitionists impressed by the reduced costs of law enforcement or by potential profits from the controlled sale of legalized drugs. Any profits, they say, would be eaten up by the social services that new addicts would require. Anyway, as Wilson writes, if taxes on legalized drugs were high, addicts would still have to commit crimes to feed their habits; and if taxes weren't high, drugs wouldn't be very profitable to the treasury.

35   The calls for legalization aren't new, of course. Still, there *is* something new about them: some of the lines, and some of the players reading them.

36   Old lines are rarely being heard these days. Conspicuously absent are the arguments of those carefree years that culminated in the 1973 recommendations of Gerald LeDain's commission on the nonmedical use of drugs, which urged Canadians to decriminalize cannabis. In those heady days, many who favoured legalization tended to talk in terms of a benign drug culture. Their arguments were infused with the climate of the Greening of America, the Age of Aquarius, the gentle dawn of a new enlightenment.

37   For people caught up in that trend, the "high" heralded a coming age of creativity and love. Drugs, particularly the "soft" drugs marijuana and hashish but also the psychedelic LSD, served as leitmotivs in the triumphant symphony of a more youthful and humane culture. Even those who doubted the miraculous somatic society — LeDain himself, in all likelihood — felt obliged to give it the benefit of their doubts. People who spoke out against the hazards of drug use (whether or not they dared to employ such phrases as "the killer weed") were regarded as antediluvian. A cautionary tone about drugs in media circles — a tone that's almost *de rigueur* in the daily press today — fifteen to twenty years ago would have exposed one to the risk of losing one's intellectual licence.

38   A cautionary tone wasn't safe even in scientific circles. In 1973, Barbara Amiel wrote an article in *Saturday Night* about Dr. Malcolm, who had been dismissed from the Addiction Research Foundation of Ontario. Malcolm, in Amiel's words, "ran afoul of what was emerging as the

dominant cult of the ARF. He disagreed with the concept of 'wise personal choice.'" This concept suggested that scientists should make no value judgments, only describe what they knew about the properties of certain chemicals so that people could make wise personal choices about their use. That included, presumably, people with little demonstrated wisdom.

Malcolm disagreed. Nor did he go along with another concept of some ARF people, namely that it wasn't scientific to say that drug dependence in itself was "an adverse effect." As a clinician who had worked with and observed addicts, Malcolm felt that "he had a responsibility to say that 'drug dependence' was an 'adverse effect' in any form." 39

The ARF's dismissal didn't disrupt Malcolm's career. His books, notably *The Case Against the Drugged Mind* and *The Tyranny of the Group*, had some influence both in Canada and in the U.S. Today he's a prominent forensic psychiatrist. However, the dismissal, whether literal or figurative, of people like Malcolm twenty years ago may have disrupted our society in significant ways. Arguably, it was our intellectual elite's quest for enlightenment, combined with our establishment's abject surrender to what the poet Schiller called "the sword of fashion," that helped spread the deadly malaise of drugs into our inner cities and suburbs. 40

By now, of course, the climate of the debate has changed. No-one argues that a "turned-on" society will lead to higher plateaus of enlightenment. Those who call for legalization in 1990 have no such illusions. Most consider drugs stupid and potentially harmful. They only think that avoidable government should be avoided; and that, while crack is the pits, invoking the genie of the state to save us from ourselves can be even more dangerous. 41

As a result many who favour legalization today, far from being associated with the youth culture of the "left," would be identified as being on the "right" of the sociopolitical spectrum. In the U.S. they include the economist Milton Friedman, the criminologist Ernest van den Haag, writers Lewis H. Lapham and William F. Buckley, Jr., and lately even former secretary of state George Shultz. In Britain it is the editorial position of *The Economist*. 42

This is, of course, by no means the position of everyone who might be described in the media as "right-wing." Prominent conservatives James Q. Wilson and George F. Will are among the most outspoken opponents of legalizing drugs, especially cocaine and heroin. At the same time, staunch civil-rights activists such as Canada's Alan Borovoy and Edward L. Greenspan help swell the ranks of those who support decriminalization. The drug debate is cutting across traditional left-right divisions today. 43

My problem with the entire debate is that I'm a somewhat callous and cussed person. Being callous, I have no interest in saving people from themselves; being cussed, I hate it when people try to save me from myself. 44

There's merit in the arguments of both sides. I find it incontestable that legalization will increase consumption; increased consumption will 45 increase abuse; and a lot of zombies can't help but lower the resilience and moral tone of society. I also feel — though it may not be *comme il faut* to say so — that drugs are more harmful for today's mass than for yesterday's class society. The perfect individual liberty I cherish may be a luxury mass societies can't quite afford.

46   Some of the drugs now spreading through our egalitarian culture were once confined mainly to the leisure or bohemian classes in the West. The damage that could be done by a Sherlock Holmes smoking his opium pipe or my great-uncle Erwin sniffing his cocaine was mitigated by their income and maybe even by their sense of noblesse oblige. No such restraints operate on kids smoking crack in the slums of Washington or in Toronto's Jane-Finch corridor today.

47   At the same time I agree with Eddie Greenspan when he points out that popular support for a presidential drug war comes mainly from citizens tired of not finding their stereos when they get home. Those who fear drugs really fear crime — and crime could better be reduced by legalizing drugs. "People feel sorry about 'junkies' wasting their lives," says Greenspan, "but what really upsets them is that addicts or pushers waste citizens' lives when they mug or shoot them." If this is the trade-off, it may not be so immoral to suggest that it's better for more voluntary abusers to overdose than for more involuntary passers-by to be shot.

48   Unfortunately, much of the debate is hypocritical. Everybody wants to crap on the other guy's drug while defending his own. Sentimental ex-hippies, for instance, have been among the first to jump on the anti-nicotine bandwagon. "If we can't smoke our grass," they seem to say, "then by golly you aren't going to smoke your cigarettes."

49   Cigarettes, of course, are unhealthy to users. They're also a nuisance to some bystanders. But nicotine, whatever else it may do, cannot alter cognition. It doesn't impair motor skills. It doesn't make users go out of their minds.

50   Referring to nicotine in the same breath with cocaine is crossing a line: the line that separates legitimate social concern from eco-facism. Curiously (or perhaps not) this line is crossed most often by those who call for lifting all bans on illicit drugs. *They* keep stressing the social harm of nicotine. It is James Q. Wilson, the ostensible regulator, who emphasizes the difference: "Tobacco shortens one's life, cocaine debases it. Nicotine alters one's habits, cocaine alters one's soul . . . . To say, as does Nadelmann, that distinguishing morally between tobacco and cocaine is 'little more than a transient prejudice' is close to saying that morality itself is but a prejudice."

51   Having quoted this, I suppose I should add one thing. I'm a smoker and I don't intend to quit.

52   Another problem with the debate is that it keeps harping on the nebulous concept of "social cost." Prohibitionists justify the state's inter-est in private habits by pointing to taxpayers' expenditures and by talking about hospital bills and early deaths. But book-keeping is a complex

matter. The true economic effects of a social problem cannot be assessed only by adding up amounts spent on its cure and control.

If an abuser gets sick and dies before his time, it's a human tragedy 53 — that's easy — but it's not necessarily a social cost. At least, not until the cost of geriatric services and pensions paid to people who linger beyond their productive years is deducted from it. No-one has calculated what it would "cost" if every year another 500,000 people lived to be ninety. Perhaps if someone did, fiscal responsibility would compel him to recommend that we force people to abstain from everything until retirement — and then oblige them to take up drinking, smoking, hang-gliding, and unsafe sex.

My final problem is that drug wars concentrate on Mr. Big, but 54 Mr. Big is a small problem. The big problem is Mr. Small. Mr. Big supplies, but it's Mr. Small who demands drugs. A traffic for which there's a demand can't be eradicated by attacking its supply alone, not even with tanks and helicopters. As long as there's a demand, there will always be someone to supply it. If you make it tough for one guy, the next one will supply it at a higher price.

Can demand be attacked? Yes, by socioeconomic and cultural changes, 55 which are slow, or with draconian measures, which are, well, draconian. Death for pushers, as in Malaysia, and seven-year minimums for first-time users might reduce a demand for drugs quite speedily. They could also turn a society into a rather nasty police state. So if we find the tempo of social change too glacial and have no stomach for getting tough, legalization may be a better option. Going after Mr. Big alone, at home or abroad, is a waste of money. Also of innocent lives, as in the case of Panama.

Perhaps luckily, Canada can't launch any invasions. Even beyond 56 that, our problems may be different — or at least delayed. Ancient and universal as addiction is, a special concern today is that illicit drugs have invaded groups that are the least equipped to cope with their effects; it's within these groups that drug use is most likely to turn into drug abuse and can lead most readily to crime and disintegration. The young constitute one such group, obviously; some minority subcultures form another. In black ghettos, for instance, crime is a necessity for users to support their habit. There are huge economic incentives — for slum dwellers, often the only incentives — to deal in illicit drugs.

Canada has proportionately the same number of young people as 57 the U.S., but most of our minority subcultures are relatively much smaller. If drugs have been less of a problem here than in America, this is one of the reasons. But things are changing. We've had new concentrations of black and Asian immigrants since the 1960s. And, like the Americans, we're seeing pushers targeting the young of all groups and classes.

"Drug use is increasing and users are getting younger," says Herb 58 Stephen, president of the Canadian Association of Chiefs of Police and police chief of Winnipeg. "Crack is just starting here. Toronto and

Vancouver have had it longer, but there was none in Winnipeg until just before Christmas. There is now. Probably the next thing will be ice."

59   If this still sounds tame by U.S. standards, it has an interesting side effect. Legalization used to be a counsel of hope. By now it has become a counsel of despair, but, while drugs are a problem in Canada, we are not yet despairing. In Canada there are fewer calls for legalization. Most people feel that things can still be nipped in the bud.

60   Chief Stephen and his fellow police chiefs stress enforcement as usual, coupled with education and rehabilitation. They oppose legalization, sure, but: "We're not even bothering to develop a position paper on it," Chief Stephen comments. "There's no real debate in this country yet."

TYPES OF WRITING:
analysis, cause and effect, comparison, direct argument

Topics for Discussion

1. How relevant is the opening example of Uncle Erwin to the current drug problem in North America? Without making any claims that legalizing drugs will turn the disadvantaged youth of North America into charming, benign figures like his uncle, what does Jonas accomplish by implication with his opening example?
2. Jonas devotes a substantial part of his article to summarizing the views of others. Can you detect any evidence of bias in the way these secondhand opinions are reported?
3. Imagine that you are Jonas and that an editor has requested that you trim your argument to about three-quarters of its present length. What parts of the essay could you cut or summarize without substantially weakening your case? Would you need to change the structure of your essay to accommodate the changes?
4. Do the concluding paragraphs suggest that Jonas's purpose in this essay may not be as straightforward as simply persuading members of his society to legalize drugs? Given the improbability of full legalization, what might Jonas more realistically be trying to promote in this essay?
5. Comment on the function of the last sentence of paragraph 8.

Topics for Writing

1. Jonas's argument concentrates on immediate effects. Write a counter-argument by following the immediate effects of legalization into the future.
2. If such drugs as marijuana and cocaine were legalized in Canada, would you use them? Your essay on this question should consider the

effects of your decision on your parents, spouse, children, close friends, and co-workers, as well as its effects on yourself — physically, mentally, socially, morally.

Where Do We Go from Here?

Martin Luther King, Jr.

1   Oppressed people deal with their oppression in three characteristic ways. One way is acquiescence: the oppressed resign of themselves to their doom. They tacitly adjust themselves to oppression, and thereby become conditioned to it. In every movement toward freedom some of the oppressed prefer to remain oppressed. Almost 2800 years ago Moses set out to lead the children of Israel from the slavery of Egypt to the freedom of the promised land. He soon discovered that slaves do not always welcome their deliverers. They become accustomed to being slaves. They would rather bear those ills they have, as Shakespeare pointed out, than flee to others that they know not of. They prefer the "fleshpots of Egypt" to the ordeals of emancipation.

2   There is such a thing as the freedom of exhaustion. Some people are so worn down by the yoke of oppression that they give up. A few years ago in the slum areas of Atlanta, a Negro guitarist used to sing almost daily: "Ben down so long that down don't bother me." This is the type of negative freedom and resignation that often engulfs the life of the oppressed.

3   But this is not the way out. To accept passively an unjust system is to cooperate with that system; thereby the oppressed become as evil as the oppressor. Noncooperation with evil is as much a moral obligation as is cooperation with good. The oppressed must never allow the conscience of the oppressor to slumber. Religion reminds every man that he is his brother's keeper. To accept injustice or segregation passively is to say to the oppressor that his actions are morally right. It is a way of allowing his conscience to fall asleep. At this moment the oppressed fails to be his brother's keeper. So acquiescence — while often the easier way — is not the moral way. It is the way of the coward. The Negro cannot win the respect of his oppressor by acquiescing; he merely increases the oppressor's arrogance and contempt. Acquiescence is interpreted as proof of the Negro's inferiority. The Negro cannot win the respect of the white people of the South or the peoples of the world if he is willing to sell the future of his children for his personal and immediate comfort and safety.

4   A second way that oppressed people sometimes deal with oppression is to resort to physical violence and corroding hatred. Violence often brings about momentary results. Nations have frequently won their independence in battle. But in spite of temporary victories, violence never brings permanent peace. It solves no social problem; it merely creates new and more complicated ones.

5   Violence as a way of achieving racial justice is both impractical and immoral. It is impractical because it is a descending spiral ending in destruction for all. The old law of an eye for an eye leaves everybody blind. It is immoral because it seeks to humiliate the opponent rather than win his understanding; it seeks to annihilate rather than to convert.

110

Violence is immoral because it thrives on hatred rather than love. It destroys community and makes brotherhood impossible. It leaves society in monologue rather than dialogue. Violence ends by defeating itself. It creates bitterness in the survivors and brutality in the destroyers. A voice echoes through time saying to every potential Peter, "Put up your sword." History is cluttered with the wreckage of nations that failed to follow this command.

If the American Negro and other victims of oppression succumb to   6
the temptation of using violence in the struggle for freedom, future generations will be the recipients of a desolate night of bitterness, and our chief legacy to them will be an endless reign of meaningless chaos. Violence is not the way.

The third way open to oppressed people in their quest for freedom is   7
the way of nonviolent resistance. Like the synthesis in Hegelian philosophy, the principle of nonviolent resistance seeks to reconcile the truths of two opposites — acquiescence and violence — while avoiding the extremes and immoralities of both. The nonviolent resister agrees with the person who acquiesces that one should not be physically aggressive toward his opponent; but he balances the equation by agreeing with the person of violence that evil must be resisted. He avoids the nonresistance of the former and the violent resistance of the latter. With nonviolent resistance, no individual or group need submit to any wrong, nor need anyone resort to violence in order to right a wrong.

It seems to me that this is the method that must guide the actions of   8
the Negro in the present crisis in race relations. Through nonviolent resistance the Negro will be able to rise to the noble height of opposing the unjust system while loving the perpetrators of the system. The Negro must work passionately and unrelentingly for full stature as a citizen, but he must not use inferior methods to gain it. He must never come to terms with falsehood, malice, hate, or destruction.

Nonviolent resistance makes it possible for the Negro to remain in   9
the South and struggle for his rights. The Negro's problem will not be solved by running away. He cannot listen to the glib suggestion of those who would urge him to migrate en masse to other sections of the country. By grasping his great opportunity in the South he can make a lasting contribution to the moral strength of the nation and set a sublime example of courage for generations yet unborn.

By nonviolent resistance, the Negro can also enlist all men of good   10
will in his struggle for equality. The problem is not a purely racial one, with Negroes set against whites. In the end, it is not a struggle between people at all, but a tension between justice and injustice. Nonviolent resistance is not aimed against oppressors but against oppression. Under its banner consciences, not racial groups, are enlisted.

If the Negro is to achieve the goal of integration, he must organize   11
himself into a militant and nonviolent mass movement. All three elements are indispensable. The movement for equality and justice can only be a

success if it has both a mass and militant character; the barriers to be overcome require both. Nonviolence is an imperative in order to bring about ultimate community

12   A mass movement of a militant quality that is not at the same time committed to nonviolence tends to generate conflict, which in turn breeds anarchy. The support of the participants and the sympathy of the un-committed are both inhibited by the threat that bloodshed will engulf the community. This reaction in turn encourages the opposition to threaten and resort to force. When, however, the mass movement repudiates violence while moving resolutely toward its goal, its opponents are revealed as the instigators and practitioners of violence if it occurs. Then public support is magnetically attracted to the advocates of nonviolence, while those who employ violence are literally disarmed by overwhelming sentiment against their stand.

13   Only through a nonviolent approach can the fears of the white community be mitigated. A guilt-ridden white minority lives in fear that if the Negro should ever attain power, he would act without restraint or pity to revenge the injustices and brutality of the years. It is something like a parent who continually mistreats a son. One day that parent raises his hand to strike the son, only to discover that the son is now as tall as he is. The parent is suddenly afraid — fearful that the son will use his new physical power to repay his parent for all the blows of the past.

14   The Negro, once a helpless child, has now grown up politically, culturally, and economically. Many white men fear retaliation. The job of the Negro is to show them that they have nothing to fear, that the Negro understands and forgives and is ready to forget the past. He must convince the white man that all he seeks is justice, *for both himself and the white man*. A mass movement exercising nonviolence is an object lesson in power under discipline, a demonstration to the white community that if such a movement attained a degree of strength, it would use its power creatively and not vengefully.

15   Nonviolence can touch men where the law cannot reach them. When the law regulates behavior it plays an indirect part in molding public sentiment. The enforcement of the law is itself a form of peaceful persuasion. But the law needs help. The courts can order desegregation of the public schools. But what can be done to mitigate the fears, to disperse the hatred, violence, and irrationality gathered around school integration, to take the initiative out of the hands of racial demagogues, to release respect for the law? In the end, for laws to be obeyed, men must believe they are right.

16   Here nonviolence comes in as the ultimate form of persuasion. It is the method which seeks to implement the just law by appealing to the conscience of the great decent majority who through blindness, fear, pride, or irrationality have allowed their consciences to sleep.

17   The nonviolent resisters can summarize their message in the following simple terms: We will take direct action against injustice without

waiting for other agencies to act. We will not obey unjust laws or submit to unjust practices. We will do this peacefully, openly, cheerfully because our aim is to persuade. We adopt the means of nonviolence because our end is a community at peace with itself. We will try to persuade with our words, but if our words fail, we will try to persuade with our acts. We will always be willing to talk and seek fair compromise, but we are ready to suffer when necessary and even risk our lives to become witnesses to the truth as we see it.

The way of nonviolence means a willingness to suffer and sacrifice. 18
It may mean going to jail. If such is the case the resister must be willing to fill the jail houses of the South. It may even mean physical death. But if physical death is the price that a man must pay to free his children and his white brethren from a permanent death of the spirit, then nothing could be more redemptive.

What is the Negro's best defense against acts of violence inflicted 19
upon him? As Dr. Kenneth Clark has said so eloquently, "His only defense is to meet every act of barbarity, illegality, cruelty and injustice toward an individual Negro with the fact that 100 more Negroes will present themselves in his place as potential victims." Every time one Negro school teacher is fired for believing in integration, a thousand others should be ready to take the same stand. If the oppressors bomb the home of one Negro for his protest, they must be made to realize that to press back the rising tide of the Negro's courage they will have to bomb hundreds more, and even then they will fail.

Faced with this dynamic unity, this amazing self-respect, this will- 20
ingness to suffer, and this refusal to hit back, the oppressor will find, as oppressors have always found, that he is glutted with his own barbarity. Forced to stand before the world and his God splattered with the blood of his brother, he will call an end to his self-defeating massacre.

American Negroes must come to the point where they can say to 21
their white brothers, paraphrasing the words of Gandhi: "We will match your capacity to inflict suffering with our capacity to endure suffering. We will meet your physical force with soul force. We will not hate you, but we cannot in all good conscience obey your unjust laws. Do to us what you will and we will still love you. Bomb our homes and threaten our children; send your hooded perpetrators of violence into our communities and drag us out on some wayside road, beating us and leaving us half dead, and we will still love you. But we will soon wear you down by our capacity to suffer. And in winning our freedom we will so appeal to your heart and conscience that we will win you in the process."

TYPES OF WRITING:
allusion, analysis, cause and effect, classification, definition, direct argument, example/illustration

Topics for Discussion

1. Discuss the way in which King uses potential violence from dissatisfied Blacks outside his movement to promote his goals.
2. Is King's assertion that there are three ways of dealing with racial discrimination an oversimplification? Would his position be weakened or strengthened if he had said more about exceptions and blends of the three approaches he describes?
3. Paragraphs 1, 4, and 7 contain pointers that help to reveal the structure of this essay. What are these pointers, and what, specifically, do they reveal? What other pointers are there following paragraph 7?
4. Locate specific examples of figurative language and poetic images, and consider the extent to which they add emotional force to King's argument in favour of nonviolent resistance.

Topics for Writing

1. Using the basic principles for bringing about change outlined here, write an essay of your own aimed at alleviating some other social injustice that has affected you personally.
2. "In the end, for laws to be obeyed, men must believe they are right." Examine the larger implications of this statement.

Death and Justice: How Capital Punishment Affirms Life

Edward I. Koch

Last December a man named Robert Lee Willie, who had been convicted 1
of raping and murdering an 18-year-old woman, was executed in the
Louisiana state prison. In a statement issued several minutes before his
death, Mr. Willie said: "Killing people is wrong. . . . It makes no difference whether it's citizens, countries, or governments. Killing is wrong."
Two weeks later in South Carolina, an admitted killer named Joseph
Carl Shaw was put to death for murdering two teenagers. In an appeal
to the governor for clemency, Mr. Shaw wrote: "Killing is wrong when I
did it. Killing is wrong when you do it. I hope you have the courage and
moral strength to stop the killing."

It is a curiosity of modern life that we find ourselves being lectured 2
on morality by cold-blooded killers. Mr. Willie previously had been convicted of aggravated rape, aggravated kidnapping, and the murders of a
Louisiana deputy and a man from Missouri. Mr. Shaw committed another
murder a week before the two for which he was executed, and admitted
mutilating the body of the 14-year-old girl he killed. I can't help wondering what prompted these murderers to speak out against killing as
they entered the death-house door. Did their newfound reverence for life
stem from the realization that they were about to lose their own?

Life is indeed precious, and I believe the death penalty helps to 3
affirm this fact. Had the death penalty been a real possibility in the
minds of these murderers, they might well have stayed their hand. They
might have shown moral awareness before their victims died, and not
after. Consider the tragic death of Rosa Velez, who happened to be home
when a man named Luis Vera burglarized her apartment in Brooklyn.
"Yeah, I shot her," Vera admitted. "She knew me, and I knew I wouldn't
go to the chair."

During my 22 years in public service, I have heard the pros and cons 4
of capital punishment expressed with special intensity. As a district leader,
councilman, congressman, and mayor, I have represented constituencies
generally thought of as liberal. Because I support the death penalty for
heinous crimes of murder, I have sometimes been the subject of emotional
outraged attacks by voters who find my position reprehensible or worse.
I have listened to their ideas. I have weighed their objections carefully. I
still support the death penalty. The reasons I maintain my position can
be best understood by examining the arguments most frequently heard
in opposition.

(1) *The death penalty is "barbaric."* Sometimes opponents of capital 5
punishment horrify with tales of lingering death on the gallows, of faulty
electric chairs, or of agony in the gas chamber. Partly in response to such
protests, several states such as North Carolina and Texas switched to

115

execution by lethal injection. The condemned person is put to death painlessly, without ropes, voltage, bullets, or gas. Did this answer the objections of death penalty opponents? Of course not. On June 22, 1984, *The New York Times* published an editorial that sarcastically attacked the new "hygienic" method of death by injection, and stated that "execution can never be made humane through science." So it's not the method that really troubles opponents. It's the death itself they consider barbaric.

6   Admittedly, capital punishment is not a pleasant topic. However, one does not have to like the death penalty in order to support it any more than one must like radical surgery, radiation, or chemotherapy in order to find necessary these attempts at curing cancer. Ultimately we may learn how to cure cancer with a simple pill. Unfortunately, that day has not yet arrived. Today we are faced with the choice of letting the cancer spread or trying to cure it with the methods available, methods that one day will almost certainly be considered barbaric. But to give up and do nothing would be far more barbaric and would certainly delay the discovery of an eventual cure. The analogy between cancer and murder is imperfect, because murder is not the "disease" we are trying to cure. The disease is injustice. We may not like the death penalty, but it must be available to punish crimes of cold-blooded murder, cases in which any other form of punishment would be inadequate and, therefore, unjust. If we create a society in which injustice is not tolerated, incidents of murder — the most flagrant form of injustice — will diminish.

7   (2) *No other major democracy uses the death penalty.* No other major democracy — in fact, few other countries of any description — are plagued by a murder rate such as that in the United States. Fewer and fewer Americans can remember the days when unlocked doors were the norm and murder was a rare and terrible offense. In America the murder rate climbed 122 percent between 1963 and 1980. During that same period, the murder rate in New York City increased by almost 400 percent, and the statistics are even worse in many other cities. A study at M.I.T. showed that based on 1970 homicide rates a person who lived in a large American city ran a greater risk of being murdered than an American soldier in World War II ran of being killed in combat. It is not surprising that the laws of each country differ according to differing conditions and traditions. If other countries had our murder problem, the cry for capital punishment would be just as loud as it is here. And I daresay that any other major democracy where 75 percent of the people supported the death penalty would soon enact it into law.

8   (3) *An innocent person might be executed by mistake.* Consider the work of Adam Bedau, one of the most implacable foes of capital punishment in this country. According to Mr. Bedau, it is "false sentimentality to argue that the death penalty should be abolished because of the abstract possibility that an innocent person might be executed." He cites a study of the 7,000 executions in this country from 1893 to 1971, and concludes that the record fails to show that such cases occur. The main point,

however, is this. If government functioned only when the possibility of error didn't exist, government wouldn't function at all. Human life deserves special protection, and one of the best ways to guarantee that protection is to assure that convicted murderers do not kill again. Only the death penalty can accomplish this end. In a recent case in New Jersey, a man named Richard Biegenwald was freed from prison after serving 18 years for murder; since his release he has been convicted of committing four murders. A prisoner named Lemuel Smith, who, while serving four life sentences for murder (plus two life sentences for kidnaping and robbery) in New York's Green Haven Prison, lured a woman corrections officer into the chaplain's office and strangled her. He then mutilated and dismembered her body. An additional life sentence for Smith is meaningless. Because New York has no death penalty statute, Smith has effectively been given a license to kill.

But the problem of multiple murder is not confined to the nation's   9
penitentiaries. In 1981, 91 police officers were killed in the line of duty in this country. Seven percent of those arrested in the cases that have been solved had a previous arrest for murder. In New York City in 1976 and 1977, 85 persons arrested for homicide had a previous arrest for murder. Six of these individuals had two previous arrests for murder, and one had four previous murder arrests. During those two years the New York police were arresting for murder persons with a previous arrest for murder on the average of one every 8.5 days. This is not surprising when we learn that in 1975, for example, the median time served in Massachusetts for homicide was less than two-and-a-half years. In 1976 a study sponsored by the Twentieth Century Fund found that the average time served in the United States for first-degree murder is ten years. The median time served may be considerably lower.

(4) *Capital punishment cheapens the value of human life.* On the contrary,   10
it can be easily demonstrated that the death penalty strengthens the value of human life. If the penalty for rape were lowered, clearly it would signal a lessened regard for the victims' suffering, humiliation, and personal integrity. It would cheapen their horrible experience, and expose them to an increased danger of recurrence. When we lower the penalty for murder, it signals a lessened regard for the value of the victim's life. Some critics of capital punishment, such as columnist Jimmy Breslin, have suggested that a life sentence is actually a harsher penalty for murder then death. This is sophistic nonsense. A few killers may decide not to appeal a death sentence, but the overwhelming majority make every effort to stay alive. It is by exacting the highest penalty for the taking of human life that we affirm the highest value of human life.

(5) *The death penalty is applied in a discriminatory manner.* This factor no   11
longer seems to be the problem it once was. The appeals process for a condemned prisoner is lengthy and painstaking. Every effort is made to see that the verdict and sentence were fairly arrived at. However, assertions of discrimination are not an argument for ending the death penalty

but for extending it. It is not justice to exclude everyone from the penalty of the law if a few are found to be so favored. Justice requires that the law be applied equally to all.

12   (6) *Thou Shalt Not Kill.* The Bible is our greatest source of moral inspiration. Opponents of the death penalty frequently cite the sixth of the Ten Commandments in an attempt to prove that capital punishment is divinely proscribed. In the original Hebrew, however, the Sixth Commandment reads, "Thou Shalt Not Commit Murder," and the Torah specifies capital punishment for a variety of offenses. The biblical viewpoint has been upheld by philosophers throughout history. The greatest thinkers of the 19th century — Kant, Locke, Hobbes, Rousseau, Montesquieu, and Mill — agreed that natural law properly authorizes the sovereign to take life in order to vindicate justice. Only Jeremy Bentham was ambivalent. Washington, Jefferson, and Franklin endorsed it. Abraham Lincoln authorized executions for deserters in wartime. Alexis de Tocqueville, who expressed profound respect for American institutions, believed that the death penalty was indispensable to the support of social order. The United States Constitution, widely admired as one of the seminal achievements in the history of humanity, condemns cruel and inhuman punishment, but does not condemn capital punishment.

13   (7) *The death penalty is state-sanctioned murder.* This is the defense with which Messrs. Willie and Shaw hoped to soften the resolve of those who sentenced them to death. By saying in effect, "You're no better than I am," the murderer seeks to bring his accusers down to his own level. It is also a popular argument among opponents of capital punishment, but a transparently false one. Simply put, the state has rights that the private individual does not. In a democracy, those rights are given to the state by the electorate. The execution of a lawfully condemned killer is no more an act of murder than is legal imprisonment an act of kidnapping. If an individual forces a neighbor to pay him money under threat of punishment, it's called extortion. If the state does it, it's called taxation. Rights and responsibilities surrendered by the individual are what give the state its power to govern. This contract is the foundation of civilization itself.

14   Everyone wants his or her rights, and will defend them jealously. Not everyone, however, wants responsibilities, especially the painful responsibilities that come with law enforcement. Twenty-one years ago a woman named Kitty Genovese was assaulted and murdered on a street in New York. Dozens of neighbors heard her cries for help but did nothing to assist her. They didn't even call the police. In such a climate the criminal understandably grows bolder. In the presence of moral cowardice, he lectures us on our supposed failings and tries to equate his crimes with our quest for justice.

15   The death of anyone — even a convicted killer — diminishes us all. But we are diminished even more by a justice system that fails to function. It is an illusion to let ourselves believe that doing away with capital

punishment removes the murderer's deed from our conscience. The rights of society are paramount. When we protect guilty lives, we give up innocent lives in exchange. When opponents of capital punishment say to the state: "I will not let you kill in my name," they are also saying to murderers: "You can kill in your *own* name as long as I have an excuse for not getting involved."

It is hard to imagine anything worse than being murdered while   16
neighbors do nothing. But something worse exists. When those same neighbors shrink back from justly punishing the murderer, the victim dies twice.

TYPES OF WRITING:
analysis, direct argument, example/illustration

Topics for Discussion

1. What would be the effect of Koch's opening examples and his frankness in dealing with them on an audience strongly opposed to capital punishment? On an audience in favour of capital punishment in some cases?
2. According to Koch, a politician, 75 per cent of Americans are in favour of capital punishment. Is he attempting to influence the remaining 25 per cent or is he directing his argument to the sympathetic majority? What makes you think so?
3. Which of the seven objections to capital punishment is Koch least successful in refuting? Which does he deal with best? Could Koch's argument be made more (or less) forceful by changing the order of his seven points?
4. In his fifth point (paragraph 11), Koch advocates fairness in the application of the death penalty through expanding its use, but he provides little indication of how he would see this done. Would his lack of comment on the details of wider application strengthen, or weaken, his argument for a general audience?
5. How successful is Koch's conclusion in bringing together the points he makes earlier in his essay?

Topics for Writing

1. Locate and explain as many fallacies of reasoning as you can in Koch's essay.
2. Choose any one of the arguments against capital punishment that Koch explores and, concentrating on that particular point, write three short essays for, or against, capital punishment: Aim the first at an audience that agrees with your position on capital punishment generally but may not have thought much about your objection. Aim the

second at an undecided audience. Aim the third at an audience opposed on principle to your position on capital punishment but not well informed about this particular objection.

Big Blue Goes Plaid

Carolyn Leitch

Sportswear is joining software in the arsenal of weapons at embattled computer giant IBM Canada Ltd. 1

Waking up to a market that prizes flexibility ahead of image, IBM is mothballing its corporate uniform of bland blue suits, white shirts and uninspired ties. 2

As part of this recent cultural house-cleaning, IBM Canada president William Etherington is encouraging employees to dress in garb that reflects the attitudes of the company's clients. 3

"The dress issue was a barrier between us and our customers," Mr. Etherington explained in an interview. 4

In an earlier era, the button-down dress code symbolized IBM's sense of professionalism and adherence to standards. Since the company was prospering, there was no reason to change. But recent surveys indicate many clients see a lack of creativity and inflexibility. 5

"For many years, that [dress code] was a very strong image for us," Mr. Etherington said. "Over time, that becomes the enemy. That's what worries me." 6

Mr. Etherington told senior managers in a recent memo that the catharsis from dropping the dress standards will "accelerate the transformation to a more free-thinking and open-to-change culture." 7

Recently, the Markham, Ont.-based computer maker has created the "new blue team" to question customers about a host of issues, including its service, quality, responsiveness and image. 8

David Williams, president of Toronto-based Loblaws Supermarkets Ltd. and National Grocer's Ltd., welcomes the change. He had started to send some of his business to IBM Canada's competitors because Big Blue was too slow to adapt. 9

When Mr. Etherington asked if he could send his new team in to find out how to win that business back, Mr. Williams was ready to accommodate. He wants more flexibility on pricing, and the ability to choose different machines and services from other suppliers. 10

"Perception is reality," Mr. Williams said, and IBM's stuffed shirts have matched their stiff policies. What's more, he said, IBM's maintenance people looked a little silly fixing a Loblaws cash register in a suit. 11

"I believe that their dress code was dictated by the sense that they were very professional," Mr. Williams said. "We don't think we're less professional because some people in our stores don't wear a suit." 12

A dress style is a powerful image in the minds of most people, says Don Hathaway, president of Toronto-based management consultants People Tech Consulting Inc. A stringent dress code creates "the implication of a conformity that perhaps isn't acceptable," he said. 13

Mr. Hathaway said business dress is becoming more relaxed, although men and women who work in the financial district still adhere to 14 a fairly strict standard. At one time, "females in trousers were frowned on. Now, thank goodness, it's disappeared."

15   Mr. Etherington said the relaxed style foreshadows wider change in the company, which is intent on becoming more agile and entrepreneurial. Reform has included flattening the corporate hierarchy and revamping the product line to offer more choice — particularly in lower price ranges — as well as adding new methods of selling and distributing the machines.

16   "Because we have so many things to change, we are demonstrating that we are changing," Mr. Etherington said.

17   That doesn't mean Hawaiian shirts have become *de rigueur* at Big Blue. A part-time employee who sells personal computers to students and homeowners over the telephone might have little reason to wear business dress. But vice-presidents will dress appropriately at meetings with bankers.

18   "You dress to your audience," Mr. Etherington said.

19   Mr. Etherington's own sartorial style varies with his plans for the day. Yesterday he met his senior managers in a casual plaid shirt. At 4:30, he planned to changed into a tuxedo for a formal dinner.

20   Curiously, IBM has never had an official dress code. When Mr. Etherington graduated from university in the 1960s, he bought a suit and hat upon joining the company because that's what he saw others wearing.

21   "We were all trying to dress like everybody else."

22   Unrelenting peer pressure, he said, has kept the code in place. The same peer pressure, Mr. Etherington is convinced, will continue to determine the lower limits.

23   Dress-down Fridays and designated casual days that raise money for charity have been very popular, he said. The staff has been quick to relax its dress since a memo went out about two weeks ago.

24   Still, some veterans haven't hung up their blue suits yet, and may not do so. "I suspect some employees will never change," Mr. Etherington said.

TYPE OF WRITING:
example/illustration

Topics for Discussion

1. What is the relationship between the diction of the first four paragraphs and IBM's new attitude towards dress?
2. Harry Bruce ("Suit, Ties Give Way to Polo Shirts, Loafers") would obviously agree with IBM's new dress policy, but do you think he would agree with the reasons for its adoption?
3. Leitch's report is written in typical newspaper style: short paragraphs, appropriate to rapid reading and narrow-column format, concentra-

tion on basic information, and use of quotations to convey opinion. Nevertheless, this style affords the writer many choices — the "angle" to be emphasized, the information to be included, the statements to be quoted. What influential advantages does the medium afford Leitch?
4. To what extent are Leitch's own views discernible in this apparently objective report about changing attitudes? How can you tell?

Topics for Writing

1. "Perception is reality," said David Williams, president of Loblaws Supermarkets and National Grocer's. After you have explained what Mr. Williams meant in this context, discuss to what extent this comment is true in a social group to which you belong.
2. Would you wear a business suit to class? Would you go to an awards banquet in jeans and a sweat-shirt? Write an essay on the subject of appropriate dress, explaining your own conclusions about the impor-tance or unimportance of appropriateness in clothing and about what considerations should determine appropriateness. Your essay should be designed to influence a specific audience (for example, your fellow students, a group of parents like yours, office workers, or professional people such as dentists or lawyers) to accept your views.
3. Compare Leitch's report to the more personal, editorial treatments of the same subject by Harry Bruce and Linda Goyette. Consider the influential effect of each piece, as well as the collective effect of having a variety of writers delivering similar messages about a subject over time.

Making Sense of War:
Demythologizing the Male Warrior

Norma Lundberg

1   On the cover of the November 1984 issue of *Esquire* magazine (a magazine subtitled "Man at His Best") is a head and shoulders photograph of a young woman, wide eyes fringed with make-up, full lips shiny with lipstick, staring at the reader. She is dressed in a torn, faded army-green T-shirt. On her head is an army helmet in camouflage colours. She is not identified by name, but we learn, from the contents page, that she represents "the greatest seductress of all time: war." This image illustrates an article on men's (*sic*) "secret passion: a lust for battle," entitled "Why Men Love War," by William J. Broyles, Jr., a Vietnam veteran.[1] According to Broyles, war is the enduring condition of man, and a sexual turn-on, since the love of war stems "from the union, deep in the core of our being, between sex and destruction, beauty and horror, love and death," and war is, for men, "at some terrible level the closest thing to what childbirth is for women: the initiation into the power of life and death."

2   As a female reader concerned about peace and nonviolence, I found the article profoundly disturbing. I was angered by the fatalism and determinism of the portrayal of "human nature" as basically violent and war-loving. I felt helpless about and depressed by the equation of sexual experience with death and violence. The comparison drawn between childbirth and war was a total aberration of the meaning of power as I understand it. I reread this article many times to try to make some sense of it that would fit in with the way I see the world, but was always left feeling frustrated: I could not "see" myself in the text. I gradually realized that it was aimed at what I would describe as the passive consumer of a masculinist militaristic ideology, and that it had the curious effect on me of imposing its authority and its authenticity at the same time as I resisted its message. Not only did the author's message disturb me, but there was something about its ability to do so, something about its nature as a piece of textual reality, that I had to deal with above and beyond simply asserting my resistance. Also, the writer incorporated mythic references in his article, drawing on them as justification for his love of war. What follows is my attempt to untangle this article to find out what gives it such power over a reader. I had to confront not only its militarism and sexism, but its authority as text and its placement in a mythology of war originating in patriarchal traditions. In doing this, I came to see this article as one piece of a discourse in which war is presented as either inevitable or necessary as part of the human condition.

3   The power of a text is something we usually take for granted. We assume as we read that the author is communicating directly with us, especially when it is written in the first person. The author's insistence,

in this case, that he is confessing to something dreadful merely serves to intensify the text's believability.

But this article by Broyles is only one piece of a larger discourse on 4 war that pervades our experience. Most readers of the *Esquire* article have likely not experienced war first hand, yet they "know" about war from stories, the news media and history lessons. We have "seen" war in films and photographs and we talk about war based on this knowledge. The war in Vietnam alone has been the subject of numerous books and articles. No single one can possibly explain at this distance in time and place what it meant and was like to be a participant in that war. Rather, they all function as pieces of the larger discourse not only on the war in Vietnam, but on the human activity we call war. Only by reading the *Esquire* article in conjunction with other literature concerning the activities of humans at war — and in particular the war in Vietnam — could I begin to see that the variety of activities that constitute "war" are not carried out by individuals in response to emotional dictates or "instincts," but are socially organized practices. This article worked as a "key" for me in unlocking the way this discourse works and in raising further questions: How does such an article help to perpetuate a male mythology of war? What does it have to do with the actual practices of war?

I would argue that what we refer to as "war" consists of a complex 5 of human activities (many of which are not distinguishable from so-called peacetime activities) and that not only the activities themselves but also the stories or myths that we tell one another about these activities, are social practices that are encouraged by the state and its agencies in the service of militarism. If we think of the myths as springing from the human unconscious to explain human actions and as being, therefore, unavoidable (as Broyles would have us believe), we run the risk of diverting attention from the way that human beings, in our daily lives, perpetuate and activate such myths. As feminists, we have a lot to gain from understanding the centrality to this mythology of war of the gender-bound metaphors of power and domination. For I think Birgit Brock-Utne's question a fundamental one: "Are we working to raise our consciousness not only on military matters, but also on the ideology of militarism and how it relates to sexism and the oppression of women?"[2]

If we read this article in isolation from other texts, as I did at first, it 6 is more difficult to break the spell of the author's authority, and the reader can become involved in a vicious circle with no exit: war is as basic as sex to human beings and human beings go to war because it is basic to our "nature." "Human nature" in the context of the article is a fundamental given, and we are told we cannot escape its dictates, cannot fully hate war even while recognizing its brutality and destructiveness. According to this logic, war is not a social phenomenon, but is a type of natural disaster affecting powerless human beings. "The truth" for Broyles is that "reasons [for war] don't matter. There is a reason for every war and a war for every reason." (p. 56) In other words, wars have no historical context, but are discrete events that recur because of our frustrated love of war.

7   Just as he writes of war as a natural and historical phenomenon, Broyles provides no personal historical context in his confessional account. Apart from writing that he served in Vietnam, he tells us nothing about himself. (The only other information about him — for example, his date of induction or educational background — is included in an editorial section of the magazine.) Broyles does not tell us where he served in Vietnam nor what his job was in the war. In fact, his entire account is devoid of information about the practices that constitute "doing war" day to day as the doing of work, in contrast with personal accounts recorded in Baker, Van Devanter and MacPherson. He only tells us he "loved" the war, much as he recognizes how "hateful" war is. He makes universal claims about the nature of war, about human nature, and spins for himself and for his readers a series of stories to explain and justify his nostalgia for Vietnam. These recollections are offered as illustrations of five "respectable . . . easy reasons" for his love of war that he then extends to "man's" love of war. These are reasons he feels comfortable with, as they do not risk disapproval from his readers. The implication is that these reasons are recognizable as the simple "facts" of war, are basic to an understanding of what war is, and are not to be disputed. In addition to these "respectable" reasons for loving war, Broyles confesses to what he calls deeper, more troubling reasons: the love of war being central to "man's" experience of being human.

8   The first reason he offers for men's love of war is that it is "an experience of great intensity . . . the human passion to witness, to see things, what the *Bible* calls the lust of the eye and the Marines of Vietnam called eye-fucking." (p. 56) Sexual metaphors are intertwined with what Broyles calls the love of war: passion, lust, eye-fucking, terrible ecstasy, endless exotic experience. The equation of sexuality with aggression, presented as an intense personal experience, is a troubling one for a woman reader, since the suggestion of violence as an integral part of sexual relationship is not, for most women (at least for this woman) a respectable reason for men to love war.

9   Helen Michalowski[3] writes of the link with sexuality as part of the brutality of military training for young men (*i.e.*, mostly under twenty-one years of age). She presents accounts of Marines in boot camp and the "systematic attacks on the recruits' sexuality." As one Marine recounts: "Once the sexual identity was threatened, psychological control achieved, and sexuality linked with military function, it was made clear that the military function was aggression. The primary lesson of boot camp towards which all behaviour was shaped, was to seek dominance. Our mission was always 'close with the enemy and destroy him.' To fail in this, as in all else, was nonmasculine. Aggression and seeking dominance, thus, was equated with masculinity."[4] The sexual thrill of war is an identification of power — aggression towards and domination — over

the "other" as a way of "proving" masculinity, and refuting the accusa-
tion of homosexuality. This practice is not conducted gratuitously, but as
part of the method of training recruits to kill. The metaphors of lust,
passion, ecstasy, and the desire to "eye fuck" what is foreign or "other"
is not an individual's natural response to situations, but a procedure for
doing a job effectively. Missing in the Broyles account is the element of
racism in the Vietnam war. The sensation of power and domination over
"the other" are features of both racism and sexism.

The game-like aspect of war is another reason Broyles offers for its   10
appeal to men. "War is a brutal deadly game, but a game, the best there
is. And men love games." (p. 56) There is an obvious (to feminists)
continuity between the games boys play, and the games men play on the
battlefield. (I am reminded of the anti-war cry: "Take the toys away from
the boys.") Mark Baker[5] refers to Vietnam as "more than just a war" but
a "ritual passage to adulthood for a generation of Americans." He refers
to boys playing war games as experiencing a tension that is "almost
sexual." Genderization is intimately linked with our identification of
certain activities as "sexual" and Baker's description illustrates this: "What
does a man do? A man stands alone against impossible odds, meets the
Apache chief in single combat to protect the manifest destiny of the
wagon train, plays guitar and gets the girl, leaps tall buildings in a single
bound, plants the flag on Iwo Jima, falls on a grenade to save his foxhole
buddies and then takes a bow to thundering applause."[6] The images are
all part of our culture's mythology of masculinity, into which the mythology of war fits comfortably. The scenario of the soldier falling on the
grenade is one that Broyles offers in his article as illustration of the
"enduring emotion of war: comradeship and brotherly love." (p. 58) His
text contains many such metaphors: cohesive groups of men experiencing
the "sexual thrill" of violence and destruction, bound closely to each other
in opposition to an enemy. This image of war experience contrasts vividly
with the accounts from other soldiers, in the Baker book, for example, of the
nausea they experienced towards the slaughter. And the myth of comradeship is called into question by an article on delayed stress in Vietnam
veterans. Heinemann[7] refers to Vietnam as "a war of individuals" — training and serving with a constantly shifting group of men in the one-year
tour of duty, with faces always changing, nameless soldiers being blown
up around the recruit, friendships tenuous. In Heinemann's account, the
war assumes no mythic proportions, and there is no sense of camaraderie:

> Your first firefight is a bloody, nasty mess, and it is a pure wonder you
> are not killed. Slowly you become accustomed to the weather and the
> work — the grinding, back-breaking humps, the going over the same
> ground day in and day out, aboard choppers and on foot. More short-
> timers leave; more fucking new guys arrive. This is the ugliest, most
> grueling, and most spiritless work you have ever done.[8]

With reference to the brutality of war-as-game, Broyles writes: "one   11
of the most troubling reasons men love war is the love of destruction, the

thrill of killing." But then he writes three pages later, "I don't know if I killed anyone in Vietnam." A man who was not certain whether he had actually killed during the war, writing of the thrill of inflicting death, seems more caught up in mythmaking than in describing any awesome actuality.

12   The metaphor or war-as-game makes a connection between another of our "everyday" activities — games, competitive sports — as "preconditioning" for wartime activities, as John Keegan observes.[9] Just as men participate in mock combat and competition on our playing fields, so a soldier like Broyles tries to achieve a high body count in combat, and expresses keen disappointment when another platoon gets a higher one.

13   Removing the "fear of freedom" is another of the respectable reasons Broyles offers for men's love of war: "it provides with its order and discipline both security and an irresistible urge to rebel against it." (p. 56) If boys become men by practicing war, they likewise rebel against "fatherly discipline." "Fatherly" seems a perverse use of a kinship term to describe the discipline of a patriarchal institution that makes young men into faceless soldiers, shaving their heads, dressing them in look-alike uniforms to remove their identities further, reminding them of their powerlessness as individuals — all in order to render them obedient to commands under combat.

14   Broyles repeatedly refers to "what war does." Yet "war" is an abstract concept, and what is done in the name of war is in actual practice done by human beings. The U.S. military, as an organized body of human beings with authority over other human beings, is barely visible in Broyles' account: it is not visibly responsible for any of the actions in Vietnam. The contrast between such a version of war, and the one put forward by John Keegan is one of idea versus practice: Broyles is caught up in the idea of war as an abstract force whereas Keegan sees war as a systematic organization to achieve certain ends. In writing about trench warfare in the Battle of the Somme, Keegan uses terminology that reflects organized activity:

> The trenches were properly house-kept and laid out as per regulations . . . organizing a proper trench routine . . . trench warfare . . . as its rules were understood.[10]

Keegan's work shows how battles were organized — an organization at variance with the notion of men (*sic*) as innately savage killers. This suggests to me that their "lust to kill," far from being natural, likewise needs to be organized and structured, so that soldiers will react as a cohesive group, a great body composed not of individuals but of "manpower," the way workers in a factory respond to start and stop whistles, to the demands of an assembly line: war as work, and the army as employer. Interestingly, Van Devanter's most militant stand against the army while she was in Vietnam was related to the working conditions and status of the nurses.[11]

For Broyles, one of the attractions of war (and the fourth reason for 15
men's love of it) is the way in which it "replaces the difficult gray areas
of daily life with an eerie serene clarity." (p. 57) Once again, he refers to
no particular practices to illustrate this, and even follows this statement
with a contradictory one: "In war you usually know who is your enemy
and who is your friend, and are given means of dealing with both. (That
was, incidentally, one of the great problems with Vietnam: it was hard to
tell friend from foe — it was too much like ordinary life.)" War — ideal-
ized war — sets up clear categories of friend and enemy, unlike "daily
life," where, according to Broyles, we do not know who we can trust and
must exercise our judgement. Broyles' contradictory statements under-
score a fundamental feature of the Vietnam war: it was the first time the
United States had been engaged directly in battle with civilians. Broyles
refers to a soldier being blown up with a command-detonated booby
trap by a ten-year-old "Vietcong" girl. Unlike the Battle of the Somme, in
Vietnam there were no front lines. In the space of three sentences, Broyles
stumbles between the ideal and the real: war's appeal is the "clarity" it
imposes with regard to categorizing others as friend or foe, yet the "great"
problem in Vietnam was the impossibility of doing just that. The ideal
and the real have become blurred because Broyles remains attached to
the abstract concept of war, and does not connect the "clarity" of categories to the structure imposed by the organization of the American
military, and the confusion between friend and enemy in Vietnam as a
feature of the organization of the North Vietnamese army. The whole
process of training American soldiers to kill was frustrated by their frequent inability to identify the enemy, yet the ideology of the clear enemy
persists in Broyles' text.

When he writes of war as "an escape from the everyday into a special 16
world" (p. 57) as another attraction of war (his fifth reason for loving it),
Broyles demonstrates little familiarity with the everyday, routine drudg-
ery of army life in Vietnam as it is recounted in the books by Baker, Van
Devanter, and MacPherson.[12] How much Broyles' detachment from the
everyday — his experience of war as a vicarious thrill, an exciting and
special world — is connected to his rank and status is difficult to determine from the scant details he provides about his duties. How much this
detachment was a feature of the war in Vietnam and how much it is a
developing feature of modern warfare is likewise difficult to assess.
Keegan refers to the growing distancing of officers from the front lines,
from the killing in battle and the "taint of guilt or social disapproval":
"the officer has, throughout the period [of the First World War] consistently and steadily withdrawn himself from the act (*i.e.*, of killing) itself."
For all that Keegan does to demonstrate the organization of battles, he
also participates in the mythology of the soldier as a self-determined
warrior, a romantic notion of the lone battler against great odds (like
Baron Macaulay's hero in "Horatius"). The officer has not "withdrawn
himself"; rather it is more likely that a feature of the social organization

of war is that officers assume a lesser role in active leadership at the front lines, while infantry are directed from a more centralized leadership higher up in the military bureaucracy.

17   The organization of the modern military is a matter of virtual speculation on my part, as I have not looked at the changing structure of command in the military. However, it is hard to imagine why the military should be exempt from the centralization of bureaucracy that has affected working life more generally. The practices that constitute the activity called war are practices that are familiar to us in our daily lives, except for the act of killing, and the myth structure of war is what makes it possible for humans to consider killing others as part of the job that is called doing battle.

18   Keegan notes the ways in which doing war fit into the daily lives of people, that is, that there is a relationship between our regular nonwar life and wartime activities. "Today, in the late twentieth century, there exists also a considerable congruence between the technology of civilian and military life."[13] There are many aspects of war technology with which the civilian population is familiar from a whole range of nonwartime artifacts and images, but also,

> Men and women employed in continuous-process industries are made indirectly familiar with many more modern battlefield phenomena: they are to a considerable degree inured to very high constant noise levels and to emissions of intense light, they work in proximity to dangerous machinery and chemicals, including poison gases, and they are involved in high-speed automatic processes — stamping, turning, reaming, cutting, moulding . . . which require perfectly timed human cooperation and imitate in many respects the actions of modern weapons systems.[14]

Rather than war being an escape from everyday life, war is an intensification of certain aspects of our everyday life. This is not to say that all our everyday activities are organized by a grand manipulator and aimed solely towards participating in wars. There is nonetheless a compatibility between our peacetime and our wartime practices, the existence of which suggests a need to examine the ability of those peacetime practices to organize our lives in ways that make "war" an acceptable way to resolve conflict and exercise domination by the ruling apparatus. For Jane Meyerding, the issue is one of "taking personal responsibility"[15] and not allowing ourselves to be manipulated into doing acts of violence, by resisting oppressive institutions. The resistance required must take cognizance of the power of the mythic structures that help to perpetuate those institutions.

19   All these "attractions" that for Broyles constitute "respectable" reasons for men to love war, are not peculiar to the war in Vietnam. The discourse of war is rife with references to its appeal as an escape from everyday life, and to the intensity of experience shared with other men. The metaphor of adventure and games is clearly linked to a gender ideology which values competition, aggression, and domination. But Broyles goes

on to confess to "deeper, more troubling reasons" for what he calls men's love of war:

> The love of war stems from the union, deep in the core of our being, between sex and destruction, beauty and horror, love and death. War may be the only way in which men touch the mythic domains in our soul. (p. 61) . . . The power of war, like the power of love, springs from man's heart. The one yields death, the other life. But life without death has no meaning; nor, at its deepest level, does life without war. Without war we could not know from what depths love rises, or what power it must have to overcome such evil and redeem us. It is no accident that men love war, as love and war are at the core of men. It is not only that we must love one another or die. We must love one another *and* die. (p. 65)

Yet these supposed universals — the love of war, the power of war — are not substantiated anywhere in his account of his own experiences. If we examine what the article reveals about his own activities in Vietnam, we get a picture of someone who participated very little in that work of the war involving direct experience of the enemy (and in virtually none of the experience of the "grunt" or infantryman). He gives the reader stories based primarily on the actions and experiences of others, and refers to these stories as having a moral, even mythic truth, rather than a literal one. The war has become an abstract concept coupled with what he names the "mythic domains of his soul." He then applies this grand abstraction — the love of war — to his experiences, which he then presents as being part of a universal male experience. These experiences, frozen in memory in the form of a text, assume the power of something tangible and durable: something real. The author's personal mythmaking procedure has been successfully reintegrated into the male mythos that fostered it.

Broyles' "deepest, darkest" revelations of why "men love war" are 20 not secrets; they are rhetorical devices. What he reveals as dark secrets are common features of the genderization process of males (certainly as it is practiced in North America), and as such, aim at making the (male) reader feel comfortable with his conditioning. The male mythology of sexual experience and the mythology of war have a lot in common. When Broyles writes that "sex is the weapon of life, the shooting sperm sent like an army of guerillas to penetrate the egg's defenses — the only victory that really matters" (p. 62), the relationship between the metaphors of sexual domination and war is quite clear. And this mythos of war is constructed by men, certainly not by women. The army nurses in Vietnam and the women who have done combat are not given any place in that mythology.[16] Nor is the mythos constructed by all men, certainly not by the infantry men shot up, mutilated and psychologically crippled (for whom Vietnam remains a nightmare, as Van Devanter's work demonstrates). The men of privilege, status, and power, like Broyles himself (Texas boy educated at Oxford, who enlisted in the Marines, founding editor of *Texas Monthly* and *California* and, for a while, editor in chief of

Newsweek), carry on the work of perpetuating the mythology, as do many men who never even served in Vietnam. In the service of a right-wing American government, they are busy reconstructing history to serve the aims of that government. "Not that even the lies aren't true, on a certain level. They have a moral, even a mythic truth, rather than a literal one. They reach out and remind the tellers and listeners of their place in the world." (p. 61) The status quo of a militaristic patriarchal tradition requires that we perpetuate the mythology of the inevitability of war.

21   We need to take apart the mythology surrounding the practices that constitute "war." We need to find out not only how such practices originated, but how they relate to our everyday lives and are reproduced there, especially in the education of our children. Otherwise, we can only react passively to the facts and fictions of the literature of war, unable to make sense of the experience, and consumed by feelings of powerlessness to act.

NOTES

1. All page numbers in parentheses, *e.g.*, (p. 56), refer to the Broyles, 1984, article. Many other references are *passim*.
2. Birgit Brock-Utne, p. 53.
3. Helen Michalowski, pp. 326-335.
4. Michalowski, p. 330.
5. Mark Baker, *Nam: The Vietnam War in the Words of the Men and Women Who Fought There.*
6. Baker, p. 5.
7. Larry Heinemann, pp. 55–63.
8. Heinemann, p. 59.
9. John Keegan, *The Face of Battle.*
10. Keegan, p. 212.
11. Lynda Van Devanter with Christopher Morgan, *Home Before Morning: The True Story of an Army Nurse in Vietnam.*
12. Myra MacPherson, *Long Time Passing: Vietnam and the Haunted Generation.*
13. Keegan, p. 324.
14. Keegan, pp. 324–325
15. Jane Meyerding, "Reclaiming Non Violence," pp. 5–15.
16. See Shelley Saywell's *Women in War.*

REFERENCES

Austin, Jacqueline. "Women Watching War." *Women's Review of Books.* Vol. 1, No. 12, September 1984, pp. 8–9.

Baker, Mark. *Nam: The Vietnam War in the Words of the Men and Women Who Fought There.* New York: Berkeley Books, 1981.

Brock-Utne, Birgit. *Educating for Peace.* Oxford: Pergamon Press, 1986.

Broyles, William, Jr. "Why Men Love War." *Esquire.* Vol. 102, No. 5, November 1984, pp. 55–65.

Chagnon, Napoleon A. *Yanomamo: The Fierce People.* Second edition, New York: Holt, Rinehart and Winston, 1977.

Hartford, Barbara, and Hopkins, Sarah, eds. *Greenham Common: Women at the Wire.* London: The Women's Press Limited, 1984.

Heinemann, Larry. "'Just Don't Fit,' Stalking the Elusive 'Tripwire' Veteran." *Harper's.* Vol. 270, No. 1619, April, 1985, pp. 55–63.

Keegan, John. *The Face of Battle.* Harmondsworth, Middlesex: Penguin, 1970.

MacPherson, Myra. *Long Time Passing: Vietnam and the Haunted Generation.* New York: Doubleday, 1984; reprinted New York: New American Library, 1985.

Meyerding, Jane. "Reclaiming Nonviolence," in Pam McAllister, *Reweaving the Web of Life: Feminism and Nonviolence.* Philadelphia: New Society Publishers, 1982, pp. 5–15.

Meyerding, Jane. "On Nonviolence and Feminism." *Trivia.* Vol. 3, No. 1, Fall 1984, pp. 60–69.

Michalowski, Helen. "The Army Will Make a 'Man' Out of You," in Pam McAllister, *Reweaving the Web of Life: Feminism and Nonviolence.* Philadelphia: New Society Publishers, 1982, pp. 326–335.

Saywell, Shelley. *Women in War.* Markham, Ontario: Viking, 1985; reprinted Markham, Ontario: Penguin, 1986.

Van Devanter, Lynda. *Home Before Morning: The True Story of an Army Nurse in Vietnam.* New York: Warner Books, 1984.

TYPES OF WRITING:
analysis, direct argument

Topics for Discussion

1. *Esquire* in the 1980s was one of the glossier men's magazines aimed at, among other things, what Lundberg points to in her piece — making the adolescent fantasies of males who were old enough and well educated enough to know better seem respectable. *Atlantis* reached an audience of intellectual feminists. What are the implications for the potential influence of these two pieces, considering where they were published?

2. Why does Lundberg review her initial intuitive and emotional responses upon reading Broyles' article before going on to explain what she thinks about it?

3. Consider the title of Lundberg's essay. Does it represent accurately what her essay is about? Does war make sense in the light of Lundberg's efforts to demythologize the male warrior?

4. What does Lundberg accomplish by calling into question Broyles's credentials to write about war — his educational background and his

personal experience of war? Why does she wait to reveal what she does know about Broyles's background until near the end of her essay?

5. What is the effect of Lundberg's comparison of Broyles's general, speculative accounts of what war may mean to certain males with realistic, detailed accounts of war from men and women who actually experienced it?

6. In what ways do Lundberg's references to and quotations from a variety of written accounts of war, most of them by men who have experienced it, lend influential force to her argument?

Topics for Writing

1. Compare Lundberg's attack on myths of the allure of war to McClung's view on a much earlier war in "The War That Ends in Exhaustion Sometimes Mistaken for Peace."

2. Most readers of Lundberg's essay will know Broyles's essay only from her account of it. Find Broyles's article in *Esquire* (available in most larger libraries) and write an essay explaining how Lundberg's depiction of what Broyles wrote makes her criticism of the myth more influential.

How the Sour Sounds of Bitchery Undermine the Sisterly Cause

Christina McCall

My daughter will be thirteen this month, and since I am a lapsed Presbyterian and her father is a non-Jewish Jew, she won't be confirmed or bat-mitzvahed on that momentous occasion. 1

All the same, it's occurred to me several times in the last few weeks that there ought to be some more portentous way to mark her rite of passage than taking her and her friends to dinner at Sam the Chinese Food Man's. There's an uneasy feeling I should be able to impart some wisdom in Lord Chesterfield's mode, if not his manner. I even went so far, one idle April evening, to try to concoct a catalogue of subjects suitable for a series of Letters To My Daughter. 2

The first topic on my list weighed on me so heavily, though, I never did get beyond it. I scribbled "#1. Beware the 'I'm A Better Woman Than You Are' trap and then stared at that maxim with astonishment, caught by the realization that even after a decade of fervid feminism — after all the sisterhood-is-beautiful slogans and all the manifestos beginning "We identify with every woman . . . with the poorest, the ugliest, the most brutally exploited" — the first thing I wanted to tell my child was that sometimes other women will try hard to undermine her. 3

Why is this, that I, who have women friends constant beyond human expectation, am writing a sentence that makes me sound like the most recalcitrant pig of a male? Maybe it's because the day before I've had my four-thousandth experience of being sand-bagged by a first-rate "I'm a better woman than you are" gamester. 4

I had met in the entrance of an expensive shop an acquaintance from another period in my life, the wife of a man who made his money in metal, and she feints for a minute ("And how is your *poor* little girl taking the separation?") while I parry ("She's fine; she loves her school and she's going to a wonderful Saturday drama class that's open to gifted children"). As a diversionary prelude to escape, I mention that the clothes inside the shop are not very interesting this season and she sees her opening immediately. "Well, I've just bought two super Sonya Rykiels, dear, but then," and her eyes dart over my torso, "I'm not sure she makes anything that would fit *you*." 5

I could live easily with such petty bitchery — and would expect my daughter to do so — if it came only from the mouths of the silly. But unfortunately, woman-to-woman putdowns are worked on all sorts of more important levels. They occur between good friends and mortal enemies, between mothers and daughters, sisters and cousins, salesclerks and customers, and are rife between women who are primarily "homemakers" and women who have "careers." 6

A woman I know, who has a demanding profession, recently mar- 7 ried a widower with two sons and has managed admirably to fill a role that's new to her. She came home exhausted one evening this winter and heard her housekeeper — a woman with two daughters, one of whom no longer speaks to her — saying to her husband loudly on the landing, "What you should have done, Mister, was marry a *real* mother, not somebody who's off gallivanting downtown when the kids come home from school. I tell you when mine were young, I was there when they came through the door." This kind of attack can be understood, if not excused, on the grounds of enraging inequities. (Almost anybody would sooner "gallivant" than tackle the kitchen floor.)

8   But the game is particularly hurtful when it's played between women who are equally privileged and presumably sisters-in-arms. A man told me the other day that the first time he encountered this situation was three or four years ago. His wife, who is witty, attractive, intelligent and has kept both her maiden name and her equanimity while coping with four children and an important media job, was talking at a party about the cost of hiring help. "A good housekeeper costs half my salary," she said ruefully. Another woman jumped in immediately, "What do you mean — half your salary. Doesn't it come out of your husband's salary too? I can see you need some consciousness raising."

9   By now this "I'm a better feminist than you" refinement of the old sorry sentence has become so prevalent in the women's movement itself that a group of feminist friends in Ottawa have made up a bitter-funny game called "I'm more left than thou," wherein the players get points according to the magnitude of oppression they've suffered or their service to the cause. (Ten points for a near rape, sixteen for a desertion and so on.)

10   All sorts of explanations are offered for female non-solidarity. Psychiatrists can trace deprivations — lack of nurturing by a strong mother figure, say — that create uncertainties that lead to envies that lead to malice. Anthropologists can maintain that women as traditional caregivers have led isolated lives and are conditioned to be wary of each other as against men who've always bonded from the time they hunted in packs. Optimistic feminists can postulate that women are in transition, subjecting themselves to multiple-role demands that are impossible to meet, and that when "liberation" is taken more for granted old jealousies will wither away like the state in the Marxist millenium.

11   My problem with these and other backward-glancing or forward-looking theories is that for my child — and for myself — I want action now. The more I think about the situation, the more my personal solution contracts to one simple sentence: Don't play the game yourself.

12   That this dictum works is made plain to me regularly in an office I know very well. A dozen women are employed there and the woman with the most important managerial job is by luck or determination a resolute non-player, not only of the I.A.B.W.T.Y.A. game, but of any other kind. She knows she is capable, and she gives everyone else her

due as being capable, too. Because of her influence, that office is the liveliest, warmest place to work I have ever seen.

In the mid-eighteenth century Lord Chesterfield could tell his son 13 that the way for a gentleman to succeed was through duplicity. In the late twentieth century, I'd like to tell my daughter that the way for a woman to thrive is through straightforward self-assertion tempered with sisterly charity — in the very best sense of that word.

TYPES OF WRITING:
example/illustration, narration, personal experience

Topics for Discussion

1. McCall is writing primarily for women and about feminism, but her essay appears in a magazine read by both men and women with varying attitudes toward the feminist movement. How does McCall's sense of her wider audience affect her approach to her subject?
2. As a point of departure for discussion, express in a single sentence of your own what McCall is advocating. Is her essential point controversial?
3. Are McCall's observations about human relations especially relevant to feminists? If yes, why and in what way? Or if no, why not?
4. How does Lord Chesterfield's advice to his son serve McCall as she considers advice she might give to her daughter? How is the Chesterfield example revealing as a point of comparison?
5. In her introductory paragraph, McCall refers to herself as "a lapsed Presbyterian" and to her daughter's father as "a non-Jewish Jew." Would these remarks offend some readers? Would their inclusion in an introductory paragraph cause McCall to lose some readers? What purpose might they serve?

Topic for Writing

1. Beginning with an appropriate occasion or incident, and using personal examples to illustrate your point, write an essay discouraging a common social practice — for example, smoking in the workplace (or, alternatively, segregating smokers), pointless telephoning at inconvenient times, or match-making by friends. As a rule, the less you like the practice you choose to write about, the easier the writing will be.

The War That Ends in Exhaustion Sometimes Mistaken for Peace

Nellie L. McClung

When a skirl of pipes came down the street,
And the blare of bands, and the march of feet,
I could not keep from marching, too;
For the pipes cried 'Come!' and the bands said 'Do,'
And when I heard the pealing fife,
I cared no more for human life!

1   Away back in the cave-dwelling days, there was a simple and definite distribution of labor. Men fought and women worked. Men fought because they liked it; and women worked because it had to be done. Of course the fighting had to be done too, there was always a warring tribe out looking for trouble, while their women folk stayed at home and worked. They were never threatened with a long peace. Somebody was always willing to go 'It.' The young bloods could always be sure of good fighting somewhere, and no questions asked. The masculine attitude toward life was: 'I feel good today; I'll go out and kill something.' Tribes fought for their existence, and so the work of the warrior was held to be the most glorious of all; indeed, it was the only work that counted. The woman's part consisted of tilling the soil, gathering the food, tanning the skins and fashioning garments, brewing the herbs, raising the children, dressing the warrior's wounds, looking after the herds, and any other light and airy trifle which might come to her notice. But all this was in the background. Plain useful work has always been considered dull and drab.

2   Everything depended on the warrior. When 'the boys' came home there was much festivity, music, and feasting, and tales of the chase and fight. The women provided the feast and washed the dishes. The soldier has always been the hero of our civilization, and yet almost any man makes a good soldier. Nearly every man makes a good soldier, but not every man, or nearly every man makes a good citizen: the tests of war are not so searching as the tests of peace, but still the soldier is the hero.

3   Very early in the lives of our children we begin to inculcate the love of battle and sieges and invasions, for we put the miniature weapons of warfare into their little hands. We buy them boxes of tin soldiers at Christmas, and help them to build forts and blow them up. We have military training in our schools; and little fellows are taught to shoot at targets, seeing in each an imaginary foe, who must be destroyed because he is 'not on our side.' There is a song which runs like this:

If a lad a maid would marry
He must learn a gun to carry.

thereby putting love and love-making on a military basis — but it goes! Military music is in our ears, and even in our churches. 'Onward Chris-

138

tian soldiers, marching as to war' is a Sunday-school favorite. We pray to the God of Battles, never by any chance to the God of Workshops!

Once a year, of course, we hold a Peace Sunday and on that day we   4
pray mightily that God will give us peace in our time and that war shall be no more, and the spear shall be beaten into the pruning hook. But the next day we show God that he need not take us too literally, for we go on with the military training, and the building of the battleships, and our orators say that in time of peace we must prepare for war.

War is the antithesis of all our teaching. It breaks all the command-   5
ments; it makes rich men poor, and strong men weak. It makes well men sick, and by it living men are changed to dead men. Why, then, does war continue? Why do men go so easily to war — for we may as well admit that they do go easily? There is one explanation. They like it!

When the first contingent of soldiers went to the war from Manitoba,   6
there stood on the station platform a woman crying bitterly. (She was not the only one.) She had in her arms an infant, and three small children stood beside her wondering.

"E would go!' she sobbed in reply to the sympathy expressed by the   7
people who stood near her. "E loves a fight — 'e went through the South African War, and 'e's never been 'appy since — when 'e 'ears war is on he says I'll go — 'e loves it — 'e does!'

"E loves it!'   8

That explains many things.   9

'Father sent me out,' said a little Irish girl, 'to see if there's a fight   10
going on any place, because if there is, please, father would like to be in it!' Unfortunately 'father's' predilection to fight is not wholly confined to the Irish!

But although men like to fight, war is not inevitable. War is not of   11
God's making. War is a crime committed by men and, therefore, when enough people say it shall not be, it cannot be. This will not happen until women are allowed to say what they think of war. Up to the present time women have had nothing to say about war, except pay the price of war — this privilege has been theirs always.

History, romance, legend and tradition having been written by men,   12
have shown the masculine aspect of war and have surrounded it with a false glory and have sought to throw the veil of glamour over its hideous face. Our histories have followed the wars. Invasions, conquests, battles, sieges make up the subject-matter of our histories.

Some glorious soul, looking out upon his neighbors, saw some   13
country that he thought he could use and so he levied a heavy tax on the people, and with the money fitted out a splendid army. Men were called from their honest work to go out and fight other honest men who had never done them any harm; harvest fields were trampled by their horses' feet, villages burned, women and children fled in terror, and perished of starvation, streets ran blood and the Glorious Soul came home victorious with captives chained to his chariot wheel. When he drove through the

streets of his own home town, all the people cheered, that is, all who had not been killed, of course.

14   What the people thought of all this, the historians do not say. The people were not asked or expected to think. Thinking was the most unpopular thing they could do. There were dark damp dungeons where hungry rats prowled ceaselessly; there were headsmen's axes and other things prepared for people who were disposed to think and specially designed to allay restlessness among the people.

15   The 'people' were dealt with in one short paragraph at the end of the chapter: 'The People were very poor' (you wouldn't think they would need to say that, and certainly there was no need to rub it in), and they 'ate black bread,' and they were 'very ignorant and superstitious.' Superstitious? Well, I should say they would be — small wonder if they did see black cats and have rabbits cross their paths, and hear death warnings, for there was always going to be a death in the family, and they were always about to lose money! The People were a great abstraction, infinite in number, inarticulate in suffering — the people who fought and paid for their own killing. The man who could get the people to do this on the largest scale was the greatest hero of all and the historian told us much about him, his dogs, his horses, the magnificence of his attire.

16   Some day, please God, there will be new histories written, and they will tell the story of the years from the standpoint of the people, and the hero will not be any red-handed assassin who goes through peaceful country places leaving behind him dead men looking sightlessly up to the sky. The hero will be the man or woman who knows and loves and serves. In the new histories we will be shown the tragedy, the heartbreaking tragedy of war, which like some dreadful curse has followed the human family, beaten down their plans, their hopes, wasted their savings, destroyed their homes, and in every way turned back the clock of progress.

17   We have all wondered what would happen if the people some day decided that they would no longer be the tools of the man higher up, what would happen if the men who make the quarrel had to fight it out. How glorious it would have been if this war could have been settled by somebody taking the Kaiser out behind the barn! There would seem to be some show of justice in a hand-to-hand encounter, where the best man wins, but modern warfare has not even the faintest glimmering of fair play. The exploding shell blows to pieces the strong, the brave, the daring, just as readily as it does the cowardly, weak, or base.

18   War proves nothing. To kill a man does not prove that he was in the wrong. Bloodletting cannot change men's spirits, neither can the evil of men's thoughts be driven out by blows. If I go to my neighbor's house, and break her furniture, and smash her pictures, and bind her children captive, it does not prove that I am fitter to live than she — yet according to the ethics of nations it does. I have conquered her and she must pay me for my trouble; and her house and all that is left in it belongs to my heirs and successors forever. That is war!

War twists our whole moral fabric. The object of all our teaching has 19
been to inculcate respect for the individual, respect for human life, honor
and purity. War sweeps that all aside. The human conscience in these
long years of peace, and its resultant opportunities for education, has
grown tender to the cry of agony — the pallid face of a hungry child
finds a quick response to its mute appeal; but when we know that hundreds are rendered homeless every day, and countless thousands are
killed and wounded, men and boys mowed down like a field of grain,
and with as little compunction, we grow a little bit numb to human
misery. What does it matter if there is a family north of the track living
on soda biscuits and turnips? War hardens us to human grief and misery.

War takes the fit and leaves the unfit. The epileptic, the consumptive, 20
the inebriate, are left behind. They are not good enough to go out to
fight. So they stay at home, and perpetuate the race! Statistics prove that
the war is costing fifty millions a day, which is a prodigious sum, but we
would be getting off easy if that were all it costs. The bitterest cost of war
is not paid by us at all. It will be paid by the unborn generations, in a
lowered vitality, the loss of a strong fatherhood, which they have never
known. Napoleon lowered the stature of the French by two inches, it is
said. That is one way to set your mark on your generation.

But the greatest evil wrought by war is not the wanton destruction 21
of life and property, sinful though it is; it is not even the lowered vitality
of succeeding generations, though that is attended by appalling injury to
the moral nature — the real iniquity of war is that it sets aside the
arbitrament of right and justice, and looks to brute force for its verdict!

In the first days of panic, pessimism broke out among us, and we 22
cried in our despair that our civilization had failed, that Christianity had
broken down, and that God had forgotten the world. It seemed like it at
first. But now a wiser and better vision has come to us, and we know
that Christianity has not failed, for it is not fair to impute failure to
something which has never been tried. Civilization has failed. Art, music,
and culture have failed, and we know now that underneath the thin
veneer of civilization, unregenerate man is still a savage; and we see
now, what some have never seen before, that unless a civilization is built
upon love, and mutual trust, it must always end in disaster, such as this.
Up to August fourth, we often said that war was impossible between
Christian nations. We still say so, but we know more now than we did
then. We know now that there are no Christian nations.

Oh, yes. I know the story. It was a beautiful story and a beautiful 23
picture. The black prince of Abyssinia asked the young Queen of England
what was the secret of England's glory and she pointed to the 'open
Bible.'

The dear Queen of sainted memory was wrong. She judged her nation 24
by the standard of her own pure heart. England did not draw her policy
from the open Bible when in 1840 she forced the opium traffic on the
Chinese. England does not draw her policy from the open Bible when

she takes revenues from the liquor traffic, which works such irreparable ruin to countless thousands of her people. England does not draw her policy from the open Bible when she denies her women the rights of citizens, when women are refused degrees after passing examinations, when lower pay is given women for the same work than if it were done by men. Would this be tolerated if it were really so that we were a Christian nation? God abominates a false balance, and delights in a just weight.

25   No, the principles of Christ have not yet been applied to nations. We have only Christian people. You will see that in a second, if you look at the disparity that there is between our conceptions of individual duty and national duty. Take the case of the heathen — the people whom we in our large-handed, superior way call the heathen. Individually we believe it is our duty to send missionaries to them to convert them into Christians. Nationally we send armies upon them (if necessary) and convert them into customers! Individually we say: 'We will send you our religion.' Nationally: 'We will send you goods, and we'll make you take them — we need the money!' Think of the bitter irony of a boat leaving a Christian port loaded with missionaries upstairs and rum below, both bound for the same place and for the same people — both for the heathen 'with our comp'ts.'

26   Individually we know it is wrong to rob anyone. Yet the state robs freely, openly, and unashamed, by unjust taxation, by the legalized liquor traffic, by imposing unjust laws upon at least one half of the people. We wonder at the disparity between our individual ideals and the national ideal, but when you remember that the national ideals have been formed by one half of the world — and not the more spiritual half — it is not so surprising. Our national policy is the result of male statecraft.

27   There is a curative power in human life just as there is in nature. When the pot boils — it boils over. Evils cure themselves eventually. But it is a long hard way. Yet it is the way humanity has always had to learn. Christ realized that when he looked down at Jerusalem, and wept over it: 'O Jerusalem, Jerusalem, how often I would have gathered you, as a hen gathereth her chickens under her wings, but *you would not.*' That was the trouble then, and it has been the trouble ever since. Humanity has to travel a hard road to wisdom, and it has to travel it with bleeding feet.

28   But it is getting its lessons now — and paying double first-class rates for its tuition!

TYPES OF WRITING:
cause and effect, direct argument, example/illustration

Topics for Discussion

1. McClung seems to be deliberately antagonistic toward men in this piece. What does this approach say about her intended audience? How might it affect her ability to exert influence in a society dominated by men and caught up in the patriotic excitement of World War I? Do you see her frank approach as a tactic or as a mistake?

2. About a third of the way through her essay, McClung dramatizes the male predilection for fighting, using two women — a young girl, identified as Irish (at the time a relatively poor immigrant group), and a mother with a pronounced lower-class British accent. Why would McClung choose these examples to demonstrate the effects of war to her Canadian audience?

3. Given that the great majority of those supporting the War would have identified themselves as Christians, why would McClung state flatly, "We know now that there are no Christian nations"?

Topics for Writing

1. Discuss the song quoted by McClung — "If a lad a maid would marry/ He must learn a gun to carry" — and her treatment of the romantic possibilities of military service in the light of Norma Lundberg's essay, "Making Sense of War: Demythologizing the Male Warrior."

2. After you have satisfied yourself that you know clearly what McClung's position is, develop an argumentative/persuasive position of your own that is completely contrary to hers.

On Euthanasia and Dying Well

E. J. McCullough

1   We have all experienced the death of family members, close friends, or acquaintances. Few of those deaths could be described as happy. We might use words like painful, lingering, lonely, or courageous, but rarely would we characterize death as a happy event. Is the term "happy death," then, an oxymoron? Are happiness and death irreconcilable? If so, we have a problem with the term "euthanasia," which in its root meaning signifies dying well or happily.

2   Euthanasia is the practice of actively terminating life in the name of compassion. If it is voluntary, it is a species of suicide. If it is involuntary, it is murder. The case I should like to make is that death can be a truly happy event, but that the notion of dying well or happily in assisted self-destruction is unacceptable.

3   The Roman philosopher Lucretius saw no problem with suicide if one's pleasures diminished and pain became intolerable. His emphasis was on feelings and personal interests. In contemporary terms we would call this consequentialism, utilitarianism, or pragmatism. The Stoic school of philosophy had a more developed ethical doctrine. Many Stoics were quite explicit about the desirability of death under difficult circumstances. "Amid the miseries of life on earth," declared Pliny the Elder, "suicide is God's best gift to man." The Roman emperor Marcus Aurelius said, "The house is smoking, and I quit it. Why do you think that this is any trouble?" The emphasis in the Stoics is on rationality: if the price of continued life is continual suffering, then it is eminently reasonable to "quit the house."

4   The Platonic and Aristotelian attitude toward death is quite different, since neither Plato nor Aristotle was prepared to deny the possibility of the continuance of life in eternity. The finest exemplar of this view is Plotinus, a disciple of both Plato and Aristotle, who said:

> When a man contrives the dissolution of the body, it is he that has used violence. . . . Suicide is an act of violence. If there be a period allotted to all by fate, to anticipate the hour could not be a happy act. . . . If everyone is to hold in another world a standing determined by the state in which he quitted this, then there must be no withdrawal as long as there is any hope of progress.

5   But the practice of euthanasia received its most severe criticism from the Roman philosopher Boethius, who wrote from the perspective of personal tragedy. Boethius argued that the circumstance he faced — his own death and the ruin of his family — necessitated a more complete response to the problem of suffering in human life. When all personal worth is destroyed, when relationships with family and friends are demolished, the only relationship left is with the divine, and in this relationship lies goodness and hope. Boethius began where Aristotle and

144

Plotinus had left off, with the conclusion that happiness is not a feeling but, to quote Aristotle, "a life lived in accordance with virtue." He went on to the view that continuity in this life is extended to relationship with God in a future life.

There are four notions of happiness implicit in this brief historical 6 account: happiness as pleasure without pain, happiness as the satisfaction of desire but including pain, happiness as a life lived in accordance with virtue, and happiness as a life lived in accordance with virtue and fulfilled in relationship with the divine.

Happiness as pleasure and the absence of pain is probably the 7 dominant view, based as it is in bodily sensations and feelings. John Stuart Mill wrote that happiness is an existence exempt as far as possible from pain and as rich as possible in enjoyment. By this he did not mean physical pleasures only, but pleasures of the mind and spirit as well. In this perception, suicide is intuitively accepted as a release from pain. The notion that happiness must include both pleasure and pain, on the other hand, is one the Stoics could have embraced quite easily. In the case of a serious imbalance of pain over pleasure, suicide is justified, but reason must provide the justification.

Happiness as the permanent state of a life lived in accordance with 8 virtue would resist the most severe temptations to suicide, for happiness of this kind disposes one to accept misfortune courageously. The fourth type of happiness — that of a life lived in accordance with virtue, supported by a sense of community and one's relationship with the divine — likewise precludes the possibility of suicide. These two notions of happiness put events in our control, whereas the first two place us at the mercy of events.

What of death? Two notions of death — as the termination of physi- 9 cal function, or as the termination of physical and psychological function — represent the nihilist's view of death as the end of life; there is no extension beyond the moment. Two other views present themselves: the fundamentalist view that death is a beginning, and the view that death is a transition. In these two notions, again, continuity of existence precludes the possibility of suicide. The nihilist holds for radical discontinuity, the fundamentalist for a modified continuity, and the non-fundamentalist for a real continuity in community and with the divine.

Given the four notions of happiness and the four notions of death, 10 can we find a place for euthanasia as a legitimate practice? According to the first two definitions of happiness and death, euthanasia is entirely acceptable. On the basis of the second two, it is not. But only the fourth definition of both happiness and death fully corresponds to our lived experience.

There is a joke about René Descartes, the seventeenth-century French 11 thinker who arrived at one of the most famous conclusions in the history of philosophy: "I think, therefore I am." When his sister offered him a cup of tea, he said, "I think not," and promptly disappeared. It is the philosophy of Descartes and his successors which has given rise to a picture of human life as episodic, discrete, and discontinuous. But history, conceptual analysis, and unacceptable alternatives lead us to the conclusion that continuity in human life is not only plausible but demonstrable. This continuity makes it possible to conceive of a happy death, and to characterize many deaths as happy. Euthanasia is not the way to a happy death or to dying well.

12   Consider my own case. In July 1990 I went for a routine checkup in order to purchase an insurance policy. I felt wonderful. I'd been working out regularly, running anywhere from three to ten miles a day. My pulse was fifty, my blood pressure was a hundred over sixty. I played tennis regularly. The doctor wanted to have a look at a spot on my arm. He also wanted to examine my prostate. The spot turned out to be a malignant melanoma. The prostate was also cancerous. CAT scans and bone scans indicated that there was probably further involvement with the lymphatic system, and possible bone cancer as well.

13   My entire plan of life was shattered, and my notions of death and dying became matters for urgent reflection. My personal ideas were radically altered. I suddenly saw death as a gift. My relationships changed: some for the worse, most for the better. In the end, I was both cured and healed.

14   There were many reasons for this: family, faith, friends, science. The common view of dying as a physical process which one undergoes passively is being radically reshaped. The pro-euthanasia movement states that we should take an active role in the process, terminating life if it is of inferior quality or involves great suffering. At the same time, modern medicine has identified the role of the dying person as an active one, one which can result in a reduction of suffering, or even a cure; having experienced the positive role one can play in pain management, I know that physical suffering can be almost totally controlled. Philosophers and theologians, too, recognize that active participation in healing — as distinct from curing — is a central feature of the intellectual and spiritual life.

15   These factors have brought us to see that dying is not a process to which we submit with resignation, but an action which we can shape in a variety of ways. Do we want to shape it by simply bringing it to an abrupt and violent end? The financial burdens imposed by the dying, and the conviction that suffering is a personal tragedy, have led the people of Holland to a national policy of assisted suicide. Perhaps twenty-five percent of people dying in Holland today die an assisted death. Is that the way we want to go? The report of the Law Reform Commission of Canada tabled in 1983 says no, but there is a steady erosion of that position in the public mind. If we are to credit the polls, more and more people accept assisted dying as an option.

16   As with abortion in its early stages of acceptance, we are now being besieged with propaganda concerning death and dying. There are three basic arguments, corresponding to three principles of moral life: the nature

of action, the social nature of death and dying, and the nature of the good. The first argument in favour of euthanasia is that we have the right to choice and autonomy in the major issues of our life, and that all rights are based on this right. This seems plausible until one notes that the decision is forced by pain. A truly free decision would be to resist those physical forces which threaten life and relationships.

The second argument is that a compassionate society should accept 17 the rights of others to self-determination, and its laws should tolerate the ethical views of others even if our own views differ. This argument centres on the right to privacy. It is the common view of politicians and many others who would neither seek euthanasia themselves nor force their opinions on others. What these people fail to understand is that laws against euthanasia play a primary teaching role in society and in the support for a life ethic. A virtuous society enshrines its virtues in laws against murder, rape, child abuse, and a variety of other vicious practices.

The third argument in favour of euthanasia is simply that it is in our 18 best interests to avoid pain and seek pleasure. But each person's sense of interest differs, and society's interests are often in conflict with the individual's.

The greatest difficulty faced by those who would make a case against 19 euthanasia comes from the steady erosion of the law. It will begin in Canada, as it began elsewhere, with the inability of the courts to prosecute people for performing an action which seems so compassionate. For that reason, the basis for the law must be made clear. There must also be a legal distinction between homicide and euthanasia, between intention and motivation, and the punishment for breach of the law must be vastly different from the punishment imposed for homicide; perhaps some form of community service would be appropriate. Finally, social circumstances must be provided to make old age a joyful experience of passage.

Our attitude to dying is a proclamation of our stance toward life. If 20 we actively participate in the process, we proclaim something of inestimable value to those we love. It becomes the most beautiful gift we can offer. "The critical difference," wrote Henri Nouwen, "has to do with how I die."

> If I die with much anger and bitterness, I will leave my family and friends behind in confusion, guilt, shame, or a sense of impotence. When I felt my death approaching, I suddenly realized how much I could influence the hearts of those whom I would leave behind. If I could truly say that I was grateful for what I had lived, eager to forgive and be forgiven, full of hope that those who loved me would continue their lives in joy and peace, and confident that Jesus would guide all who had belonged to my life — if I could do that, I would, in the hour of my death, create more spiritual freedom than I had been able to create in all the years of my life.
>
> I realized with new intensity that dying is the most important act of living. It involves a choice to bind with guilt or to set free with gratitude. The choice is between a death that gives life and a death that kills.

21   Euthanasia is an act of violence. It kills not only the person who dies but the spirit of those left behind. My own experience has been one of unbounded love. My students wrote poems for me; my colleagues held a healing service; my family prayed fervently; my friends — religious and atheist alike — held my hands and embraced me in a manner I can only understand as a divine gift. It would not have comforted me in my worst moments if someone had offered to assist me by a violent act in my passage.

22   Healing is the action of making whole. It is paradoxical that this divine gift may come at a time when our bodies cannot be made whole except in the sense of witnessing to the sacred and mysterious moment when we give the best of ourselves to others. Dying is an active gift, a healing gift, and a proclamation to the world. Contrast that with the violence of killing, even in the name of compassion, and there is no doubt where wisdom lies.

> An aged man is but a paltry thing,
> A tattered coat upon a stick, unless
> Soul clap its hands and sing, and louder sing
> For every tatter in its mortal dress. . . .
> — W. B. Yeats, "Sailing to Byzantium"

23   Take the hands of the sick and the dying, the aged amongst you, the "paltry things." Take their hands and tell them that you love them, and euthanasia as an issue will disappear. The dying will stay for your sake. They will see dying as the last and most beautiful act of a soul yearning for ecstasy, full of hope, leaving a legacy of love.

TYPES OF WRITING:
analysis, cause and effect, definition, direct argument, personal experience

Topics for Discussion

1. Although McCullough's essay is primarily an argument proceeding carefully from one logical point to the next, he becomes openly emotional, almost sentimental, in several places. Identify these passages and discuss how they help or hinder the argument McCullough is advancing.
2. What is the function of paragraph 6 in relation to the first five? And what do paragraphs 7 and 8 do?
3. How do your answers to question 2 help you to answer question 1?
4. What is the importance of the final sentence of paragraph 10?
5. In paragraph 2, McCullough makes two key distinctions about euthanasia, briefly, and almost bluntly. Is this an effective approach to such a complex matter? Does it help, or hinder, his attempt to persuade his readers?

Topics for Writing

1. Drawing on your own experience of death — that of a family member, a close friend, or someone in public life to whom you felt a strong attachment — write an essay agreeing or disagreeing with McCullough.
2. Drawing on what you have learned from McCullough's method of identifying, analyzing, and refuting conceptions of and justifications for euthanasia, write an essay in which you take a strong stand on a controversial topic such as abortion, animal rights, or universal healthcare.

French Is a Must for Canadians

Hugh MacLennan

1   The old proverb about people who live in glass houses applies perfectly to me when I write about bilingualism in Canada. I can't blame my fellow Canadians of the English language for being unable to speak French because I speak it brokenly myself, and my ears are painfully slow to catch it from others. I read French reasonably well, but that is not the same thing at all. In a country like ours I should be able to speak it almost as well as English. My inability to do so is a constant shame to me, and I recognize it as the severest educational handicap in my entire life.

2   To remedy that loss now would require at least six months, possibly a year. I would have to live with a French family and reduce my thinking processes to the elementary ideas which would be the only ones I could express in a language I have yet to master. At my time of life — I am fifty-three — I cannot afford that year or half-year, nor can I afford the temporary retrogression it would impose on my mind.

3   So the handicap abides, debarring me from reaching a true equality with my French-speaking friends. Being Montrealers, their English is as good as my own, and I cannot practise my broken French on a bilingual *Canadien* without mutual embarrassment.

4   I am also debarred from participating with courtesy in many of the gatherings where most of the company is *Canadien*. Surely it is improper to require a dozen men and women to forsake their own language for the benefit of the one person in the room who cannot speak it. Beyond this again, my weakness in the senior language of Canada is a private poverty, for French is the most precise instrument of speech the world has known since the death of ancient Greek.

5   If I speak at some length about my own case, it is only because I am typical of so many English-speaking Canadians. Barely three percent of them born outside the province of Quebec are bilingual. I would not be surprised if many of that three percent had either a French-speaking parent or had been living side by side with *Canadien* families when they were young. Certainly they could not become bilingual in any English-language Canadian public school. In this land of ours, more than nine times out of ten the bilingual person is either an immigrant or a *Canadien* who speaks English.

6   The reasons for this situation are various, and once again my own case is a good illustration. I grew up in Halifax, a city where no French is spoken. When I went to school, instruction in that language did not begin until Grade Nine. Too little of it came too late to do any good. It was taught without conversation by teachers who, I suspect, would have had difficulty ordering a meal in a Paris restaurant.

7   After two years of plodding along in the grammar of a living language taught as though it were dead, I abandoned French and took up

Greek. I could not carry both French and Greek in the same curriculum and, on the whole, this was a wise decision. I was to learn a lot of Greek, but I could not have learned how to speak French in the system then in use in Nova Scotia.

Always I hoped that a chance of learning French from French-speak- 8 ing people would come, but it never did. When I was a student in Europe it was essential for me to learn German for my research work. This precluded any chance of learning French in a French family.

Later, to my surprise, I found myself a resident of Montreal, and 9 here the situation was curious. In Montreal there is no *apparent* need to learn French in order to communicate; the Montreal *Canadiens* all speak English, at least the ones you meet in stores and buses. Nor, in my case, was there any opportunity to master the language. I was now very busy working, often night and day, on two professions simultaneously. Time passed and I neared middle age.

The best I could do was to use scraps of time to study French grammar 10 and for a few years go to an instructor twice a week for French conver- sation. It was better than nothing. I learned to read the language with reasonable fluency and to speak it after a fashion. Nor do I mean to suggest that it is impossible for a person to acquire French at middle age. It would do much good if more of us tried.

In middle life most men are too occupied with their professions or 11 businesses to find the necessary time. Two cabinet ministers in two separate federal governments have lamented to me the fact that although they would sooner acquire French than almost anything else, their sixteen- hour working day leaves them no opportunity.

There is the further difficulty that when a man has grown up it is 12 much harder to learn a foreign language, and it is especially hard to learn French.

Few *Canadiens* seem to realize the truth of this latter sentence. The 13 difficulty with French stems from its perfection, and this you can see when you contrast it with English. The spelling of English is horribly confusing to foreigners because the spelling was set before the pronun- ciations established themselves. But English grammar is much easier than French grammar, and the standards of speech in North American English are so loose that English of the average North American can almost be called a *lingua franca*.

We English-speaking North Americans tolerate sloppy sentence 14 structures, overwhelming doses of slang, a general vagueness of expres- sion, and a lack of style which make many of us sound uncouth even to foreigners who have had to learn English as a second language.

With French this is not the case. There seems to be no basic French as 15 there is a basic English or a basic German. You can get by in German or English with a very small vocabulary, but in French you have to speak the language pretty well in order to speak it at all. This makes French exceptionally difficult for an adult to pick up.

16   Finally, French is more difficult to catch with the ear than English or German because of the *liaison* within the phrase and the extreme rapidity with which a Frenchman can deliver himself of groups of personal pronouns. When I served as the sole English-speaking member of the original Montreal *Conseil des Arts*, I well remember an occasion where a *Canadien* colleague read the minutes. They were printed before me and I was reading them myself, but as he ran through them I realized he could speak almost as swiftly as the eye could follow the printed word.

17   For these reasons I say feelingly that the achievement of a true bilingualism in Canada is not going to come easily. But we can certainly do better than we are doing now. The matter is so important to our national existence that the most radical plans should be considered for improving the situation.

18   The last point — that bilingualism is vital to our national existence — is not self-evident, as anyone knows who has followed the attempts of educational boards to introduce conversational French into the curriculum of an English-speaking province. Recently in Ontario, where a partial attempt was made, the cry went up: "What is the *use* of French if we don't live in Quebec?"

19   The use is twofold. On the one hand, the study of a language like French is rewarding in itself and gives a superlative training to a student in the precise handling of his own language. On the other hand, an interest in bilingualism may well be the sole measure which can save Canada from absorption by the United States.

20   This country of ours is a dual one or it is nothing: the essence of Canadian nationhood lies in this very fact, that it is a political fusion of the two elements in North American history which refused to belong to the United States. More than we realize, we Canadians of both languages are committed to the Canadian experiment. I teach the young three hours a week and I know from experience that Canada means much more to them than a place where they can earn a living and raise families. The yearning of our ancestors for a home of their own may not be visible in today's high-pressure prosperity, but it lies underneath the surface.

21   If any Canadian politician went to the electorate with an annexation program he would be annihilated at the polls. To be, at least to an extent, masters of our own future is one of the strongest collective aims in the Canadian people today. Forty years hence this nation — if it still is a nation — will have a population of forty million. If that weight of numbers will not make Canada a world power, it will certainly make her a world force. But not as things are going now. As things are going now, we English Canadians are well on the way to being absorbed culturally, while Quebec is in greater danger of cultural isolation than ever before.

22   Therefore, I truly believe that a rapid and large increase in bilingualism is the best remedy in Canada against this blind drift into a limbo none of us really want. If as many as twenty-five percent of the English-speaking Canadians in the next generation were bilingual, Canada would

not only come closer together in her various parts; she would attain a measure of inner self-confidence she now lacks. She would become a unique nation which the world would eye with respect, and to which we would be intensely proud to belong. That seems a vision worth striving for.

The question is, how can the vision be translated into reality? What 23 active factors are necessary to bring it about?

The first is a genuine desire on the part of the English-speaking 24 provinces to learn French. This desire is not likely to grow unless it is fostered, unless the necessity of bilingualism is pointed out in the strongest possible terms. But if the desire comes into being, and the necessity is recognized, then the problem becomes a technical one. And technical problems have one great attraction: if you try hard enough, you can generally solve them.

Granted a willingness to learn French properly, the next step would 25 be the admission of the scientific truth so often advanced by Dr. Wilder Penfield of McGill — that the time to learn a language is in childhood. Dr. Penfield insists that he is on firm scientific ground when he says that any normal child can learn at last three languages by the age of twelve, providing he is given the right environment and training.

At that age, and not at the high-school age, the child's reason is still 26 unawakened. But his imitative faculties and his memory are at their highest stretch. Words, phrases, and the basic sounds and logic of a language can pass effortlessly into the child's subconscious if they are fed into it at an early age.

Hence it follows that the time to begin French instruction in Canada 27 is not in Grades Seven and Eight but in Grade One. Nor is one hour a day sufficient. We should follow the same method used in some parts of Quebec and in all parts of Nova Scotia in the schools for French-speaking children. In the morning *all* instruction — not merely in language but in arithmetic, geography, and history — should be given in English; in the afternoon all instruction should be given in French. For the sake of variety, of course, the schedule should be switched back and forth: in the morning during one week, French; in the afternoon, English, and vice versa.

I know this sounds drastic, but what other course can we follow and 28 make sense? Nor would this method have to be followed into the high school. If it were followed for the first eight years, we would actually have a bilingual youth, and in the high schools French could be taught on the hour-a-day basis to students who knew enough of the language to study its literature as they study English literature.

For this system to succeed, one further requirement would have to 29 be fulfilled. Elementary-school teachers would have to be bilingual. In order to obtain enough instructors, at least in the beginning, it would be necessary to recruit teachers from Quebec or from French-speaking people in Ontario and the Maritimes. It is a *canard* spread about by university professors from France that the *Canadien* cannot speak proper French. What difference does it make if his accent is not Parisian? Do we say the Americans cannot speak English because they do not sound like Oxonians?

30   Here, briefly put, is the plan I suggest: bilingual teaching of *all* subjects in the grade schools. I have no illusion that this plan will be received with enthusiasm in the English-speaking provinces, or that it would be easy to put into effect. But if bilingualism is ever to be achieved in Canada, this is the only way in which it can be done.

TYPES OF WRITING:
comparison, direct argument, personal experience

Topics for Discussion

1. What is the effect of MacLennan's confessional opening with its reference to his failure to master French as a "constant shame" and his "severest educational handicap"? Does his essay supply clues to why he would feel the need to make so strong a statement?
2. Is MacLennan's praise of French at the expense of his own first language a rhetorical tactic or a symptom of the guilt he apparently feels regarding this issue? Is it likely to influence the English-speaking Canadians he is addressing to adopt bilingual education?

Topics for Writing

1. Since MacLennan's essay was published in 1960, a great deal has been said, both for and against bilingualism. What is your view about the subject? In writing your essay, try to be as honest about your own motives and reasons as MacLennan was about his.
2. Direct an essay arguing for or against MacLennan's solution toward the teachers' union in an English-speaking province. Keep in mind that unilingual teachers might well feel threatened by MacLennan's plan to import bilingual teachers from Quebec.
3. The experience that MacLennan describes in the first two sentences of paragraph 4 may be one that you have experienced yourself: French-speaking Montrealers will regularly switch to English in a group situation even if only one member of the group does not understand French. What do you think of this? Whatever your view of the situation may be, try to deal with alternative views thoughtfully and fairly.

Indian Self-Government and Sovereignty in Canada

Ovide Mercredi

The issue of sovereignty in terms of self-rule for a people is not so much   1
a legal or constitutional issue, but a moral and political problem for all
Canadians. I say that not to be disrespectful to you, but to give you a
perspective which you did not see nor hear in the constitutional process.

The structure of the constitutional talks was on the basis of the legal   2
and constitutional debate, and did not address the primary issue, which
in my view is moral and political.

Let me explain it this way. You have a right to freedom which you   3
cherish. You understand it thoroughly in the context of individual freedom, and you will do anything to defend it. More than that, what you
tend to forget is that the individual right to freedom does not stand by
itself. It derives from some collective right of freedom that we have as
equals, and when you look within your own history in this country since
Confederation, you have fought for and defended your freedom in two
world wars. But it wasn't the individual right that you were defending,
but the collective right of freedom to your institutions of government, to
your democracy. What I fail to understand, as an aboriginal person, is
how you cannot somehow translate that passion which you have for
freedom into our context as aboriginal people.

What we are seeking is not so much recognition of an individual's   4
freedom within the context of Canada, although we know that we have
to strive for our civil and individual rights as well within your society,
but essentially the collective expression of the freedom of the collectivity,
the people themselves, to decide through their own general will, the
expression of their institutions, of how they choose to live and where
they choose to go collectively as a people. I ask you what is so difficult
about that?

All that we are looking for is what you already have, what you enjoy   5
as a people, which is your institutions that you collectively agree to, such as
parliament, such as provincial legislatures, such as your judicial system.
You take these institutions, not for granted, but you accept them as the
collective expression of your freedom as a people. So when we talk about
the right of self-government, we are not talking about the right that you
have to tell me, and my people, how we are to conduct our affairs. I
don't agree that you have the right to tell me, an indigenous person, how
I have to conduct my affairs. There lies the moral issue. When we try to
enter into dialogue with your government, and we put forward processes
and ideas of how we might entertain negotiations or discussions, your
governments continually put obstructions in front of us and they rely
on the rule of law. They rely on the constitution, your constitution, as
justification for refusing to sit down with us and engage in meaningful

dialogue on how we could express ourselves through our institutions of self-government in this country. When your governments refuse to talk to us, it becomes a political issue.

6   Where we are heading right now in this country is a collision course where you and I would lose, where there will be no winners. What we have to do is to take lessons from our ancestors, yours and mine. Those who had at least a vision, whether they believed it or not, that the proper way to deal with the aboriginal people is through discussion, negotiations, and the making of treaties. In this country there was no Indian war between us and the government of Canada other than the resistance of the Metis people in Saskatchewan. There has never been a deployment of the army in this country against the aboriginal people until very recently in Kahnawake and Kanesatake. That happened, in my view, because people have lost the vision that your ancestors and mine had — that we should resolve our differences through political discussion, and that we should come to some consensus on the issues that we face together.

7   We have a rich heritage in this country, a very rich heritage — the treaty-making process. Why is it that contemporary Canadians and their governments have forgotten about it? Is it because you are so ethnocentric in your views that you fail to see that the actions of your government amount to white supremacy? That is a strong suggestion, but think about it. From my perspective as an aboriginal person, when I am told, as I have been told by officials in the government, that they will not engage in discussions on the right to self-government until there is a constitutional amendment that recognizes explicitly our right to govern ourselves, then I know there is a great obstacle that I cannot do anything about. When we engage in discussions with them and we try to move issues forward, and I'll give you some examples, they place before you the suggestion that there are only two jurisdictions in this country, the provincial government and the federal government, and you wonder to yourself: at what point in your history as an indigenous person did your people surrender the right to govern themselves? Where in our history is there a document that tells you that I gave you the right to tell me how I am to live? Where in our entire history is there a scrap of paper that suggests that our people have abandoned their right to exist as a distinct people, or for that matter that they have relinquished their own self-government so they can adopt and embrace yours as superior forms of institutions of government?

8   I will tell you what sovereignty is not, so that you will have at least some understanding of why we also, like you, cherish our freedoms. First of all, it is not the Indian Act. It is not parliament sitting down deciding in assembly in one session to pass a law that tells me that I can do this but I can't do that. That is not sovereignty, that is not self-government and that is not self-rule. That is someone telling you what to do. Our people are operating under a system of government that is not

traditional. The reason for that is that somewhere after Confederation some of your people decided in parliament that they would impose a system of government called the Chief and Council system, where they would delegate powers to the Indian people, but they would not recognize the law-making ability of the Indian people. They would just delegate some by-law making powers which would not become law until the Minister of Indian Affairs approved them. That is not sovereignty. That is delegated authority. That is the municipalization of our people's right to self-government, and has been rejected by our people.

When we had discussions during the constitutional process, many of the premiers, including the prime minister, were totally amazed at our assertion that we have a continuing right, a pre-existing right, to govern ourselves. That does not derive from your parliament. The source of authority comes from the people, our own history, our own nations, our own culture. If you examine your own institutions and how you formed as a nation, you understand what I am saying to you. All we want is to express ourselves in the same way that you are able to do, subsequent to Confederation throughout this country what Canadians were able to do as they formed provinces, and eventually we'll do in the northern parts of our country because Meech Lake did not pass.

When we speak about self-government, our biggest problem in dealing with politicians, the premiers and the prime minister, is that somehow it is absurd for us to think that we can govern ourselves, that it is absurd for us to imagine or even dream about governmental powers equivalent to provincial powers. The reason why people feel, in my view, that it is not permissible for us to express ourselves through our own institutions is the conclusion that we are not ready to govern ourselves. That is a moral issue and has nothing to do with law or constitutional change. That has to do with attitudes, belief, morality. When you form opinions about us, as your government has done, that we are still not ready for self-government and that we need to be brought along a little more, that we still need a department of Indian Affairs to nudge us along, then you can appreciate what I am trying to say to you — that it is not a constitutional problem, it is not a legal problem, it is a moral problem.

If we can begin to address these issues and put aside these double standards that operate all the time — the double standard that tells me you can have your institutions of government but I cannot, the double standard that tells me you can elect your own representative to make laws for you but I cannot — if we can get rid of them we would have removed one major obstacle towards what we need to do.

What is it that we need to do? We need to come to some common understanding on how we are going to co-exist in this country. We need to talk about how we are going to share the resources of this country. We need to talk about how we are going to share power. We need to talk about how we are going to jointly deal with individual rights, but for us to get there, the moral issues have to be dealt with first, because otherwise, if we go back to the constitutional table, we will still be dealing with resistance to our rights, our freedoms.

13   You have a very rich heritage as a democracy. Many of us have studied your system of government. We know you much more than you know us because we are, just like you, a product of your educational system. We have studied Greek and Roman philosophy. We have studied Western civilization; we have memorized in your schools the historical events of your people. We know you exceedingly well, and we know that you cherish law and order, that you cherish the rule of law. We know that over the centuries your governments have evolved to where they are now, including your courts, and that throughout the history of your court system there have been periods when major developments took place, such as for example the recognition and protection of individual rights, concepts like due process and natural justice.

14   We are offended when the attorney-general of Ontario tells the Indian lawyers in their assembly last year that it is not possible to have Indian tribal courts because of the Charter of Rights and Freedoms. I say to you: when did you become the standard for human rights? Perhaps we can do better if we create our own courts. Maybe we will interpret individual rights in a social context so that it is not possible for a person who is found guilty not to be accountable for the harm committed. Give us a chance to deal with issues like social problems. Give us a chance to deal with these problems in the courts, because the courts refuse to take on that added responsibility because your lawyers and judges are on a pedestal in your society, and they cannot condescend to deal with the social problems they find in court; they leave that to social workers and psychologists.

15   There is something to be said, even in the context of experimentation, for you to abandon your tendency to put obstacles in our path to self-government, because what might happen, very possibly, is that we might create laws, we might create courts, that would become models, and new standards where human rights might have a different expression and meaning. So don't throw your Charter of Rights and Freedoms at us as an obstacle, because we will not say to you that we will not accept that. To think there is only one way of looking at human rights is very ethnocentric.

16   When I went to Geneva on the rights of the child, when the convention was being drafted in its final stages, I was very surprised that the western civilizations are still bullying totally everybody in the world and imposing their concepts of the rights of the child without taking into account the different cultures that exist. What I saw was not an exchange as I expected in the United Nations between different cultures to develop a standard of children's rights, but what exists here in this country, a western civilization imposing its political will on others. My question is how a dominant society can possibly justify continuing to bully the aboriginal people to toe the line and to be like everybody else because it is in their interest, and if they don't they will be held accountable for it.

I conclude by saying that we haven't given up on this country. We 17
are looking for a way of arriving at consensual arrangements so that we
can co-exist, where you can respect my collective rights as we respect
yours, so that individual rights can be enjoyed by me in your society as
you ought to be able to enjoy them within the context of my society as
well. That is what we have to work for, that is where we have to go in
the next 20–50 years.

We don't need confrontation, we don't need police officers enforcing 18
the political will by force, because that is what happened in Oka in my
view. We need processes, guidelines and discussion. We have to get
away from these simple-minded politicians who talk about the rule of
law. The rule of law has become a battle cry with the federal government
and the premier of Quebec, and they think that Canadians are completely
behind them now because they want law and order. But there is no law
and order without justice, for justice is the foundation of law and order
and what is absent in their battle cry is justice. Until your government
begins to deal with justice for our people we will not make very much
progress in this country.

I may have sounded preachy, sometimes I get that way, but let me 19
tell you something that really struck me the other day. Like you, I have
to get ready for winter and I was working outside. My daughter, who
looks very much Indian, was playing with some children from the
neighborhood — two white boys and a young lady, named Jill, who is
very impressed with me. Every opportunity she gets she introduces me
to her friends as one of *the* Indian leaders in Canada. On this occasion,
she said to the boys, "He is one of the top Indian leaders in the world,"
and one of them asked, "How is he going to get out of jail?" I didn't
interfere with them, but I heard one of the girls say, "You will never
understand." What we have to do is make sure that we understand each
other. I know you because I have studied you. It would be nice if somehow you would force yourselves to study us, to understand us, and
maybe there's hope for this country so that a hundred years from now
there is not another Indian leader, "the best in the world," standing here
preaching to you, but proclaiming, not denouncing, the greatness of this
country.

TYPES OF WRITING:
analysis, definition, direct argument

Topics for Discussion

1. At the beginning of his essay, Mercredi tells us that, in his view, "the
   primary issue . . . is moral and political." Does he succeed in separating the moral and political issue from the legal and constitutional

one? What is the moral side of the issue, as Mercredi conceives it? What is the political problem, and how is it distinct from law?

2. Discuss the functions of the first two sentences of paragraph 6: How do these two sentences follow from the previous five paragraphs? How are these sentences calculated to appeal to the reader? How (if at all) do they prepare the reader for the arguments that follow?

3. In paragraph 6, Mercredi states that the country is heading on a collision course, and in the next paragraph he refers to "the treaty-making process." How are these two points related? What persuasive tactic is Mercredi using here?

4. Mercredi takes a strong stand throughout this piece, and at various points he warns that change on the part of the dominant Canadian society is urgent. Yet he also resists being outright threatening or antagonistic. Locate instances where Mercredi attempts to avoid provoking an angry or frightened reaction from his non-Native audience. How and how well do these work?

5. Is the anecdote in Mercredi's last paragraph an effective conclusion? Why or why not?

Topics for Writing

1. "I don't agree that you have the right to tell me, an indigenous person, how I have to conduct my affairs" (paragraph 5). After you have placed this statement in its context, use it as a starting point for an essay in which you try to persuade your reader either that Mercredi is right in what he says about Indian self-government, or that he is wrong.

2. "To think there is only one way of looking at human rights is very ethnocentric." Write an essay arguing for or against the idea that Western concepts of human rights should be promoted in other parts of the world for the good of the people living there.

The Story of Service

Jessica Mitford

There was a time when the undertaker's tasks were clearcut and rather   1
obvious, and when he billed his patrons accordingly. Typical late l9th
century charges, in addition to the price of merchandise, are shown on
bills of the period as: 'Services at the house (placing corpse in the coffin),
$1.25', 'Preserving remains on ice, $10', 'Getting Permit, $1.50'. It was
customary for the undertaker to add a few dollars to his bill for being 'in
attendance', which seems only fair and right. The cost of embalming was
around $10 in 1880. An undertaker, writing in 1900, recommends these
minimums for service charges: Washing and dressing, $5; embalming,
$10; hearse, $8 to $10. As historians of the trade have pointed out: 'The
undertaker had as yet to conceive of the value of personal services offered
professionally for a fee, legitimately claimed.' Well, he has now so conceived with a vengeance.

When weaving in the story of service as it is rendered today,   2
spokesmen for the funeral industry tend to become so carried away by
their own enthusiasm, so positively lyrical and copious in their declara-
tions, that the outsider may have a little trouble understanding it all.
There are indeed contradictions. Preferred Funeral Directors International
has prepared a mimeographed talk designed to inform people about
service: 'The American public receive the services of employees and pro-
prietor alike, nine and one half days of labor for every funeral handled,
they receive the use of automobiles and hearses, a building including a
chapel and other rooms which require building maintenance, insurance,
taxes and licenses, and depreciation, as well as heat in the winter, cool-
ing in the summer and light and water.' It goes on to say that while the
process of embalming takes only about three hours, yet, 'it would be
necessary for one man to work two forty-hour weeks to complete a
funeral service. This is coupled with an additional forty hours service
required by members of other local allied professions, including the work
of the cemeteries, newspapers, and of course, the most important of all,
the service of your clergyman. These some 120 hours of labor are the
basic value on which the cost of funerals rests.'

Our informant has lumped a lot of things together here. To start   3
with 'the most important of all, the service of your clergyman', the average religious funeral service lasts no more than 25 minutes. Furthermore,
it is not, of course, paid for by the funeral director. The 'work of the
cemeteries' presumably means the opening and closing of a grave. This
now mechanized operation, which takes 15 to 20 minutes, is likewise not
billed as part of the funeral director's costs. The work of 'newspapers'?
This is a puzzler. Presumably reference is made here to the publication
of an obituary notice on the vital statistics page. It is, incidentally, surprising to learn that newspaper work is considered an 'allied profession'.

4   Just how insurance, taxes, licences and depreciation are figured in as part of the 120 man-hours of service is hard to tell. The writer does mention that his operation features '65 items of service'. In general, the funeral salesman is inclined to chuck in everything he does under the heading of 'service'. For example, in a typical list of 'services' he will include items like 'securing statistical data' (in other words, completing the death certificate and finding out how much insurance was left by the deceased), 'the arrangements conference' (in which the sale of the funeral to the survivors is made), and the 'keeping of records', by which he means his own bookkeeping work. Evidently there is some confusion here between items that properly belong in a cost-accounting system and items of *actual* service rendered in any given funeral. In all likelihood, idle time of employees is figured in and prorated as part of the 'man-hours'. The up-to-date funeral home operates on a 24-hour basis, and the mimeographed speech contains the heartening news:

5   'The funeral service profession of the United States is proud of the fact that there is not a person within the continental limits of the United States who is more than two hours away from a licensed funeral director and embalmer in case of need. That's one that even the fire fighting apparatus of our country cannot match.'

6   While the hit-or-miss rhetoric of the foregoing is fairly typical of the prose style of the funeral trade as a whole, and while the statement that 120 man-hours are devoted to a single man- (or woman-) funeral may be open to question, there really is a fantastic amount of service accorded the dead body and its survivors.

7   Having decreed what sort of funeral is right, proper and nice, and having gradually appropriated to himself all the functions connected with it, the funeral director has become responsible for a multitude of tasks beyond the obvious one of 'placing corpse in the coffin' recorded in our 19th century funeral bill. His self-imposed duties fall into two main categories: attention to the corpse itself, and the stagemanaging of the funeral.

8   The drama begins to unfold with the arrival of the corpse at the mortuary.

9   Alas, poor Yorick! How *very* surprised he would be to see how his counterpart of today is whisked off to a funeral parlour and is in short order sprayed, sliced, pierced, pickled, trussed, trimmed, creamed, waxed, painted, rouged and neatly dressed — transformed from a common corpse into a Beautiful Memory Picture. This process is known in the trade as embalming and restorative art, and is so universally employed in the United States and Canada that the funeral director does it routinely, without consulting corpse or kin. He regards as eccentric those few who are hardy enough to suggest that it might be dispensed with. Yet no law requires embalming, no religious doctrine commends it, nor is it dictated by considerations of health, sanitation, or even of personal daintiness. In no part of the world but in Northern America is it widely used. The

purpose of embalming is to make the corpse presentable for viewing in a suitably costly container; and here too the funeral director routinely, without first consulting the family, prepares the body for public display.

Is all this legal? The processes to which a dead body may be subjected 10 are after all to some extent circumscribed by law. In most states, for instance, the signature of next of kin must be obtained before an autopsy may be performed, before the deceased may be cremated, before the body may be turned over to a medical school for research purposes; or such provision must be made in the decedent's will. In the case of embalming, no such permission is required nor is it ever sought. A textbook, *Principles and Practices of Embalming*, comments on this: 'There is some question regarding the legality of much that is done within the preparation room.' The author points out that it would be most unusual for a responsible member of a bereaved family to instruct the mortician, in so many words, to *'embalm'* the body of a deceased relative. The very term 'embalming' is so seldom used that the mortician must rely upon custom in the matter. The author concludes that unless the family specifies otherwise, the act of entrusting the body to the care of a funeral establishment carries with it an implied permission to go ahead and embalm.

Embalming is indeed a most extraordinary procedure, and one must 11 wonder at the docility of Americans who each year pay hundreds of millions of dollars for its perpetuation, blissfully ignorant of what it is all about, what is done, how it is done. Not one in ten thousand has any idea of what actually takes place. Books on the subject are extremely hard to come by. They are not to be found in libraries or bookshops.

In an era when huge television audiences watch surgical operations 12 in the comfort of their living rooms, when, thanks to the animated cartoon, the geography of the digestive system has become familiar territory even to the nursery-school set, in a land where the satisfaction of curiosity about almost all matters is a national pastime, the secrecy surrounding embalming can, surely, hardly be attributed to the inherent gruesomeness of the subject. Custom in this regard has within this century suffered a complete reversal. In the early days of American embalming, when it was performed in the home of the deceased, it was almost mandatory for some relative to stay by the embalmer's side and witness the procedure. Today, family members who might wish to be in attendance would certainly be dissuaded by the funeral director. All others, except apprentices, are excluded by law from the preparation room.

A close look at what does actually take place may explain in large 13 measure the undertaker's intractable reticence concerning a procedure that has become his major *raison d'être*. Is it possible he fears that public information about embalming might lead patrons to wonder if this trip is really necessary? If the funeral men are loath to discuss the subject outside the trade, the reader may, understandably, be equally loath to go on reading at this point. For those who have the stomach for it, let us part the formaldehyde curtain and find out what happens. Others should skip to [paragraph 29].

14   The body is first laid out in the undertaker's morgue — or rather, as the trade prefers, Mr. Jones is reposing in the preparation room — to be readied to bid the world farewell.

15   The preparation room in any of the better funeral establishments has the tiled and sterile look of a surgery, and indeed the embalmer-restorative artist who does his chores there is beginning to adopt the term 'dermasurgeon' (appropriately corrupted by some mortician-writers as 'demi-surgeon') to describe his calling. His equipment, consisting of scalpels, scissors, augers, forceps, clamps, needles, pumps, tubes, bowls and basins, is crudely imitative of the surgeon's, as is his technique, acquired in a nine- or twelve-month post-high-school course in an embalming school. He is supplied by an advanced chemical industry with a bewildering array of fluids, sprays, pastes, oils, powders, creams, to fix or soften tissue, shrink or distend it as needed, dry it here, restore the moisture there. There are cosmetics, waxes and paints to fill and cover features, even plaster of Paris to replace entire limbs. There are ingenious aids to prop and stabilize the cadaver: a Vari-Pose Head Rest, the Edwards Arm and Hand Positioner, the Repose Block (to support the shoulders during the embalming), and the Throop foot positioner, which resembles an old-fashioned stocks.

16   Mr. John H. Eckels, president of the Eckels College of Mortuary Science, thus describes the first part of the embalming procedure: 'In the hands of a skilled practitioner, this work may be done in a comparatively short time and without mutilating the body other than by slight incision — so slight that it scarcely would cause serious inconvenience if made upon a living person. It is necessary to remove the blood, and doing this not only helps in the disinfecting, but removes the principal cause of disfigurements due to discoloration.' This is a plucky try at reassurance, although some living persons might think it *would* cause a rather serious inconvenience to remove their blood.

17   Another textbook discusses the all-important time element: 'The earlier this is done, the better, for every hour that elapses between death and embalming will add to the problems and complications encountered. . . .' Just how soon should one get going on the embalming? The author tells us: 'On the basis of such scanty information made available to this profession through its rudimentary and haphazard system of technical research, we must conclude that the best results are to be obtained if the subject is embalmed before life is completely extinct — that is, before cellular death has occurred. In the average case, this would mean within an hour after somatic death.' For those who feel that there is something a little rudimentary, not to say haphazard, about this advice, a comforting thought is offered by another writer. Speaking of fears entertained in early days of premature burial, he points out: 'One of the effects of embalming by chemical injection, however, has been to dispel fears of live burial.' How true; once the blood is removed, chances of live burial are indeed remote.

To return to Mr. Jones, the blood is drained out through the veins 18 and replaced by embalming fluid pumped in through the arteries. As noted in *Principles and Practices of Embalming*, 'every operator has a favorite injection and drainage point — a fact which becomes a handicap only if he fails or refuses to forsake his favorites when conditions demand it'. Typical favourites are the carotid artery, femoral artery, jugular vein, subclavian vein. There are various choices of embalming fluid. If Flextone is used, it will produce a 'mild, flexible rigidity. The skin retains a velvety softness, the tissues are rubbery and pliable. Ideal for women and children.' It may be blended with B. and G. Products Company's Lyf-Lyk tint, which is guaranteed to reproduce 'nature's own skin texture . . . the velvety appearance of living tissue'. Suntone comes in three separate tints: Suntan; Special Cosmetic Tint, a pink shade 'especially indicated for young female subjects'; and Regular Cosmetic Tint, moderately pink.

About three to six gallons of a dyed and perfumed solution of form- 19 aldehyde, glycerin, borax, phenol, alcohol and water are soon circulating through Mr. Jones, whose mouth has been sewn together with a 'needle directed upward between the upper lip and gum and brought out through the left nostril', with the corners raised slightly 'for a more pleasant expression'. If he should be bucktoothed, his teeth are cleaned with Bon Ami and coated with colourless nail polish. His eyes, meanwhile, are closed with flesh-tinted eye caps and eye cement.

The next step is to have at Mr. Jones with a trocar, a long, hollow 20 needle attached to a tube. It is jabbed into the abdomen, poked around the entrails and chest cavity, the contents of which are pumped out and replaced with 'cavity fluid'. This done, and the hole in the abdomen sewn up, Mr. Jones's face is heavily creamed (to protect the skin from burns which may be caused by leakage of the chemicals), and he is covered with a sheet and left unmolested for a while. But not for long — there is more, much more, in store for him. He has been embalmed, but not yet restored, and the best time to start the restorative work is eight to ten hours after embalming, when the tissues have become firm and dry.

The object of all this attention to the corpse, it must be remembered, 21 is to make it presentable for viewing in an attitude of healthy repose. 'Our customs require the presentation of our dead in the semblance of normality . . . unmarred by the ravages of illness, disease or mutilation,' says Mr. J. Sheridan Mayer in his *Restorative Art*. This is rather a large order since few people die in the full bloom of health, unravaged by illness and unmarked by some disfigurement. The funeral industry is equal to the challenge: 'In some cases the gruesome appearance of a mutilated or disease-ridden subject may be quite discouraging. The task of restoration may seem impossible and shake the confidence of the embalmer. This is the time for intestinal fortitude and determination. Once the formative work is begun and affected tissues are cleaned or removed, all doubts of success vanish. It is surprising and gratifying to discover the results which may be obtained.'

22   The embalmer, having allowed an appropriate interval to elapse, returns to the attack, but now he brings into play the skill and equipment of sculptor and cosmetician. Is a hand missing? Casting one in plaster of Paris is a simple matter. 'For replacement purposes, only a cast of the back of the hand is necessary; this is within the ability of the average operator and is quite adequate.' If a lip or two, a nose or an ear should be missing, the embalmer has at hand a variety of restorative waxes with which to model replacements. Pores and skin texture are simulated by stippling with a little brush, and over this cosmetics are laid on. Head off? Decapitation cases are rather routinely handled. Ragged edges are trimmed, and head joined to torso with a series of splints, wires and sutures. It is a good idea to have a little something at the neck — a scarf or high collar — when time for viewing comes. Swollen mouth? Cut out tissue as needed from inside the lips. If too much is removed, the surface contour can easily be restored by padding with cotton. Swollen necks and cheeks are reduced by removing tissue through vertical incisions made down each side of the neck. 'When the deceased is casketed, the pillow will hide the suture incisions . . . as an extra precaution against leakage, the suture may be painted with liquid sealer.'

23   The opposite condition is more likely to present itself — that of emaciation. His hypodermic syringe now loaded with massage cream, the embalmer seeks out and fills the hollowed and sunken areas by injection. In this procedure the backs of the hands and fingers and the under-chin area should not be neglected.

24   Positioning the lips is a problem that recurrently challenges the ingenuity of the embalmer. Closed too tightly, they tend to give a stern, even disapproving, expression. Ideally, embalmers feel, the lips should give the impression of being ever so slightly parted, the upper lip protruding slightly for a more youthful appearance. This takes some engineering, however, as the lips tend to drift apart. Lip drift can sometimes be remedied by pushing one or two straight pins through the inner margin of the lower lip and then inserting them between the two front upper teeth. If Mr. Jones happens to have no teeth, the pins can just as easily be anchored in his Armstrong Face Former and Denture Replacer. Another method to maintain lip closure is to dislocate the lower jaw, which is then held in its new position by a wire run through holes which have been drilled through the upper and lower jaws at the midline. As the French are fond of saying, *il faut souffrir pour être belle.**

25   If Mr. Jones has died of jaundice, the embalming fluid will very likely turn him green. Does this deter the embalmer? Not if he has intestinal fortitude. Masking pastes and cosmetics are heavily laid on, burial garments and casket interiors are colour-correlated with particular care,

---

*In 1963, *Mortuary Management* reports a new development: 'Natural Expression Formers', an invention of Funeral Directors Research Company. 'They may be used to replace one or both artificial dentures, or over natural teeth; have "bite-indicator" lines as a closure guide . . . Natural Expression Formers also offer more control of facial expression.'

and Jones is displayed beneath rose-coloured lights. Friends will say, 'How *well* he looks.' Death by carbon monoxide, on the other hand, can be rather a good thing from the embalmer's viewpoint: 'One advantage is the fact that this type of discoloration is an exaggerated form of a natural pink coloration.' This is nice because the healthy glow is already present and needs but little attention.

The patching and filling completed, Mr. Jones is now shaved, washed 26 and dressed. Cream-based cosmetic, available in pink, flesh, suntan, brunette and blond, is applied to his hands and face, his hair is shampooed and combed (and, in the case of Mrs. Jones, set), his hands manicured. For the horny-handed son of toil special care must be taken; cream should be applied to remove ingrained grime, and the nails cleaned. 'If he were not in the habit of having them manicured in life, trimming and shaping is advised for better appearance — never questioned by kin.'

Jones is now ready for casketing (this is the present participle of the 27 verb 'to casket'). In this operation his right shoulder should be depressed slightly 'to turn the body a bit to the right and soften the appearance of lying flat on the back'. Positioning the hands is a matter of importance, and special rubber positioning blocks may be used. The hands should be cupped slightly for a more lifelike, relaxed appearance. Proper placement of the body requires a delicate sense of balance. It should lie as high as possible in the casket, yet not so high that the lid, when lowered, will hit the nose. On the other hand, we are cautioned, placing the body too low 'creates the impression that the body is in a box'.

Jones is next wheeled into the appointed slumber room where a few 28 last touches may be added — his favourite pipe placed in his hand or, if he was a great reader, a book propped into position. (In the case of little Master Jones a Teddy bear may be clutched.) Here he will hold open house for a few days, visiting hours 10 a.m. to 9 p.m.

All now being in readiness, the funeral director is discreetly scurrying 29 around to see that all goes as it should. A staff conference is called to make sure that each assistant knows his precise duties. Mr. Wilber Krieger writes: 'This makes your staff feel that they are a part of the team, with a definite assignment that must be properly carried out if the whole plan is to succeed. You never heard of a football coach who failed to talk to his entire team before they go on the field. They have drilled on the plays they are to execute for hours and days, and yet the successful coach knows the importance of making even the bench-warming third-string substitute feel that he is important if the game is to be won.' The winning of *this* game is predicated upon glass-smooth handling of the logistics. The funeral director has notified the pallbearers whose names were furnished by the family, has arranged for the presence of clergyman, organist, and soloist, has provided transportation for everybody, has organized and listed the flowers sent by friends. In *Psychology of Funeral Service* Mr. Edward A. Martin points out: 'He may not always do as much as the family thinks he is doing, but it is his helpful guidance that they appreciate in knowing they are proceeding as they should. . . . The important thing is how well his services can be used to make the family believe they are giving unlimited expression to their own sentiment.'

30   The religious service may be held in a church or in the chapel in the funeral home; the funeral director vastly prefers the latter arrangement, for not only is it more convenient for him but it affords him the opportunity to show off his beautiful facilities to the gathered mourners. After the clergyman has had his say, the mourners queue up to file past the casket for a last look at the deceased. The family is *never* asked whether they want an open-casket ceremony; in the absence of their instruction to the contrary, this is taken for granted. Consequently well over 90 per cent of all American funerals feature the open casket — a custom unknown in other parts of the world. Foreigners are astonished by it. An Englishwoman living in San Francisco described her reaction in a letter to the writer:

31   'I myself have attended only one funeral here — that of an elderly fellow worker of mine. After the service I could not understand why everyone was walking towards the coffin (sorry, I mean casket), but thought I had better follow the crowd. It shook me rigid to get there and find the casket open and poor old Oscar lying there in his brown tweed suit, wearing a suntan makeup and just the wrong shade of lipstick. If I had not been extremely fond of the old boy, I have a horrible feeling that I might have giggled. Then and there I decided that I could never face another American funeral — even dead.'

32   The casket (which has been resting throughout the service on a Classic Beauty Ultra Metal Casket Bier) is now transported by a hydraulically operated device called Porto-Lift to a balloon-tyred, Glide Easy casket carriage which will wheel it to yet another conveyance, the Cadillac Funeral Coach. This may be lavender, cream, light green — anything but black. Interiors, of course, are colour-correlated, 'for the man who cannot stop short of perfection'.

33   At graveside, the casket is lowered into the earth. This office, once the prerogative of friends of the deceased, is now performed by a patented mechanical lowering device. A 'Lifetime Green' artificial grass mat is at the ready to conceal the sere earth, and overhead, to conceal the sky, is a portable Steril Chapel Tent ('resists the intense heat and humidity of summer and the terrific storms of winter . . . available in Silver Grey, Rose or Evergreen'). Now is the time for the ritual scattering of earth over the coffin, as the solemn words 'earth to earth, ashes to ashes, dust to dust' are pronounced by the officiating cleric. This can today be accomplished 'with a mere flick of the wrist with the Gordon Leak-Proof Earth Dispenser. No grasping of a handful of dirt, no soiled fingers. Simple, dignified, beautiful, reverent! The modern way!' The Gordon Earth Dispenser (at $5) is of nickel-plated brass construction. It is not only 'attractive to the eye and long wearing'; it is also 'one of the "tools" for building better public relations' if presented as 'an appropriate

non-commercial gift' to the clergyman. It is shaped something like a saltshaker.

Untouched by human hand, the casket and the earth are now united.   34

It is in the function of directing the participants through this maze of   35
gadgetry that the funeral director has assigned to himself his relatively
new role of 'grief therapist'. He has relieved the family of every detail,
he has revamped the corpse to look like a living doll, he has arranged for
it to nap for a few days in a slumber room, he has put on a well-oiled
performance in which the concept of *death* has played no part whatsoever — unless it was inconsiderately mentioned by the clergyman who
conducted the religious service. He has done everything in his power to
make the funeral a real pleasure for everybody concerned. He and his
team have given their all to score an upset victory over death.

Dale Carnegie has decreed that in the lexicon of the successful man   36
there is no such word as 'failure'. So have the funeral men managed to
delete the word 'death' and all its associations from their vocabulary.
They have from time to time published lists of In and Out words and
phrases to be memorized and used in connection with the final return
of dust to dust; then, still dissatisfied with the result, have elaborated
and revised the lists. Thus a 1916 glossary substitutes 'prepare body'
for 'handle corpse'. Today, though, 'body' is Out and 'remains' for
'Mr. Jones' is In.

'The use of improper terminology by anyone affiliated with a mor-   37
tuary should be strictly forbidden,' declares Edward A. Martin. He suggests a rather thorough overhauling of the language; his deathless words
include: 'service, not funeral; Mr., Mrs., Miss Blank, not corpse or body;
preparation room, not morgue; casket, not coffin; funeral director or
mortician, not undertaker; reposing room or slumber room, not laying-
out room; display room, not showroom; baby or infant, not still-born;
deceased, not dead; autopsy or post-mortem, not post; casket coach, not
hearse; shipping case, not shipping box; flower car, not flower truck;
cremains or cremated remains, not ashes; clothing, dress, suit etc., not
shroud; drawing room, not parlor'.

This rather basic list was refined in 1956 by Victor Landig in his *Basic*   38
Principles of Funeral Service. He enjoins the reader to avoid using the
word 'death' as much as possible, even sometimes when such avoidance
may seem impossible; for example, a death certificate should be referred
to as a 'vital statistics form'. One should speak not of the 'job' but rather
of the 'call'. We do not 'haul' a dead person, we 'transfer' or 'remove'
him — and we do this in a 'service car', not a 'body car'. We 'open and
close' his grave rather than dig and fill it, and in it we 'inter' rather than
bury him. This is done not in a graveyard or cemetery but rather in a
'memorial park'. The deceased is beautified, not with makeup, but with
'cosmetics'. Anyway, he didn't die, he 'expired'. An important error to
guard against, cautions Mr. Landig, is referring to 'cost of the casket'.
The phrase 'amount of investment in the service' is a wiser usage here.

39   Miss Anne Hamilton Franz, writing in *Funeral Direction and Management*, adds an interesting footnote on the use of the word 'ashes' to describe (in a word) ashes. She fears this usage will encourage scattering (for what is more natural than to scatter ashes?) and prefers to speak of 'cremated remains' or 'human remains'. She does not like the word 'retort' to describe the container in which cremation takes place, but prefers 'cremation chamber' or 'cremation vault', because this 'sounds' better and softens any harshness to sensitive feelings'.

40   As for the Loved One, poor fellow, he wanders like a sad ghost through the funeral men's pronouncements. No provision seems to have been made for the burial of a Heartily Disliked One, although the necessity for such must arise in the course of human events.

TYPES OF WRITING:
analysis, description, example/illustration, humour, narration

Topics for Discussion

1. Consider how the first seven paragraphs serve to introduce the remainder of the essay. Upon what concerns do these paragraphs focus the reader's attention? How? Do these paragraphs make you want to read on? Why or why not?
2. How does paragraph 8 function in the essay? How is its brevity appropriate for this function?
3. Mitford makes her case about embalming practices by accumulating factual details, quotations, and terminology, and letting these speak for themselves. But she also reveals her attitude and leads her readers through her choice of words and her tone. Locate and consider the effects of passages in which Mitford implies criticism through her choice of words rather than by stating her case directly.
4. What influential advantage does Mitford derive from naming her sample cadaver?
5. How does Mitford's treatment of the euphemisms common in the undertaking business reinforce her more general criticism of the way death is handled in contemporary North America?

Topics for Writing

1. Researching your subject as necessary, use Mitford's methods to criticize some unpleasant practice, such as trapping fur-bearing animals, industrial chicken raising, cosmetic surgery, or medical research on animals.
2. In this essay Mitford is plainly trying to influence a wide audience — but to what ends? What primary and secondary changes of behaviour

and attitude might Mitford hope to accomplish? In answering this question it will be helpful to distinguish between appeals to reason and appeals to emotion.

3. Drawing on what you have learned from studying Mitford's treatment of jargon and euphemisms in the funeral industry, write an essay criticizing a typical attitude of some other profession or special-interest group as it is revealed in specialized language and images.

The Noose, the Chair and the Needle

Ruth Morris

1   Polls show 68 percent of Canadians favour a return to hanging; sound-
ings suggest about 2/3 of our present parliament, given a free vote,
would endorse a return to capital punishment. Gloomy figures for those
of us who don't want to see Canada join the US and Turkey as the only
Western nations carrying out the death penalty.

2   The good news is that the same polls show these beliefs to be based
largely on an absence of accurate information:

- 80% of Canadians have read nothing on the issue;
- Canadians believe the violent crime rate to be seven times what it
  actually is, and that the murder rate has been increasing since 1976
  — it has not;
- Most who advocate a return to capital punishment still belive deterrence works, and are unaware of extensive research which fails to
  show any evidence of the effectiveness of deterrence.

3   The answer then appears to be in education and lobbying, by those
of us who know and care about the issue.

ARGUMENTS AGAINST THE DEATH PENALTY

4   There are six major reasons for opposing the death penalty:

- DISCRIMINATION: Everywhere, racial minorities and the poor are
  far more likely than others to get executed.
- MISTAKES: Beyond a shadow of a doubt, many innocent people
  have been executed.
- LOTTERY: The tiny proportion of those executed compared to the
  numbers of victims of all kinds of social ills, including victims of
  murder, makes capital punishment the most barbaric lottery of
  them all.
- MORAL-RELIGIOUS: Regardless of anything else, we cannot practice capital punishment because of what it does to us when we engage in willful, premeditated social murder.
- DETERRENCE: There is no evidence that deterrence works.
- POLITICAL OPPRESSION: Amnesty International and others oppose capital punishment because, around the world, more people
  are executed for their political and religious beliefs or behavior than
  for any other reason.

5   Let's look at these arguments one by one.

DISCRIMINATION

One searched in vain for the execution of any member of the affluent strata of our society.
　　　　　　　　　　　　　　　　— U.S. Supreme Court Justice Douglas

In the US, chances are 3–10 times greater of being executed for killing a　6
white than a black person. Such discrimination goes back to the Middle Ages. An upper class person killing a lower status one was often not even guilty of an offence. Yet to kill one's social superiors led to death; worse still the grosser forms of execution have traditionally been reserved for killing those above us in the social ladder.

　　Today, more than 90% of those on death row could not afford to hire　7
their own lawyers. Lest anyone imagine discrimination is foreign to Canadian courts, my own 1982 study of Toronto bail courts showed substantial racial discrimination, making it harder for blacks than whites to be released on bail; and a number of studies on natives and prisons show rank discrimination by Canadian courts against native people (*Canadian Dimension*, 19 #5, December 1985).

　　There is no question that if we reinstitute capital punishment, we　8
will not be selecting the nastiest and most dangerous Canadians to execute. We will be executing almost exclusively: *POOR* people, *BLACK* people, *NATIVE* people, and *OTHER MINORITIES*. It is no coincidence that the otherwise very moderate National Association for the Advancement of Colored People (NAACP) in the USA has pioneered the fight against capital punishment. They know whose necks are on the line. For myself, even if all other arguments were nonexistent, I could not condone capital punishment, knowing it has operated everywhere and at all times as the ultimate expression of racial hatred and economic oppression.

MISTAKES

A recent American Civil Liberties Union study cites 343 cases in US　9
history where people were clearly wrongfully convicted of offences punishable by death. Twenty-five of these people were executed. University of Florida criminologist Radelet identified over 100 innocent individuals who were at one time condemned to die.

　　In Canada in the past two years, both John Wildman and Donald　10
Marshall have been released from prison after serving years for murders they did not commit. Had we had capital punishment, they too might have died.

　　To this, Ernest van den Haag, Fordham professor of jurisprudence,　11
says "The infrequency of improper executions . . . buttresses the case for capital punishment . . . 25 wrongful executions, if true, is a very acceptable number." He adds that playing golf or football causes accidental death, and concludes triumphantly that we have in these few errors of capital punishment "a net gain in justice." I suppose we are all entitled

to our own ideas of justice. But I don't think many *Dimension* readers are willing to pay the price Prof. Van den Haag thinks so acceptable for the "benefits" capital punishment confers.

LOTTERIES

12 The best way to explain this argument is to look at some figures:

1. Of 20,000 homicides a year, fewer than 150 people will be given a death sentence.
2. The chances of receiving the death penalty are many times greater in certain jurisdictions and under certain judges, than elsewhere.

13   Far from being a systematic form of justice, the death penalty is a lottery, and one of the few in which the underprivileged are favored to win. What they win is a ticket to state-supplied death.

14   Another significant way of looking at it is this: If it is violent and unnatural death we fear, our chances of losing a loved one to drunk driving are 2 ½ times as great as to murder; and we are 6 times as likely to lose someone to industrial accident as to murder. If we seriously believe capital punishment for murder is the best mode of prevention, who's for capital punishment for drunk drivers? Or for industrial tycoons with lax safety codes?

MORAL-RELIGIOUS

15 We become the choices we make. Every time we make a choice for violence, we become more violent and hating people. Every time we make a choice for nonviolence, we become more loving, nonviolent people. We cannot hide behind having someone else pull the electric switch or drop the trap for us: the choice for capital punishment affects each one of us who consents to it, affects even more each one who advocates it. And in making that choice as a society, we create a more violent, immoral society.

16   It is not enough to say, "They killed, so we may." The Bible has a powerful verse, "Vengeance is mine, saith the Lord." Whatever that means, it clearly means that to tamper with vengeance in this world is to set ourselves up as Gods. To usurp the right to judge, in the absolute way capital punishment does, is to indulge in the ultimate destructive arrogance of power. It is also to yield absolutely to the violence we deplore. When we execute a murderer, we are finally saying, "You have shown us that violence is the only true power. You have taught us that violence is stronger than anything else, and so we follow your example, and we too choose ultimate violence." In so doing, every one of us becomes a little more like everything in that murderer which we deplore.

"Why do we kill people who kill people, to show that killing people 17
is wrong?" Capital punishment is not just a sick non sequitur. It is morally a wrong train, and it takes us in a direction which damages our own
attempts to become better people, and a more wholesome, caring society.

DETERRENCE

Since the abolition of capital punishment in Canada, the homicide rate 18
has decreased from 3.09 per 100,000 to 2.74. Comparisons of neighbouring
states in the US with and without capital punishment show no consistent
differences. My own favorite story on deterrence happened in 17th century
England. They had to discontinue public hangings of pickpockets: not
out of humanity, but because too many pickpockets were operating in
the crowd, watching the public hangings.

There is no clear evidence that capital punishment deters others from 19
murder. The logic of this is apparent when we consider that contrary to
popular belief, the average murderer is not a fiend lurking in a dark
alley premeditating bestial murder, but a member of one's own household, or a close friend, acting out a spontaneous passion. Murderers
don't add up the odds and weigh their bets rationally: they act out of
spontaneous emotions in situations of high pressure. Calculating the
temper of the local judiciary and the current legislation are not part of
the thinking of many of them.

POLITICAL OPPRESSION

As you read this, countless people around the world are being impris- 20
oned, tortured, and otherwise oppressed for their political beliefs. As
long as capital punishment exists, it will be used as an instrument of
political oppression — as a means of exterminating opposition. We always
imagine we would never do that, but the use of the state as a weapon of
oppression is inherent in our inability to know objectively our own capacity to abuse power. I remember well one prisoner in Ontario who
spent the last half of his sentence in a maximum security prison because
he wrote a poem critical of prison which was read at an Easter service by
his chaplain.

Among the people who would have been spared had the state not 21
thought it had the right to take life officially are Socrates, Jesus Christ,
Joan of Arc, Martin Neimoller, and Thomas à Becket. Pretty good
company.

THE OTHER SIDE OF THE COIN:
FEAR AND REVENGE

22 Ranged against all these arguments are the powerful forces of our fear of violence: in ourselves, in others, and in the world around us. Killing people through capital punishment expresses our inner rage not only at murder, but at all the social ills we cannot attack, all the personal injuries we cannot revenge, and all the violence and wrong we see around us. Killing a few "dangerous killers" relieves us a little of our fear that the world is becoming more violent and out of control. Capital punishment is one of the few socially acceptable outlets for our fear and anger. But if we are truly concerned about violence, there are some much more obvious and effective remedies than capital punishment.

- GUN CONTROL: Even the weak gun control laws of 1976 in the USA have saved over 500 lives.
- FAMILY CRISIS INTERVENTION: We could spend more money on intervention in potentially violent situations, and could also identify children, on their way toward being future helpless purveyors of violence.
- REDUCTION OF OVERT TV VIOLENCE: The National Coalition on Violent Entertainment estimates this generation of TV viewers will see 600 times more assaults, 500 times more rapes, and 300 times more murders than their predecessors. This increases perception of our society as violent, and increases our fear and anger about it. A study by Dr. Geruner of Annenberg School of Communications has shown that heavy TV viewers are more right-wing than light viewers, because of this distorted view of reality. Moreover, over 2000 separate studies link media violence to negative effects on children.
- MEANINGFUL VICTIM SERVICES: Victims do need help; a recognition that what has happened to them is tragic and wrong; a release from blame; people to listen patiently; opportunities to grieve; compensation for damages and burdens; and the right to information about the facts affecting them. These sound obvious, yet they are rarely available to victims now. With these supports victims need not turn to blind vengeance.

23 Despite the odds quoted at the beginning of this article, we can remain an abolitionist state in Canada. The Coalition Against the Return of the Death Penalty included nearly 30 religious and activist groups, and has put together an excellent action package which includes most of the points in this article, and many more.

24 Above all, we need to let our MPs, newspapers, and the public know there are those of us who don't want to step back toward blind vengeance. And if you're poor, black or native, and unlucky, the life you save may well be your own.

TYPES OF WRITING:
analysis, classification, direct argument

Topics for Discussion

1. Is it possible to decide where Morris stands on the issue of capital punishment from the outset of her essay? How? If it is not possible, why not?
2. Why does Morris concentrate on facts rather than opinion in introducing her views?
3. What does Morris's approach to her audience and subject suggest about the periodical in which her essay appears?
4. Morris refers to examples that are historically and geographically remote from contemporary Canada. How might these references lend force to her argument in the eyes of (1) a sympathetic audience, and (2) an audience undecided about capital punishment?
5. How does the concluding section, "The Other Side of the Coin: Fear and Revenge," strengthen Morris's argument, even though some of the points, such as television violence, are not closely related to her primary area of concern? Why do you think she chose to place this section at the end of her essay?

Topics for Writing

1. Concentrating on a point considered by both Koch in "Death and Justice: How Capital Punishment Affirms Life," and Morris in this essay, compose a short argument of your own for or against capital punishment.
2. Pretend you are Morris and that you have been given an opportunity to present your views on capital punishment to a general audience, in which, as your opening shows, the majority will favour capital punishment but will not be very well informed about it. Adapt your essay for this sceptical, mildly hostile general audience.

Swiftwings

Farley Mowat

1 It was known to the Nascopie Indians of Ungava as *swiftwings*, in recognition of its superlative powers of flight. Other native peoples knew it by a variety of names, none more appropriate than the one given it by aboriginal Patagonians. They called it by a word best translated as *cloud of wonder* because of its autumnal appearance in flocks of such overwhelming magnitude that they darkened the Patagonian skies.

2 Poles distant from Patagonia, the Inuit of the tundra plains bordering the Arctic Ocean from Bathurst Inlet west to Alaska's Kotzebue Sound knew it, too. They called it *pi-pi-piuk* in imitation of its soft and vibrant whistle, which was their certain harbinger of spring. As late as 1966, an old Inuk living on the shores of Franklin Bay could still tell me what it had been like when pi-pi-piuk returned from whatever distant and unknown world had claimed it during the long winter months.

3 "They came suddenly, and fell upon us like a heavy snow. In my father's time it was told they were so many on the tundra it was like clouds of mosquitoes rising in front of a walking man. Their nests and eggs were in every tussock of grass. At the end of the hatching moon there were so many of their young scurrying about it was as if the moss itself was moving. Truly, they were many! But when I was still a child, they were few. And one spring they did not come."

4 It was in that same year, he told me, that his people first heard about the incomprehensible slaughter in which we, the *Kablunait*, had immured ourselves — the First World War. When the pi-pi-piuk failed to reappear in subsequent years, the Inuit speculated that perhaps they had been destroyed by us in one of our inexplicable outbursts of carnage.

5 "One need not look too far to find the cause which led to the destruction of the Eskimo Curlew. On its breeding grounds in the far north it was undisturbed. And I cannot believe that during its migrations it was overwhelmed by any great catastrophy at sea which could annihilate it . . . several other birds make similar long ocean flights without disaster. There is no evidence of disease, or failure of food supply. No, there is only one cause: slaughter by human beings; slaughter in Labrador and New England in late summer and fall; slaughter in South America in winter and slaughter, worst of all, from Texas to Canada in spring."

6 So wrote Dr. A. C. Bent, dean of American ornithologists in the 1920s. His was a verdict that must have taken some courage to express since the good doctor had himself killed tens of thousands of birds, including Eskimo curlews, both in pursuit of sport and in the name of science.

7 Curlews are of the sandpiper and plover kind, collectively known as wading birds or shorebirds because most of them haunt shorelines and shallows. However, the erect, long-legged, and long-necked curlews with

their gracefully down-curving beaks are as much at home in upland meadows, pampas, prairies, and tundra plains as they are by the sea.

The Eskimo curlew, which I shall hereafter call by its Nascopie name, was the smallest of the three North American curlews. It stood only about a foot high and weighed no more than a pound, but it was by all odds the most successful of the three. Although it seems to have mated for life, it was nevertheless intensely social, living in close company with millions of its fellows in what was, in effect, a single close-knit nation. 8

Because no one region could feed its multitudes for long, it was a nomadic nation possessed of flying and navigational skills that enabled its members to avail themselves of the resources of two continents in the course of an annual migration of phenomenal length and complexity. 9

This journey began on the tundra breeding grounds where the perpetual daylight of the brief summer season resulted in an explosive reproduction of insect and other small forms of life. The eggs of the swiftwings were timed to hatch just as this outburst reached its peak so that the young birds, which were able to run about and forage for themselves within minutes of their hatching, had ample food available. Nevertheless, there was not enough to feed both them and their millions of parents. The adults mostly subsisted through the weeks of nest-building, egg-laying, and brooding on reserves of fat acquired during their northbound migration; but by the time the eggs hatched, these inner resources were running low and could not be replenished locally without endangering the survival of the young. 10

The swiftwings had evolved the answer to this problem. Before the young were even out of their natal down, the adults drew together in enormous flocks and flew away. To us this might seem heartless, even brutal, but it was not. Although flightless, the young were fully capable of caring for themselves — so long as food was plentiful. The departure of their parents helped ensure that this would be the case. 11

As early as mid July, horizon-filling flights of hungry adults departed on their search for sustenance. Because of their enormous and concentrated numbers they needed equally immense and concentrated food supplies, not only to satisfy their urgent current needs, but also to build new reserves of body fat with which to fuel their ongoing odyssey. 12

The munificent larder they required did not lie close at hand. To reach it, they had to cross the continent from west to east, flying roughly 3,000 miles. Their objective was Labrador and Newfoundland, where extensive stretches of open heathland nurtured (and still does) a low-growing species of bush that quite literally carpeted hundreds of thousands of square miles — a bush with juicy, pea-sized berries that begin to ripen as early as the middle of July. This fecund plant is known to science as *Empetrum nigram*, but to the residents of Newfoundland and Labrador it was, and remains, the curlew berry. It was the principal support of the swiftwings in late summer. They fed upon it with such 13 gusto that their bills, legs, heads, breasts — even their wing feathers — became royally stained with rich purple juice.

14   The arrival of the feeding flocks left an indelible impression on human observers. In 1833, Audubon witnessed their arrival on the south coast of Labrador. "They came . . . in such dense flocks as to remind me of the passenger pigeon . . . flock after flock passed close around our vessel and directed their course toward the mountainous tracts in the neighbourhood." In 1864, a Dr. Packard watched the arrival of a single flock, "which may have been a mile long and as broad . . . [the cries of the birds] sounded at times like the wind whistling through the ropes of a thousand-ton vessel; at others like the jingling of a multitude of sleigh-bells." And in 1884, Lucien Turner observed them in northern Labrador with an artist's eye. "Each flock flew in a wedge shape, the sides of which were constantly swaying back and forth like a cloud of smoke . . . or in long dangling lines which rise or twist spirally . . . At other times the leader plunges downward followed by the remainder of the flock in graceful undulations, becoming a dense mass, then separating into a thin sheet spread wide again . . . reforming into such a variety of shapes that no description would suffice . . . [the flocks] alight on level tracts from Davis Inlet to the Gulf of St. Lawrence, each day adding to their number until the ground seems alive with them. They feed on the ripening berries, becoming wonderfully fat in a few days."

15   "Wonderfully fat" expressed it perfectly. After only a week on the berry grounds the birds had become so plump that, if shot in flight, the corpses often split like over-ripe peaches when they struck the ground. And they *were* shot, everywhere that men lived along the coasts of Labrador and Newfoundland.

16   In the 1770s, so Captain Cartwright noted in his journal, a hunter could count on killing 150 curlews in a single day with only the crude muzzleloader of those times. A century later, Labrador hunters with improved firearms were routinely killing thirty curlews at a shot. Most fishermen kept loaded guns in their boats and on their fishing stages, "and shot indiscriminately into the great flocks as they wheeled by."

17   These "liveyers," as the local people called themselves, were not the only curlew hunters. During the latter part of the nineteenth century, many foreigners visited Labrador to enjoy the curlew hunt. In 1874, ornithologist Dr. Eliot Coues described a typical entertainment of this sort. "Although six or eight gunners were stationed at the spot and kept up a continual round of firing upon the poor birds, they continued to fly distractedly about our heads, notwithstanding the numbers that every moment fell."

18   If local residents found powder too expensive or in short supply, they stalked the swiftwings at night on their roosting grounds, dazzling them into immobility with bull's-eye lanterns, then striking them down "in enormous numbers" with clubs and flails. Hardly an outport family

in Newfoundland and Labrador failed to begin the winter with several casks of curlews preserved in salt or in the birds' own rendered fat.

There was commercial slaughter, too. Employees of the Hudson's 19 Bay Company at Sandwich Bay annually put up tens of thousands of curlews in hermetically sealed tins, which were shipped to London and Montreal to be consumed as a gourmet specialty. A government official who visited Sandwich Bay in the late 1800s reported seeing 2,000 curlews hung up like bunches of enormous grapes in the company warehouse — the result of one day's shooting.

Meantime, what of the young that had been left behind? As soon as 20 their flight feathers and wing muscles were sufficiently developed, they, too, took to the high skies and performed the seemingly miraculous feat of rejoining their parents on the berry barrens of Labrador and Newfoundland.

Toward the end of July, the united flocks began to leave the berry 21 grounds, drifting restlessly southward, some pausing briefly on the Magdalen Islands where they were once reported in millions and on Prince Edward Island before moving down the Nova Scotia peninsula.

Gunners waited for them everywhere. In the 1760s, hunters on 22 Lunenburg common frequently killed a bushel-basket-full with a single musket shot. They killed for the pot or for the market. A century later a new breed of gunner, the self-styled sportsman, joined in the fusillade. One English visitor to Prince Edward Island did not think curlews "offered a very high order of sport." Nevertheless, they provided an opportunity to enjoy oneself: "The weather at this season is so charming, the labour so light, and the birds such delightful eating that the pursuit is worth it. And sometimes they do give very pretty sport as they wheel over the decoys. I once shot one on a marsh; its companion took a short flight then re-alighted beside the dead bird, quietly waiting there until I had reloaded my gun and was ready for him. This simple pair had probably just arrived from the remote north where that cruel, devouring monster, man, had never set foot. A short stay in Prince Edward Island teaches these birds a lesson." There were many such lessons to be learned, and the cost of learning was appallingly high.

Early in August the southward trickle swelled to a mighty torrent 23 and now there was no hesitation. Except for brief interruptions due to bad weather, the winged river maintained an almost unbroken flow until early September saw the last of the young birds leave Newfoundland and Labrador.

The massed millions of swiftwings did not usually follow the New 24 England coast southward but streamed off the coasts of Newfoundland and Nova Scotia heading over the open Atlantic directly for that portion of South America lying between the mouths of the Amazon and the Orinoco Rivers — a sea passage of nearly 3,000 miles. Superb fliers that they were, they appear to have made this journey non-stop; but supposing they did encounter heavy weather, it would have been no tragedy, for they were able to land on water and take off again when conditions improved. Severe easterly gales sometimes deflected part of the high-flying stream over the New England coast, with the result that hundreds of thousands of swiftwings unexpectedly alighted on shores, marshes, even on farmers' meadows.

25   New Englanders looked upon such visitations as manna from the skies. They called the visitors dough-birds because they were so plump. According to a nineteenth-century account, "their arrival was the signal for every sportsman and market hunter to get to work, and nearly all that reached our shores were shot." Such enormous numbers landed on Nantucket Island one autumn in the 1840s that the supply of shot and powder was exhausted and, to the disappointment of the residents, the butchery had to be "interrupted." A Cape Cod sportsman, irritated by the activities of the market hunters, complained: "Those birds which may come, can not, if they would, remain any longer than is absolutely necessary for they are so harassed immediately after landing that the moment there occurs a change in weather favourable to migration they at once depart." Dr. Bent remembered "hearing my father tell of the great shooting they used to have when I was a small boy, about 1870. As he has now gone to the happy hunting ground I cannot give the exact figures, but he once saw a wagon loaded full of 'dough birds' shot in one day."

26   Sportsmen of those times differed little from those of today except that they had more living targets available to them. They believed, as they still do, that hunting for sport was not only beyond reproach, but was almost a duty if one was to qualify as a proper man.

27   A number of them published books describing their successes and extolling the virtues of those who dedicated themselves to "this natural and healthy outdoor pursuit." Nevertheless, they wrote with some equivocation. The verb "to kill" was almost never used. Instead, their prey was "captured," "collected," or even "brought to hand." Blood did not flow upon the pages of these books. The emphasis was on the skill, sense of fair play, and gentlemanly conduct of the author, and on his honest affection for and admiration of the God-given beauties of nature, which were the real reasons he enjoyed the sport.

28   Sportsmen of those days kept careful account of their shooting scores, either in their own "game books" or in the record books of the sporting clubs to which many of them belonged. Most such clubs owned or leased their own hunting hotels and controlled great stretches of beach and marshland exclusively reserved for the guns of their members. One such was the Chatham Hotel on Long Island, patronized by New York sportsmen. It provided almost unlimited opportunities to practise gunners' skills and sportsmanship on the vast flocks of shorebirds, including curlews, that frequented the eastern seaboard beaches during migrations. The Chatham prided itself on enabling its well-heeled members to establish and maintain reputations as "number one, first class, sportsmen."

One such member was a Mr. James Symington, who chalked up the following score in the Club's record book in just three autumnal days in 1897.

beattle-heads (black-bellied plover)	393
jack curlews	55
golden plover	18
mud snipe (dowitcher)	674
jack snipe	37
calico bird (turnstone)	7
redbreast (knot)	149
peeps (small sandpipers and plover)	382
	Total 1,715

Not all sportsmen shot wading birds for the same lofty reasons. 29 Some did so — if one can credit this — as *practice* for shooting at clay pigeons. According to one of them: "It was my habit to indulge myself in a few hours gunning on the beaches before engaging in friendly competition at the [trap shooting] Club. Nothing so exercises one's abilities in this regard as to meet the challenges of those swift, elusive birds, particularly those of the plover family."

When the mighty river of southbound swiftwings eventually reached 30 the South American coast, it vanished. Nothing is known about its subsequent movements until it reappeared over Paraguay and Uruguay, winging steadfastly southward toward its wintering grounds on the rolling pampas stretching from central Argentina south to Patagonia. Here the swiftwings at last came to rest after a journey from their Arctic breeding grounds of nearly 10,000 miles.

By the nineteenth century it had become a broken rest. From the 31 Falkland Islands north to Buenos Aires, the great flocks were harried from place to place by ranchers, settlers, and sportsmen who slaughtered them not alone for food and fun, but even to provide cheap food for pigs.

With the coming of the northern spring, the survivors reformed and 32 the shimmering pampas air again filled with the flash of wings. We know little about the northward journey after the departure from Argentina in late February until the flocks darkened the dawn skies of the Gulf coast of Texas a few weeks later. I suspect that both spring and autumn migrations flew through the centre of the southern continent, taking advantage of the food to be found on the vast plateau prairies of the interior such as the campos of Brazil, where they would have encountered few people of European origin, and few guns.

After their return to our continent the flocks drifted slowly northward, 33 pacing the march of spring across the greening immensity of the Great Plains. Here was food in plenty to restore them after the long flight from the Argentine and to build the reserves that would be vital to a successful breeding season on the High Arctic nesting grounds. The preferred food at this season was insects, especially grasshoppers. The curlews were remarkably adept at harvesting these, as a report written in 1915 attests.

34   "The Eskimo Curlew was a bird of such food habits that it is a distinct loss to our agriculture that it should have disappeared. During the invasion of the Rocky Mountain grasshopper [in the 1870s] it did splendid work in the destruction of grasshoppers and their eggs. Mr. Wheeler states that in the later seventies these birds would congregate on land which had not yet been plowed and where the grasshoppers' eggs were laid, reach down into the soil with their long bills and drag out the egg capsules which they would then devour with their contents of eggs and young hoppers, until the land had been cleared of the pests . . . A specimen examined in 1874 had 31 grasshoppers in its stomach . . . the bird also often alighted on plowed ground to feed on the white grubs and cutworms."

35   Some idea of the effect the curlews' appetites must have had on insect pests is suggested by Professor Lawrence Bruner's description of the size of the flights that visited Nebraska during the late 1860s. "Usually the heaviest flights occurred coincident with the beginning of the corn-planting time, and enormous flocks would settle on the newly plowed fields and on the prairies where they searched industriously for insects. The flocks reminded the settlers of the flights of passenger pigeons [which they had seen in the East] and thus the curlews were given the name of 'prairie pigeons.' The flocks contained thousands of individuals and would form dense masses of birds extending for a quarter to half a mile in length and a hundred yards or more in width. When such a flock would alight the birds would cover 40 or 50 acres of ground."

36   The vital service rendered by the curlews to settlers trying to farm the plains, particularly in Oklahoma, Kansas, and Nebraska, was, to say the least, ill-requited. Along with Texas, these three states became one enormous slaughterhouse for the swiftwings. Here, where they had been and would have continued to be of enormous assistance to the agricultural efforts of the human invaders, their race was ultimately destroyed.

37   Professor Myron Swenk described how their annihilation was brought about: "During the [spring] flights the slaughter of these poor birds was appalling and almost unbelievable. Hunters would drive out from Omaha and shoot the birds without mercy until they had literally slaughtered a wagonload of them, the wagon being actually *filled*, and with the sideboards on at that. Sometimes when the flights were unusually heavy and the hunters well supplied with ammunition, their wagons were too quickly and easily filled, so whole loads of the birds would be dumped on the prairie, their bodies forming piles as large as a couple of tons of coal, where they would be allowed to rot while the hunters proceeded to refill their wagons with fresh victims and thus further gratify their lust for killing. The compact flocks and tameness of the birds made this slaughter possible, and at each shot usually dozens of the birds would fall. In one specific instance a single shot from an old muzzle-loader into

a flock of these curlews brought down 28 birds while for the next half mile every now and then a fatally wounded bird would drop to the ground . . . So dense were the flocks when the birds were turning in their flight one could scarcely throw a brick or missile into it without hitting a bird.

"There was no difficulty getting close to the sitting birds, perhaps 38 within 25 or 35 yards, and at this distance the hunters would wait for them to rise on their feet, which was the signal for the first volley of shots. The startled birds would rise and circle a few times, affording ample opportunity for further murderous discharges of the guns, and sometimes would re-alight in the same field, when the attack would be repeated. Mr. Wheeler has killed as many as 37 birds with a pump gun at one rise. Sometimes the bunch would be seen alighting on a field 2 or 3 miles away, when the hunters would at once drive to that field with a horse and buggy, relocate the birds, and resume the fusillade and slaughter."

This kind of butchery, be it noted, was done solely in the name of 39 sport! However, by the 1870s, commercial gunners in the East had so savaged the passenger pigeon (which had been the staple of the wild bird market, and whose numbers had been thought to be infinite) that the public appetite for edible wild birds could no longer be sated by it.

The penetration of the railroads through the prairie states at about 40 this same time stimulated "some smart fellows" in Wichita, Kansas, into filling the gap with the corpses of "prairie pigeons." The first carload-lots of spring-killed curlews, preserved on ice, reached New York in 1872 and were snapped up at such high prices that the fate of the re-maining swiftwings was sealed forthwith.

During the spring of 1873, the butchery of curlews on the Great 41 Plains mushroomed to a massacre of such proportions that, by 1875, no large curlew flocks were to be seen crossing Texas. In the spring of 1879, the last great flights were seen in Kansas; and by 1886, puzzled gunners in Labrador, Newfoundland, Nova Scotia, and New England were won-dering where the great flocks had gone.

One of the most widely accepted explanations for the rapid disap- 42 pearance of what had been one of North America's most abundant birds was that it had been exterminated by western farmers using poisoned bait to protect their seed corn from "the depredations of these insatiable pests." As an exculpation, this one was typical of our attempts to vindicate the mass destruction visited by us on other forms of life. And in this case, as in most, it was a blatant lie. Far from eating the farmers' seed, the curlews had been of great assistance in helping the crop to grow at all.

The annihilation of the swiftwings for short-term gain, together with 43 the reduction to relict levels of the millions of associated insect-eating birds that once checked insect plagues on the western plains of Canada and the United States, has cost grain farmers an estimated $10-$15 billion since 1920 in losses suffered directly from such insect infestations and as the price paid in attempts to curb such visitations through the use of chemical poisons and other means.

44   That cost is ongoing. It must continue to be paid, presumably in perpetuity, not just by Great Plains farmers and those of the campos and pampas of South America, but by all of us. The wanton destruction of the Eskimo curlew provides a classic example, not only of the ruthlessness of modern man, but also of his imperishable stupidity.

45   During the final years of the nineteenth century, only a very few flocks remained to run the gamut of the guns as they made their way north through the Dakotas and the Canadian prairies to the relative security of the Mackenzie Valley corridor. Along the Arctic coast the Inuit waited, and they, too, wondered what had happened to the pi-pi-piuk that had once come spiralling down upon the tundra as thick as falling snow.

46   At the turn of the century, Nascopie Indians walking across the caribou barrens, ankle-deep in a carpet of ripe curlew berries, wondered what had happened to the multitudes of swiftwings that had once gorged themselves on those high plains.

47   The last curlews to be seen in the Halifax market were sold there in the fall of 1897; by 1900, Newfoundland and Labrador fishermen were complaining that "you can't get a taste of a curlew anywhere." In 1905, a sportsman named Green, who for decades past had shot over Miscou Island in Bay Chaleur, expressed "a pang of regret shared by all naturalists, sportsmen and epicures, for the curlew is rapidly disappearing."

48   On the pampas of Patagonia, gauchos hefted their *bolas* as they searched in vain for the flocks that did not come — flocks that had once descended in such masses that a single throw of the leaden balls might kill a dozen birds.

49   The swiftwings were failing fast but, as Dr. Bent noted, "No one lifted a finger to protect them until it was too late." In fact, Dr. Bent's ornithological peers did just the opposite. As the curlews became rare in life, so did their "specimen" value soar. Scientists began to compete fiercely with each other to acquire the skins of those few that still remained. According to the well-known American naturalist, Dr. Charles Townsend, a flock of eight swiftwings appeared at Sandwich Bay in the fall of 1912. Seven were promptly killed and the skins of five were gratefully received in the name of science at Harvard by yet another famous American ornithologist, William Brewster, who added them to the enormous collection of "study skins" in the university's collection. To quote again from Dr. Bent: "The last kills in Nebraska were made in 1911 and 1915. On March 11, 1911 . . . two birds were shot by Mr. Fred Gieger . . . they are at present in the collection of Mr. August Eiche . . . No Eskimo Curlews were noted in 1914 but a single bird was killed south of Norfolk, Nebraska on the morning of April 17, 1915. It came into the possession of Mr. Hoagland, who had it mounted."

50   By 1919, the skin of a swiftwing was worth $300, and with such a

price on their heads the few remaining survivors had little chance. In 1924 and 1925, the last two individuals ever to be seen in the province of Buenos Aires were both collected for Argentina's Museo Naçional de Historia Natural.

By then, Dr. Bent had already epitomized the "natural history" of 51 the swiftwings. "The story of the Eskimo Curlew is just one more pitiful tale of the slaughter of the innocents. It is a sad fact that the countless swarms of this fine bird . . . which once swept across our land are gone forever, sacrificed to the insatiable greed of man."

Gone forever? Not quite . . . not yet. In 1932, a single bird was killed 52 at Battle Harbour on the Labrador coast for the University of Michigan's collection. Another was collected on Barbados in 1963. In addition, there have been several sight records, mostly in the Northwest Territories and in Texas, where one was photographed in 1962.

There remains at least the possibility that a handful still survive — 53 some authorities think as many as twenty — but they are little more than spectral beings, no more able to fill the wind with their swift wings than the dead can rise again.

TYPES OF WRITING:
cause and effect, definition, description, example/illustration, narration

Topics for discussion

1. Mowat introduces the English name of the curlew only in paragraph 5 and waits until paragraph 7 to begin a conventional introduction to his subject. What rhetorical advantage does he gain by placing the information contained in the first six paragraphs at the beginning of the essay?
2. At two points in this essay (after paragraphs 6 and 29), the double-spacing between paragraphs indicates a structural division. Describe briefly what Mowat does in each of the three parts and explain how the three-part structure adds to the force of the ideas he presents.
3. How does Mowat's reliance on quotations add credibility and force to his position?
4. How does Mowat shape the reader's perceptions of "sportsmen" near the end of his second section? What advantage does his approach offer over a more direct, more overtly critical attack?

Topics for Writing

1. How is this essay persuasive? The answer to this question is rather simple, but your essay in reply to the question should go into some detail about the different parts of the essay's structure and about the strategies Mowat uses to get the reader's sympathy.

2. In the light of increased knowledge about such matters as migration patterns, animal and bird populations, hibernation, breeding grounds, and so on, hunting associations today argue that hunting is necessary to stabilize and thus preserve populations of wild animals and birds. Write an essay arguing for the necessity of controlled hunting in Canada, or in a specific area, or arguing that hunting should be banned.

The Temple of Fashion

Joyce Nelson

"The act of acquiring has taken the place of all other actions, the sense of having has obliterated all other senses," the British art critic and cultural historian John Berger observed in his 1972 book *Ways of Seeing*. By the mid-1970s, acquisition had achieved the status of a new religion in the West. The appearance of a new advertising buzzword, *spirit*, was a clear signal of this development. 1

Once Coca-Cola had merely claimed to add "life" to our lives. Now everything from a cola through a department store and a hotel chain to a fashion designer began to make even bolder assertions. In slogans such as "the Pepsi Spirit," "Simpson's Spirit," "the Spirit of Hyatt," and Yves Saint-Laurent's "New Spirit of Masculinity," advertisers proclaimed the new religion of buying. More recently, the word *soul* has entered the advertising lexicon as another religious additive to enhance acquisition. 2

In such a context, shopping malls have become the cathedrals of our time: vast horizontal-Gothic places of worship that draw the faithful together in communal rites central to the new religion. While the Prime Movers in this religion are the TV God and its consort, the advertising industry, the shopping cathedrals are themselves temples of technomagic where steps move effortlessly beneath one's feet, doors open automatically, celestial Muzak hymns permeate the atmosphere, and the wave of a credit card completes the sacred transaction. Isolated from the mundane reality of urban existence, the shopping mall is sacred space, climate-controlled and patrolled, devoted to the ease of acquisition: the meaning of life in the postwar West. 3

This religion has evolved its own holy days (such as Boxing Day solstice) and holy seasons (Back-To-School octave). It also has its important sites of pilgrimage (in Canada, the West Edmonton Mall and Toronto's Eaton Centre), although every North American city has its lesser malls where the same litany of brand names holds out the promise of salvation. Nevertheless, this is a religion in which both faith and good works are necessary. This facet of the religion is nowhere more apparent than in the domain of Fashion, whose side chapels in each shopping cathedral remind us that last season's profession of faith is up for renewal. 4

According to the arcane hermeneutics of the Fashion Bible, one risks damnation by last year's colour or the slightest oversight of tie, lapel, or faux nail. Thus, the Gospels according to Armani and Alfred Sung, Ralph Lauren and Christian Dior are continually being reinterpreted for our edification and enlightenment. While slogans such as Calvin Klein's "Eternity for Men" and Alfred Sung's "Timeless" collection evoke an eschatological promise signifying the end-time of shopping, it is a central tenet within the religion (and certainly dogma in Fashion) that our indulgences are never plenary. "Shop Till You Drop" is the vulgar — but correct — grasp of this aspect of consumer theology. 5

189

6   Fortunately, the high priests of Fashion (particularly the college of ecclesiastics gathered at *Women's Wear Daily*) continually disseminate guidance on each chapter and verse of the Fashion Bible. Their perennial lists of "Best Dressed" and "Worst Dressed" remind us that even those not banished to the purgatory of obscurity risk hellfire by sinning against Fashion commandments that are perpetually under revision.

7   For this reason, there exists a wealth of inspirational literature and illustrated texts to assist us in our salvific efforts. *Vogue, Esquire, Gentleman's Quarterly*, and *Flare* provide not only the necessary iconography for the consumer aspirant's meditation but also details on those Fashion sins (venial and mortal) that can impede our progress. The pages of such inspirational texts also offer devotional readings on the lives of the Fashion saints: popular saints of the past like St. Marilyn and St. James Dean; current beatified exemplars like Madonna and Billy Idol; and our living martyr to Fashion, Elizabeth Taylor. But such devotional reading and contemplation are only preparations for the greater liturgies of the mall.

8   Window shopping brings the congregation into closer proximity to the Fashion priesthood and the means of redemption, but before we enter any of the mall's side chapels there is usually an impressive form of statuary to mediate our passage. Modern mannequins have evolved with the mall itself, becoming increasingly elaborate, detailed, and even startling in their effect.

9   The old form of mannequin (like the old form of storefront) was, for the most part, simply uninspiring: its wig askew, its coiffure outmoded, its facial expression vague and nondescript, its limbs akimbo or missing, its stand ridiculous or pathetic. Only by the greatest leap of faith could the consumer attain the proper buying spirit through a glance at such a guardian of the portals.

10   The new mannequins, on the other hand, are appropriate statuary for the impressive cathedrals that surround them. Figures of anatomical perfection, these statues with their erect nipples, painted fingernails, detailed eye makeup, stunning hairdos, high cheekbones, and long sinewy legs remind us at a glance just what it is that we, as mundane Fashion consumers, aspire to. While the male statuary is somewhat less intimidating, it too bespeaks the contemporary codes of the Fashion cult: chiselled jaws, muscled but sleek torsos, long-legged figures of power.

11   But it is the faces of the new statuary that are most significant in their religious function: aloof, haughty, disdaining, beyond appeal. Inspiring neither solace nor prayer, these figures at the portals are part of the shrines of envy and are meant to inspire a certain measure of fear.

12   To gaze at one of these detailed figures is an oddly unsettling experience (though in truth they are meant to be only glimpsed in passing). Typically, the statue is posed so that its haughty gaze is directed above or away from us, as though we were quite obviously beneath contempt. At the same time, the statue's fetish of forever-perfect and hyperrealistic

detail cruelly reminds us of our own imperfections. Whether we are fully conscious of the effect or not, we enter the chapels of Fashion subtly diminished and suitably envious.

Such feelings enhance the redemptive power of the array of apparel 13 within. Each article of clothing promises to increase our status and transform us in turn into objects of envy, in our own eyes and the imagined eyes of others. Here, the numinous brand name confers its accretion of socially envious connotations, religiosity, and sacred trust. This veneer laid upon mere cloth by the high priests of Fashion is necessary for passing through the challenging ritual of the changing room.

Within this confessional enclosure, one is confronted by the attendant 14 mirror revealing all the sins of the flesh that mar one's progress: the cellulite thighs, the body hair, the paunch, the girth, the less-than-perfect contours reminding us that the spirit is willing but the flesh is weak. Making promises to join the modernday *flagellantes* in a daily workout routine, we proceed to put on the desired article of clothing that promises to miraculously transform our lives.

The moment of beholding ourselves dressed in the desired brand 15 name has also been prefigured and prepared by the statue at the chapel's portal. Like it, we must harden our gaze, overlook that small inner voice of protest about the price, and focus on a future vision of ourselves as the envied possessor of this article of apparel that most of the faithful will have already seen (and desired) in the inspirational Fashion texts. We know that the envious others will recognize at a glance that we have joined the elect.

Where once it was possible for the faithful to identify, from a mo- 16 mentary glimpse, the habit of a Franciscan friar or Benedictine nun, so now the congregation is steeped in the familiar cut and style of various designer looks. Indeed, one can dress oneself entirely from head to foot in Ralph Lauren or YSL, Lee or Esprit. As the most dedicated of the Fashion faithful realize, it is the brand, not the cloth, that clothes us. So the slogan says, "Life's Necessities: Food, Shelter and Lee Jeans."

As we become the objects of our own devotion, the high point in the 17 shopping mall liturgy approaches: the transforming ritual of the credit card. Through its instantaneous magic, we momentarily redeem ourselves and enter the ecstasy of acquisition, consuming and consumed by the bliss of possession.

It is precisely this ease of acquisition that is fundamental to the new 18 religion. The technomagic of the credit card is in keeping with the whole aura of effortlessness that pervades the mall. Indeed, the many objects on display seem magically conjured out of nothing to fulfil the promise of advertising images' sleight-of-hand. For all intents and purposes, these millions of objects seem to have no origin, no history of labour and creation. Only the shopping agnostic would think to consider such questions as: who made these things, and under what conditions?

For example, most of our brand-name clothing is made by Third 19

World garment workers, primarily women, who are grossly underpaid and exploited by North American contractors paying as little as ten cents an hour for the labour. In the export-processing zones of the Philippines, Thailand, Hong Kong, Mexico, Indonesia, and dozens of other countries, non-unionized workers typically work sixteen-hour days for the most meagre of wages, assembling the host of products that fill our malls. Even Canada's high priest of Fashion, Alfred Sung, employs Hong Kong labour to work at a fraction of Canadian wages in sewing the apparel of the elect.

20   But the religion of acquisition excludes any knowledge of the actual work that goes into the making of our products. For most of the consumer faithful, these millions of objects simply appear "as seen on TV" or in the photo magazines: as though untouched by human hands, as though the image itself (like an idea in the mind of God) had somehow spawned its progeny, as it were, "in the flesh." Like Doubting Thomases, we touch and buy their tangibility to reaffirm our faith. Thus, while some have dubbed this new religion the Church of Perpetual Indulgence, it may more accurately be described as the Church of the Wholly Innocent: wilfully apolitical, purposely unknowing, steeped in the mystification and technomagic of our time.

TYPES OF WRITING:
analogy, comparison, description, example/illustration

Topics for Discussion

1. Throughout her essay Nelson employs an extended metaphor, a figure of speech, which implicitly compares the world of fashion — its designers, the malls, the fashion magazines — with Christianity — its saints, the churches, the sacred writings. Does this comparison lend credibility to Nelson's ideas about fashion? If so, how?
2. Does Nelson's controlling metaphor seem forced in places? Would her views about fashion have been more or less convincing if she had relied less on the comparison of fashion and religion?
3. Nelson points out some of the obvious devices and strategies used by those in the fashion world to persuade us that we should buy their products. In spite of this obviousness, many of us still buy these products. Why?
4. In paragraph 19, Nelson briefly points out that much of our brand-name clothing is made by third-world workers who are poorly paid. Why does she not expand on this seemingly important fact? Is this lack of explanation a weakness in her essay?
5. What, finally, is the persuasive intent of this essay? Do you believe that Nelson's criticisms of the fashion industry will persuade a signifi-

cant proportion of her readers to reconsider their buying habits? If not, why?

Topics for Writing

1. After you have read the essays by Harry Bruce, Linda Goyette, and Carolyn Leitch, compose an extended essay in which each of these writers reflects on what Nelson says about fashion. Their reflections will be the result of your imagination, of course, but they should be based on a careful reading of each of the three essays.
2. Do you agree with Nelson that "it is the brand, not the cloth, that clothes us" (paragraph 16)? Your response will attempt to persuade your reader that, based on your experience and that of your friends, Nelson is, on the whole, either right or wrong.
3. Compare Jessica Mitford's treatment ("The Story of Service") of the way the funeral industry attempts to manipulate its image, and through its image its customers, with Nelson's representation of the fashion industry.

To Kill a People —
Dash Their Dream

Peter C. Newman

1   Great art, really great art, whatever its format, must be guided by an invisible hand: the spontaneous blossoming of humanity caught in a moment's creative impulse. That's even more true of a great people, like Newfoundlanders. Spontaneity is their middle name.

2   To be a Newfie is to be a survivor. A survivor, not with any negative connotation of trying to outlive others, but in an exhilarating, nose-thumbing sense of tempting the fates that have never stopped trying to bring you down. That great spirit — that feeling of Darwinian pride that has allowed Newfoundlanders to claim with brassy validity that they are a race apart — is in jeopardy.

3   They are about to become an endangered species. Dash a people's dreams often enough and you eventually kill their culture that depends for its sustenance on perpetuating the way of life that gave it birth.

4   The human tragedy currently playing itself out on the Rock has no precedent in Canadian history. It threatens not only the livelihood of 27,000 jobless and temporarily idled fishers and plant workers and their families, but it could be the end of a unique way of living. Fishing, as anyone knows who has done it even as a sport, is a serious business that gets into your blood, doubly so if your living depends on it. Richard Cashin, the former fishermen's union president who headed the Atlantic Fisheries Task Force that issued its eloquent report last December, put it best when he wrote: "The sea is to those who fish what land is to those who farm. The relationship of the harvester to the elements — the sea or the land — is more than economic, it is organic. It is how one gains a sense of place, of belonging and of accomplishment."

5   It's not news that there are no cod to be caught off Newfoundland — or any other part of the Atlantic coast — because of overfishing. What is news is that previous gloomy predictions by industry experts may have been too optimistic. According to the fisheries task force, the optimism of the early 1980s in Atlantic Canada has turned to despair as catches for the valuable groundfish actually declined by 90 per cent over the past five years and miscalculations by federal scientists about the fish stocks became obvious. The report estimates that it will take at least seven years for the depleted stocks to recover. And if they do recover, future levels in the groundfish catch will be considerably lower — at least one-third lower than those experienced in the 1980s. As a result, the task force is recommending a reduction in both groundfish harvesting and processing capacity of up to 50 per cent.

6   In other words, the ground fisheries are not just dormant but dead for the foreseeable future as a major source of employment. And the 27,000 Newfoundlanders who are currently receiving or are eligible to

194

receive relief through Ottawa's $772-million assistance program are living on a knife edge. The program is due to run out on May 15 and even if it's extended, as it will be in modified form, Canadian taxpayers can't be expected to carry the province forever.

The loss of jobs isn't equivalent to a factory closing in Ontario or a 7
sawmill bankruptcy in British Columbia. Most of Newfoundland's outports depend *entirely* on the fishery, so that collapse of the resource means ruin of the community. And that, in turn, will mean the enforced resettlement of its people. To the Newfies who have lived through its previous manifestations, it's a deadly concept that echoes sentiments of the Holocaust. Although the rest of Canada hardly noticed, between 1953 and 1975, the inhabitants of some 300 small communities were "resettled." That was a polite term for the agony of being wiped off the maps by bureaucratic edicts issued in Ottawa and St. John's, with compensation of as little as $400 paid to house owners and families who were uprooted and forced to move into larger centres, or more frequently, to emigrate to an uncertain future in Upper Canada. To be poor with the high-spirited dignity only the Newfies can muster is one thing; to be forced out of your birthplace and have to sever your essential touchstones is quite another.

Apart from the obvious difficulty of finding alternative employment 8
in a shrinking economy while equipped with few transferable skills, Newfoundlanders face a severely limited job market. Even the $5-billion Hibernia offshore oil drilling project will not produce more than 1,000 permanent new jobs in the province. Nor will it add to tax revenues: 97 per cent of the project's petroleum royalties will flow directly to Ottawa.

About the only alternative is a plan being pushed by the Newfound- 9
land & Labrador Rural Development Council, a group of 59 community associations that co-ordinates local economic initiatives. "In order to be successful," says council president Woodrow Mullett, "economic development can't be imposed from outside. People have to be able to play a role in the process and help determine what sorts of activities are best suited to their conditions. You can't just dump something on them from out of the blue and expect them to reorder their lives accordingly." Sample community projects include: building a pioneer village in Wiltondale; setting up an Arctic char hatchery at Daniel's Harbour; starting an eiderdown industry at Main Brook; opening a silviculture training centre at Gander Bay; examining a fish silage plant at Leading Tickles; erecting the mother of all compost heaps in Lockston; and converting the old CN line across the province into a tourist walking trail. It's not much but there isn't a great deal more available.

The value of any culture ultimately depends not on good books or 10
great art, but on the passage of a people's seed from one generation to the next, on their link to the soil and the sea. The Newfoundlanders' life force is expressed less in words than in deeds — in the compassion and humor they feel for one another when there is nothing else available to

share. That's what is really at stake in Newfoundland these days. And that's why Canadians who don't live on the Rock should not begrudge the relatively modest tax burden to keep our most vibrant culture alive and kicking.

TYPES OF WRITING:
analysis, direct argument

Topics for Discussion

1. What hint is there in Newman's title that his essay has a persuasive aim?
2. Newman's introductory paragraph is composed of three generalizations. To what extent does he later elaborate on these general statements?
3. Contrast Newman's first three paragraphs, his introduction, with his final paragraph, his conclusion. To what extent does his conclusion deal with the issue he raises in his introduction?
4. At the beginning of his essay Newman stresses the importance of his subject through expressions such as "great art," "creative impulse," "a great people," "that great spirit," "a race apart," and "an endangered species." Yet his final sentence refers to "the relatively modest tax burden." Did you find this last sentence somewhat anti-climactic? If so, explain why. If not, explain how Newman prepares his readers for this conclusion and how it contributes to his overall argument.

Topics for Writing

1. "The loss of jobs isn't equivalent to a factory closing in Ontario or a sawmill bankruptcy in British Columbia. Most of Newfoundland's outports depend *entirely* on the fishery, so that collapse of the resource means ruin of the community." Attempt to persuade readers that Newman's statement is too sweeping, that there are small towns elsewhere in Canada that also depend entirely on one industry, and that the loss of this industry can be just as devastating as the loss of fisheries in Newfoundland.
2. "To be a Newfie is to be a survivor." Choosing a word that would best characterize the people in the place where you grew up, write an essay explaining not only how this term is appropriate but also how it is vital to the identity of the province, region, or community that helped form your own identity.

Do We Have the Right to Die?

Patrick Nowell-Smith

I

"I am 79 years of age, in relatively vigorous health and constantly amused 1
with life while it lasts. But I saw my mother and my father, years apart,
in the same chronic care hospital suffering helplessly for months when
they might have been quietly released; and this makes me dread a similar
fate unless the law is changed so that one can choose, if still able, to slip
away in dignity from the inhumane methods many hospitals employ
today to keep one from dying a natural death."

This letter is typical of many that I have received since I started, with 2
a few friends, to form a euthanasia society in Canada. Most people, if
they think about their own death at all, say that they would like to die in
their sleep or to be struck down by a sudden heart attack; but in Canada
today that will not be their fate. Seventy per cent of us will die in hospitals
or other institutions. Many have shown an interest in the euthanasia
society because they have heard of booklets such as Exit's *A Guide To Self
Deliverance* and they want information not for immediate use but for the
comfort of knowing that if life becomes intolerable they will be able to
die in a manner of their own choosing. "The keys of my prison," wrote
John Donne, "are in mine own hands."

The legal position in Canada is clear — at least on paper. Suicide is 3
not a crime; but it is a crime to "aid and abet" suicide, and a doctor who
hands a patient a lethal dose or who tells a patient how to kill himself
faces the possibility of a fourteen year sentence. To be sure, the law on
paper is not always the same as the law in practice; there has been no
test case in Canada, but recently in England, where the law is similar,
those who have helped others to die at their own request, though found
guilty as the law requires, have suffered only a nominal penalty. We
must also remember the number of cases which do *not* get into the
courts. We don't know how many doctors respond with compassion to
pleas like that of my correspondent. How could we? Doctors are not
likely to advertise the fact that they break the law. One of the major
reasons for changing the law is to relieve them of the threat of criminal
or civil actions if they want to help their patients.

The fundamental question is not whether, as the law stands, we 4
have a right to die but whether, morally speaking, we ought to have this
right. DO we have a moral right to die at a time and in a manner of our
choosing and, if necessary, to be assisted? Such a right does not figure
prominently in traditional lists of rights such as those of the American or
French revolutionaries; in fact it doesn't figure at all, and this is not
surprising. Most people for most of their lives want to go on living

197

however hard their lives may be; and it was only in very special circumstances, such as those in which Socrates and Seneca were placed, that it even made sense to ask "Do I really want to go on living or not?" Certainly we all ask this question from time to time in a temporary mood of depression; but the mood passes, and if others have dissuaded or restrained us we are grateful.

5   But now all this has changed; modern medicine can and does prolong almost indefinitely the lives of those who before would have died a natural death, even when there is no hope that the patient will eventually lead a tolerable life. In this situation the individual is compelled to live against his will. This stands the traditional theory of rights on its head. For the traditional theory starts with the premise that individuals have needs and interests — things that they want to be or do or have — and legal rights are introduced as legal devices for the satisfaction of needs and the protection of interests. Since the interest of one person will often conflict with those of another, not all interests can be protected; as a society we must choose which interests to protect by law, which to permit without legal protection, and which to deny. On the traditional theory of liberal democracy this choice is made on the basis of the greatest liberty for each compatible with the same liberty for all. I may move my arm in any way I like provided that the space which I wish my fist to occupy is not occupied by your nose.

6   In theory, then, the burden of proof lies not on those who would defend the right to choose death but on those who would deny it. Are there any good reasons for maintaining the present system under which it is murder to kill someone at his or her request and a lesser crime even to assist suicide? First there is the argument from religion. Murder and suicide are both strongly condemned by the Judaeo-Christian tradition we have inherited, still the dominant tradition in our society. But ours is a secular society in which people are free to follow any religion or none at all but not free to force their religious convictions on others. Here a distinction needs to be made between positive and negative rights; a *positive* right to die suggests that someone — probably a doctor or nurse — has a duty to take positive action, and it is sometimes argued that if euthanasia were legalized people could be required to kill or to assist suicide even if it were against their principles to do so. But no one in the euthanasia movement advocates a positive legal right to death. What we want is the *negative* right, and this requires only that we are *permitted* to assist suicide, that no one who does so is guilty of a crime. It is the pro-lifers, not the supporters of euthanasia who insist on forcing their own moral and religious convictions on others.

7   Leaving religion aside, it might be said that human life is sacred and must on no account be taken; and this is a stance that might be taken by a person of any religious convictions or none at all. But the trouble with this position is that very few people actually hold it; some allow killing the enemy in war as an exception, others capital punishment. On what

grounds, then, should they refuse to make an exception in favour of those who choose to die? And what are the grounds for holding *all* human life sacred? Why should the life of a human being, when it is devoid of any of the attributes that make it human, when it is in fact no different from that of a vegetable, be considered any more sacred than the life of a vegetable?

The argument from the sanctity of human life is, in short, not so 8 much an argument as a refusal to think about the question. "The sanctity of human life" is a slogan, and ancient slogans do not solve modern problems. In bygone days those who survived childhood diseases and avoided violent deaths died naturally when the will to live had gone. They did not share my correspondent's fears because the technology for keeping people alive against their wills did not exist. But new technology forces us to think afresh not only about the moral but also about the conceptual issues involved. In the old days a person was either alive or dead, and it was easy to tell the difference. Not so today. Is a person in an irreversible coma, totally unconscious and unable to relate to others, alive or dead? We hesitate to say; and this is not because we do not know how to describe this and other cases but because the *concepts* of life and death are no longer clear. And if we decide to say that a person whose vital functions are kept going by artificial means is still alive, there remains the question whether such a body is still a human being, with all the moral implications of that status still intact. In all this I am not suggesting that new technology or anything else could change the foundations of morality. Justice and benevolence have always been duties and always will be; what changes is the application of these moral concepts. If a doctor decides to prolong life, he needs to ask "to whom (or what) am I being either just or benevolent?"

II

I shall return later to the serious arguments against legalizing euthana- 9 sia, but it is important to realize that the debate between pro-lifers and the supporters of the right to die is not, and cannot be conducted at an entirely rational level. Deep emotions and traditionally entrenched psychological attitudes are involved. The taboos against murder and suicide are among the strongest in the Judaeo-Christian system. Some societies, for example European society in the fifteenth century, have been obsessed by death; ours goes to the opposite extreme and banishes both death and aging from consciousness as much as possible. This is itself unfortunate since it is well established that people who have thought for some time about their own coming death tend to "die better" than those who have not, so that we should be encouraged rather than discouraged from the contemplation of our mortality.

Rational discussion of these issues is also made more difficult by the 10 prevailing attitude of the medical profession and by the fact that laymen tend to attribute to doctors and especially to psychiatrists an expertise which they simply do not have. How this situation has come about it would take a whole History of Medicine since 1900 to explain, but the sociological facts are not in doubt. When should a life that could be saved be terminated? When should a person who wishes to die be helped to do so? Such questions, involving as they do estimates of the consequences of alternative decisions, are partly factual and to that extent best left to experts. But basically they are *moral* questions and the blunt fact is that most doctors have no training in medical ethics and are incompetent to answer them. Bio-medical ethics is a growing field of study in the United States, but Canadian medical schools have been slow to follow this example. In the Fall of 1980 some students at the University of Toronto Medical School requested courses in medical ethics. When this request was refused, they organized a course in their own time and at their own expense. It is not recognized as a credit course. The medical establishment seems to believe either that there are no moral problems in the practice of medicine or that, if there are, they can be solved without special training.

11   This is delicate ground on which to tread, but an analysis of one example may help to illustrate the problem. Interviewed by a journalist from the *Toronto Sun*, Dr. Harley Smyth is reported to have said that the case against mercy killing is simple. "You cannot ask a doctor to be a killer as well as a healer." If that is really the case, it is indeed simple; but it is not, as Dr. Smyth seems to think, conclusive. What has keeping someone alive for a few more weeks when there is no possibility of recovery to do with *healing?* The slogan works on our emotions by referring to a doctor who would perform an act of mercy killing as a "killer," thus conjuring up images of Jack the Ripper and the hired hit man. In a different context (whether or not to allow a severely deformed neonate to die) Dr. Smyth is reported to have seen "an alarming trend in medicine in which doctors are going beyond the purely medical question of asking themselves 'can this life be lived?' which they have every right to deal with, to the moral question 'should this life be lived?' which is not properly their decision." He went on to say, "A doctor is entitled to his opinion on whether a particular life ought to be lived. But if he presents his opinion as authority to the parents at a time when they are already on the ropes emotionally, he is breaking a fundamental trust."

12   Short though it is, this passage invites a number of comments. First, the trend of which Dr. Smyth writes is not new. It has been with us ever since laymen acquired the habit of shifting moral decisions which are properly theirs onto the shoulders of doctors by treating doctors as authorities rather than as technical advisers. Second, if a doctor has answered in the affirmative the "purely medical question," the moral question whether the life ought to be saved or not arises and must be answered by somebody. The problem is, by whom? In the United States there is a growing

tendency to answer "by the courts"; but there are many reasons for hoping that the creeping legalism characteristic of life south of the border will not invade Canada. Let us keep such decisions in the hands of parents and doctors as much as we can. But should it be the parent or the doctor? Dr. Smyth's position seems to be unclear. On the one hand, though entitled to an opinion, the doctor must not present it "as authority." He or she must recognize that the decision is not properly the doctor's. But Dr. Smyth never says firmly that the decision is the parents'; and if they are "already on the ropes emotionally," they are hardly capable of rational choice.

Reading between the lines I get the impression that Dr. Smyth, reluctantly assuming the burden of taking a decision he knows is not properly his, takes the immense step from deciding that the neonate's life can be saved to the decision to save it. That he is assuming responsibility for a moral decision is disguised by his way of posing the question as "can/should this life be lived?" rather than as "can/should *I* save this baby's life?" 13

III

By far the most powerful arguments against voluntary euthanasia are drawn from the idea that, one way or another, mistakes will be made and abuses will occur. There are too many variations on this theme to permit discussion of them all; but most of them rely on the idea that we can never be sure that a request for death is fully voluntary, and here again what is needed is a bit of conceptual analysis, a commodity usually in short supply. Briefly, to say that a choice is fully voluntary is to say that it is not made under coercion, that the agent was fully informed as to its consequences, and that he was in his right mind. People might be nagged or inveigled into requesting death in ways that, though more subtle than a gunman's threats, are nevertheless coercive. As to full information, what a patient really wants to know is the probability of relief from the painful or distressing condition which led him to request death in the first place. Certainty is, of course, not to be had; but in many cases a doctor is in a position to make a soundly based estimate of the chances of recovery. The frequently used argument that relief should always be denied on the grounds that a new miracle drug might come along at any time is as cruel as it is dishonest. 14

It is the third criterion of voluntariness that is most difficult to apply. When is a person "in his right mind"? No sharp line can be drawn. This, like other criteria, is a matter of degree and however we assess rationality there will always be borderline cases. The concept of rationality is, like that of baldness, inherently indeterminate. Some people are obviously bald, others as obviously not bald; but there is a grey area between where we cannot be sure. And, as in the case of the concept of life and death, this is not because there is any doubt about the facts. Counting 15 the hairs on his head would avail us nothing; our difficulty arises from the indeterminacy of the concept itself. So it is with the concept of rationality; it is not so much that we might make a mistake, declaring someone rational when he is not or *vice versa*, as that the concept itself is indeterminate.

16   When this type of situation arises, the one thing that we must *not* do is to declare by fiat that some type of choice is intrinsically irrational and hence can never be free. Yet this is precisely what is often done. An article in *Maclean's* is entitled "Suicide: An Irrational Act Rationalized"; clearly the implication is that suicide must *always* be irrational by definition, and since this view is often taken by psychiatrists it enjoys an undeserved popularity. Why people should regard psychiatrists as specially competent to define rationality is another large question in social history; but the view itself is absurd. For to be rational is to choose means likely to achieve whatever end you have in mind and to choose ends that you have a fair chance of achieving; and on this definition it will often be rational to choose death: death in preference to dishonour, death rather than life with the knowledge that one's existence is a burden to oneself and to others, death, perhaps, simply because one finds life intolerably boring. To make this last choice would certainly be unusual, but that does not make it irrational.

17   Declaring the wish to die irrational by definition is not only a device for running away from the problem, it can be, and is used as a device for depriving us of a right we already have. In Common Law everyone has a right to refuse treatment. To use this fact as an argument against the necessity for legislative change is in itself somewhat callous. "So you want to die? Very well; you can refuse intravenous feeding. It won't be long before you're dead." But the definition of suicide as irrational denies us even this macabre option. Since to choose death is automatically to be irrational anyone who chooses death can be declared incompetent and deprived of his right to refuse treatment by due process.

18   Nevertheless we must honestly face the fact that if public opinion comes to recognize a moral right to die — and polls in many countries indicate that we have come a long way in this direction — and if this change is reflected in legislation, some mistakes will be made and some abuses will occur. There will be cases in which a patient is allowed to die because his disease is held to be incurable when in fact it is not, and there will be cases in which a person's decision to die will be accepted as fully voluntary when, in one way or another, it was not. These considerations, always advanced when a radical proposal to change the law is made, are never decisive. If we admit that mistakes will be made, we must also admit that our present legal system is imperfect. In other areas of law, for example contract, we have techniques for deciding whether or not consent is voluntary, and there is no reason why these techniques could not be incorporated in new legislation about the right to die. The

possibilities of error and abuse must be weighed in the balance against the absolute certainty of needless suffering under our present laws.

TYPES OF WRITING:
analysis, definition

Topics for Discussion

1. Is Nowell-Smith writing in hopes of influencing an audience that disagrees with his position, one that is in sympathy with his views, or one that is undecided? Why do you think so? What kind of influence might this essay have on the intended audience?
2. Nowell-Smith might have said more about the financial implications of assisted suicide. What might he have added about financial implications — for hospitals, doctors, relatives, insurance companies, and government departments responsible for health care — associated with prolonging, or ending, the lives of incurably sick people? Why might he have decided to play down this side of the question?
3. How do terms such as "quietly released," "slip away in dignity," "natural death," and "self-deliverance" function in this essay? What is the effect of designating the opposing sides in the debate "pro-lifers" and "the supporters of the right to die"?

Topics for Writing

1. Drawing on the views of North American attitudes toward death presented in essays in this book, as well as on your own experience of the way death is depicted on television and in the movies, write an essay promoting honesty about the subject.
2. What, in your opinion, is the answer to the question in Nowell-Smith's title?
3. Nowell-Smith states that "the burden of proof lies not on those who would defend the right to choose death but on those who would deny it." In his essay he argues for the right to choose death, whereas E. J. McCullough, in "On Euthanasia and Dying Well," denies this right. Your essay will discuss which of these two essays you find the more persuasive, and why.

A Hanging

George Orwell

1   It was in Burma, a sodden morning of the rains. A sickly light, like yellow tinfoil, was slanting over the high walls into the jail yard. We were waiting outside the condemned cells, a row of sheds fronted with double bars, like small animal cages. Each cell measured about ten feet by ten and was quite bare within except for a plank bed and a pot of drinking water. In some of them brown silent men were squatting at the inner bars, with their blankets draped round them. These were the condemned men, due to be hanged within the next week or two.

2   One prisoner had been brought out of his cell. He was a Hindu, a puny wisp of a man, with a shaven head and vague liquid eyes. He had a thick, sprouting moustache, absurdly too big for his body, rather like the moustache of a comic man in the films. Six tall Indian warders were guarding him and getting him ready for the gallows. Two of them stood by with rifles and fixed bayonets, while the others handcuffed him, passed a chain through his handcuffs and fixed it to their belts, and lashed his arms tight to his sides. They crowded very close about him, with their hands always on him in a careful, caressing grip, as though all the while feeling him to make sure he was there. It was like men handling a fish which is still alive and may jump back into the water. But he stood quite unresisting, yielding his arms limply to the ropes, as though he hardly noticed what was happening.

3   Eight o'clock struck and a bugle call, desolately thin in the wet air, floated from the distant barracks. The superintendent of the jail, who was standing apart from the rest of us, moodily prodding the gravel with his stick, raised his head at the sound. He was an army doctor, with a grey toothbrush moustache and a gruff voice. "For God's sake hurry up, Francis," he said irritably. "The man ought to have been dead by this time. Aren't you ready yet?"

4   Francis, the head jailer, a fat Dravidian in a white drill suit and gold spectacles, waved his black hand. "Yes sir, yes sir," he bubbled. "All iss satisfactorily prepared. The hangman iss waiting. We shall proceed."

5   "Well, quick march, then. The prisoners can't get their breakfast till this job's over."

6   We set out for the gallows. Two warders marched on either side of the prisoner, with their rifles at the slope; two others marched close against him, gripping him by arm and shoulder, as though at once pushing and supporting him. The rest of us, magistrates and the like, followed behind. Suddenly, when we had gone ten yards, the procession stopped short without any order or warning. A dreadful thing had happened — a dog, come goodness knows whence, had appeared in the yard. It came bounding among us with a loud volley of barks, and leapt round us wagging its whole body, wild with glee at finding so many human beings together. It was a large woolly dog, half Airedale, half

pariah. For a moment it pranced round us, and then, before anyone could stop it, it had made a dash for the prisoner, and jumping up tried to lick his face. Everyone stood aghast, too taken aback even to grab at the dog.

"Who let that bloody brute in here?" said the superintendent angrily. 7 "Catch it, someone!"

A warder, detached from the escort, charged clumsily after the dog, 8 but it danced and gambolled just out of his reach, taking everything as part of the game. A young Eurasian jailer picked up a handful of gravel and tried to stone the dog away, but it dodged the stones and came after us again. Its yaps echoed from the jail walls. The prisoner, in the grasp of the two warders, looked on incuriously, as though this was another formality of the hanging. It was several minutes before someone managed to catch the dog. Then we put my handkerchief through its collar and moved off once more, with the dog still straining and whimpering.

It was about forty yards to the gallows. I watched the bare brown 9 back of the prisoner marching in front of me. He walked clumsily with his bound arms, but quite steadily, with that bobbing gait of the Indian who never straightens his knees. At each step his muscles slid neatly into place, the lock of hair on his scalp danced up and down, his feet printed themselves on the wet gravel. And once, in spite of the men who gripped him by each shoulder, he stepped slightly aside to avoid a puddle on the path.

It is curious, but till that moment I had never realised what it means 10 to destroy a healthy, conscious man. When I saw the prisoner step aside to avoid the puddle, I saw the mystery, the unspeakable wrongness, of cutting a life short when it is in full tide. This man was not dying, he was alive just as we were alive. All the organs of his body were working — bowels digesting food, skin renewing itself, nails growing, tissues forming — all toiling away in solemn foolery. His nails would still be growing when he stood on the drop, when he was falling through the air with a tenth of a second to live. His eyes saw the yellow gravel and the grey walls, and his brain still remembered, foresaw, reasoned — reasoned even about puddles. He and we were a party of men walking together, seeing, hearing, feeling, understanding the same world; and in two minutes, with a sudden snap, one of us would be gone — one mind less, one world less.

The gallows stood in a small yard, separate from the main grounds 11 of the prison, and overgrown with tall prickly weeds. It was a brick erection like three sides of a shed, with planking on top, and above that two beams and a crossbar with the rope dangling. The hangman, a grey-haired convict in the white uniform of the prison, was waiting beside his machine. He greeted us with a servile crouch as we entered. At a word from Francis the two warders, gripping the prisoner more closely than ever, half led, half pushed him to the gallows and helped him clumsily up the ladder. Then the hangman climbed up and fixed the rope round the prisoner's neck.

12   We stood waiting, five yards away. The warders had formed in a rough circle round the gallows. And then, when the noose was fixed, the prisoner began crying out on his god. It was a high, reiterated cry of "Ram! Ram! Ram! Ram!", not urgent and fearful like a prayer or a cry for help, but steady, rhythmical, almost like the tolling of a bell. The dog answered the sound with a whine. The hangman, still standing on the gallows, produced a small cotton bag like a flour bag and drew it down over the prisoner's face. But the sound, muffled by the cloth, still persisted, over and over again: "Ram! Ram! Ram! Ram! Ram!"

13   The hangman climbed down and stood ready, holding the lever. Minutes seemed to pass. The steady, muffled crying from the prisoner went on and on, "Ram! Ram! Ram!" never faltering for an instant. The superintendent, his head on his chest, was slowly poking the ground with his stick; perhaps he was counting the cries, allowing the prisoner a fixed number — fifty, perhaps, or a hundred. Everyone had changed colour. The Indians had gone grey like bad coffee, and one or two of the bayonets were wavering. We looked at the lashed, hooded man on the drop, and listened to his cries — each cry another second of life; the same thought was in all our minds: oh, kill him quickly, get it over, stop that abominable noise!

14   Suddenly the superintendent made up his mind. Throwing up his head he made a swift motion with his stick. "Chalo!" he shouted almost fiercely.

15   There was a clanking noise, and then dead silence. The prisoner had vanished, and the rope was twisting on itself. I let go of the dog, and it galloped immediately to the back of the gallows; but when it got there it stopped short, barked, and then retreated into a corner of the yard, where it stood among the weeds, looking timorously out at us. We went round the gallows to inspect the prisoner's body. He was dangling with his toes pointed straight downwards, very slowly revolving, as dead as a stone.

16   The superintendent reached out with his stick and poked the bare body; it oscillated. Slightly. "*He's* all right," said the superintendent. He backed out from under the gallows, and blew out a deep breath. The moody look had gone out of his face quite suddenly. He glanced at his wrist-watch. "Eight minutes past eight. Well, that's all for this morning, thank God."

17   The warders unfixed bayonets and marched away. The dog, sobered and conscious of having misbehaved itself, slipped after them. We walked out of the gallows yard, past the condemned cells with their waiting prisoners, into the big central yard of the prison. The convicts, under the command of warders armed with lathis, were already receiving their breakfast. They squatted in long rows, each man holding a tin pannikin, while two warders with buckets marched round ladling out rice; it seemed quite a homely, jolly scene, after the hanging. An enormous relief had come upon us now that the job was done. One felt an impulse to sing, to break into a run, to snigger. All at once everyone began chattering gaily.

The Eurasian boy walking beside me nodded towards the way we had come, with a knowing smile: "Do you know, sir, our friend (he meant the dead man), when he heard his appeal had been dismissed, he pissed on the floor of his cell. From fright. — Kindly take one of my cigarettes, sir. Do you not admire my new silver case, sir? From the boxwallah, two rupees eight annas. Classy European style." 18

Several people laughed — at what, nobody seemed certain. 19

Francis was walking by the superintendent, talking garrulously: "Well, sir, all hass passed off with the utmost satisfactoriness. It wass all finished — flick! like that. It iss not always so — oah, no! I have known cases where the doctor wass obliged to go beneath the gallows and pull the prisoner's legs to ensure decease. Most disagreeable!" 20

"Wriggling about, eh? That's bad," said the superintendent. 21

"Ach, sir, it iss worse when they become refractory! One man, I recall, clung to the bars of hiss cage when we went to take him out. You will scarcely credit, sir, that it took six warders to dislodge him, three pulling at each leg. We reasoned with him. 'My dear fellow,' we said, 'think of all the pain and trouble you are causing to us!' But no, he would not listen! Ach, he wass very troublesome!" 22

I found that I was laughing quite loudly. Everyone was laughing. Even the superintendent grinned in a tolerant way. "You'd better all come out and have a drink," he said quite genially. "I've got a bottle of whisky in the car. We could do with it." 23

We went through the big double gates of the prison, into the road. "Pulling at his legs!" exclaimed a Burmese magistrate suddenly, and burst into a loud chuckling. We all began laughing again. At that moment Francis's anecdote seemed extraordinarily funny. We all had a drink together, native and European alike, quite amicably. The dead man was a hundred yards away. 24

TYPES OF WRITING:
description, narration, personal experience

Topics for Discussion

1. What general impression does Orwell create of the person about to be executed? What is the influential effect of this impression?
2. How does atmosphere contribute to the overall effect of this piece?
3. Why does Orwell describe a hanging that was quick and uncomplicated while referring to more difficult executions only in second-hand accounts?
4. Orwell generally concentrates on describing what happens and rarely reveals his own reactions directly. Only in the paragraph beginning "It is curious" does he focus mainly on himself. Why would Orwell concentrate his reactions in one paragraph? Why would he position

this paragraph in the middle of his account rather than using it as an opening or a conclusion?

Topics for Writing

1. Analyze the role of the dog in this essay, paying particular attention to its function as a source of sympathy for the prisoner.
2. Write an essay discouraging some organized, socially acceptable activity by revealing how it actually works through description and narration. You might choose a beauty pageant, a rodeo, line-dancing, a boxing match, or anything that you find morally or aesthetically offensive.

Rock As Art

Camille Paglia

Rock is eating its young. Rock musicians are America's most wasted   1
natural resource.

Popular music and film are the two great art forms of the twentieth   2
century. In the past twenty-five years, cinema has gained academic prestige. Film courses are now a standard part of the college curriculum and
grants are routinely available to noncommercial directors.

But rock music has yet to win the respect it deserves as the authentic   3
voice of our time. Where rock goes, democracy follows. The dark poetry
and surging Dionysian rhythms of rock have transformed the consciousness and permanently altered the sensoriums of two generations of
Americans born after World War Two.

Rock music should not be left to the Darwinian laws of the market-   4
place. This natively American art form deserves national support. Foundations, corporations and Federal and state agencies that award grants
in the arts should take rock musicians as seriously as composers and
sculptors. Colleges and universities should designate special scholarships
for talented rock musicians. Performers who have made fortunes out of
rock are ethically obligated to finance such scholarships or to underwrite
independent agencies to support needy musicians.

In rock, Romanticism still flourishes. All the Romantic archetypes of   5
energy, passion, rebellion and demonism are still evident in the brawling,
boozing bad boys of rock, storming from city to city on their lusty,
groupie-dogged trail.

But the Romantic outlaw must have something to rebel against. The   6
pioneers of rock were freaks, dreamers and malcontents who drew their
lyricism and emotional power from the gritty rural traditions of white
folk music and African-American blues.

Rock is a victim of its own success. What once signified rebellion is   7
now only a high-school affectation. White suburban youth, rock's main
audience, is trapped in creature comforts. Everything comes to them
secondhand, through TV. And they no longer have direct contact with
folk music and blues, the oral repository of centuries of love, hate, suffering and redemption.

In the Sixties, rock became the dominant musical form in America.   8
And with the shift from singles to albums, which allowed for the marketing of personalities, it also became big business. The gilded formula
froze into place. Today, scouts beat the bushes for young talent, squeeze
a quick album out of the band, and put them on the road. "New" material
is stressed. Albums featuring cover tunes of classics, as in the early Rolling Stones records, are discouraged.

From the moment the Beatles could not hear themselves sing over   9
the shrieking at Shea Stadium in the mid-Sixties, the rock concert format
has become progressively less conducive to music-making. The enor-

mous expense of huge sound systems and grandiose special effects has left no room for individualism and improvisation, no opportunity for the performers to respond to a particular audience or to their own moods. The show, with its army of technicians, is as fixed and rehearsed as the Ziegfeld Follies. Furthermore, the concert experience has degenerated. The focus has switched from the performance to raucous partying in the audience.

10   These days, rock musicians are set upon by vulture managers, who sanitize and repackage them and strip them of their unruly free will. Like sports stars, musicians are milked to the max, then dropped and cast aside when their first album doesn't sell.

11   Managers offer all the temptations of Mammon to young rock bands: wealth, fame, and easy sex. There is not a single public voice in the culture to say to the musician: You are an artist, not a money machine. Don't sign the contract. Don't tour. Record only when you are ready. Go off on your own, like Jimi Hendrix, and live with your guitar until it becomes part of your body.

12   How should an artist be trained? Many English rock musicians in the Sixties and early Seventies, including John Lennon and Keith Richards, emerged from art schools. We must tell the young musician: Your peers are other artists, past and future. Don't become a slave to the audience, with its smug hedonism, short attention span and hunger for hits.

13   Artists should immerse themselves in art. Two decades ago, rock musicians read poetry, studied Hinduism, and drew psychedelic visions in watercolors. For rock to move forward as an art form, our musicians must be given the opportunity for spiritual development. They should be encouraged to read, to look at paintings and foreign films, to listen to jazz and classical music.

14   Artists with a strong sense of vocation can survive life's disasters and triumphs with their inner lives intact. Our musicians need to be rescued from the carpetbaggers and gold-diggers who attack them when they are young and naïve. Long, productive careers don't happen by chance.

TYPES OF WRITING:
cause and effect, direct argument

Topics for Discussion

1. When Paglia says that "Rock is eating its young" she does not, of course, mean this literally. What, then, does she mean? How is this arresting opening related to the sentence that follows?
2. Paglia makes some very sweeping generalizations — such as the one that opens paragraph 2 — without supporting them by references to statistics or authorities who have written on her subject. Would Paglia's

essay be more persuasive if she were more concerned with proof? Why might she have chosen not to compose a more conventionally reasoned argument?

3. What does Paglia mean when she says in paragraph 4 that "rock music should not be left to the Darwinian laws of the marketplace"? How do the connotations of the terms "Darwinian laws" and "the marketplace" assist Paglia in influencing readers to accept her views?

4. Is it contradictory to argue in one paragraph that needy rock musicians should be supported by granting agencies and scholarships while devoting the next paragraph to the Romantic rebellion of "the brawling, boozing bad boys of rock, storming from city to city on their lusty, groupie-dogged trail"? Is Paglia suggesting that the average needy garage band will be improved by concentrating on obtaining arts grants instead of producing hit records? How does this shift from dependency on grants to extravagant social rebellion make sense in the context of Paglia's entire essay?

Topics for Writing

1. "Popular music and film are the two great art forms of the twentieth century." Although such a generalization would be extremely difficult to prove, do your best, basing your essay at least in part on your own experience and that of your friends. Or, if you disagree, argue that some other art form — the novel, theatre, car design, computer software, video games, comic books — is at least as important as rock or film.

2. Paglia proposes to tell young musicians, "Don't become a slave to the audience." Write an essay of your own, either supporting Paglia's view, or arguing instead that rock, notwithstanding the enormity of the industry built around it, is essentially a folk art that draws its vitality, as well as its evolving forms, in large part from the artists' responses to their audiences.

What Is Poverty?

Jo Goodwin Parker

1   You ask me what is poverty? Listen to me. Here I am, dirty, smelly, and with no "proper" underwear on and with the stench of my rotting teeth near you. I will tell you. Listen to me. Listen without pity. I cannot use your pity. Listen with understanding. Put yourself in my dirty, worn out, ill-fitting shoes, and hear me.

2   Poverty is getting up every morning from a dirt- and illness-stained mattress. The sheets have long since been used for diapers. Poverty is living in a smell that never leaves. This is a smell of urine, sour milk, and spoiling food sometimes joined with the strong smell of long-cooked onions. Onions are cheap. If you have smelled this smell, you did not know how it came. It is the smell of the outdoor privy. It is the smell of young children who cannot walk the long dark way in the night. It is the smell of the mattresses where years of "accidents" have happened. It is the smell of the milk which has gone sour because the refrigerator long has not worked, and it costs money to get it fixed. It is the smell of rotting garbage. I could bury it, but where is the shovel? Shovels cost money.

3   Poverty is being tired. I have always been tired. They told me at the hospital when the last baby came that I had chronic anemia caused from poor diet, a bad case of worms, and that I needed a corrective operation. I listened politely — the poor are always polite. The poor always listen. They don't say that there is no money for iron pills, or better food, or worm medicine. The idea of an operation is frightening and costs so much that, if I had dared, I would have laughed. Who takes care of my children? Recovery from an operation takes a long time. I have three children. When I left them with "Granny" the last time I had a job, I came home to find the baby covered with fly specks, and a diaper that had not been changed since I left. When the dried diaper came off, bits of my baby's flesh came with it. My other child was playing with a sharp bit of broken glass, and my oldest was playing alone at the edge of a lake. I made twenty-two dollars a week, and a good nursery school costs twenty dollars a week for three children. I quit my job.

4   Poverty is dirt. You say in your clean clothes coming from your clean house, "Anybody can be clean." Let me explain about housekeeping with no money. For breakfast I give my children grits with no oleo or cornbread without eggs and oleo. This does not use up many dishes. What dishes there are, I wash in cold water and with no soap. Even the cheapest soap has to be saved for the baby's diapers. Look at my hands, so cracked and red. Once I saved for two months to buy a jar of Vaseline for my hands and the baby's diaper rash. When I had saved enough, I went to buy it and the price had gone up two cents. The baby and I suffered on. I have to decide every day if I can bear to put my cracked, sore hands into the cold water and strong soap. But you ask, why not

hot water? Fuel costs money. If you have a wood fire it costs money. If you burn electricity, it costs money. Hot water is a luxury. I do not have luxuries. I know you will be surprised when I tell you how young I am. I look so much older. My back has been bent over the wash tubs every day for so long, I cannot remember when I ever did anything else. Every night I wash every stitch my school age child has on and just hope her clothes will be dry by morning.

Poverty is staying up all night on cold nights to watch the fire, 5 knowing one spark on the newspaper covering the walls means your sleeping children die in flames. In summer poverty is watching gnats and flies devour your baby's tears when he cries. The screens are torn and you pay so little rent you know they will never be fixed. Poverty means insects in your food, in your nose, in your eyes, and crawling over you when you sleep. Poverty is hoping it never rains because diapers won't dry when it rains and soon you are using newspapers. Poverty is seeing your children forever with runny noses. Paper handkerchiefs cost money and all your rags you need for other things. Even more costly are antihistamines. Poverty is cooking without food and cleaning without soap.

Poverty is asking for help. Have you ever had to ask for help, knowing 6 your children will suffer unless you get it? Think about asking for a loan from a relative, if this is the only way you can imagine asking for help. I will tell you how it feels. You find out where the office is that you are supposed to visit. You circle that block four or five times. Thinking of your children, you go in. Everyone is very busy. Finally, someone comes out and you tell her that you need help. That never is the person you need to see. You go see another person, and after spilling the whole shame of your poverty all over the desk between you, you find that this isn't the right office after all — you must repeat the whole process, and it never is any easier at the next place.

You have asked for help, and after all it has a cost. You are again 7 told to wait. You are told why, but you don't really hear because of the red cloud of shame and the rising black cloud of despair.

Poverty is remembering. It is remembering quitting school in junior 8 high because "nice" children had been so cruel about my clothes and my smell. The attendance officer came. My mother told him I was pregnant. I wasn't, but she thought that I could get a job and help out. I had jobs off and on, but never long enough to learn anything. Mostly I remember being married. I was so young then. I am still young. For a time, we had all the things you have. There was a little house in another town, with hot water and everything. Then my husband lost his job. There was unemployment insurance for a while and what few jobs I could get. Soon, all our nice things were repossessed and we moved back here. I was pregnant then. This house didn't look so bad when we first moved in. Every week it gets worse. Nothing is ever fixed. We now had no money. There were a few odd jobs for my husband, but everything went for food then, as it does now. I don't know how we lived through three years and three babies, but we did. I'll tell you something, after the last baby I destroyed my marriage. It had been a good one, but could you keep on bringing children in this dirt? Did you ever think how much it costs for any kind of birth control? I knew my husband was leaving the day he left, but there were no good-byes between us. I hope he has been able to climb out of this mess somewhere. He never could hope with us to drag him down.

9   That's when I asked for help. When I got it, you know how much it was? It was, and is, seventy-eight dollars a month for the four of us; that is all I ever can get. Now you know why there is no soap, no needles and thread, no hot water, no aspirin, no worm medicine, no hand cream, no shampoo. None of these things forever and ever and ever. So that you can see clearly, I pay twenty dollars a month rent, and most of the rest goes for food. For grits and cornmeal, and rice and milk and beans. I try my best to use only the minimum electricity. If I use more, there is that much less for food.

10   Poverty is looking into a black future. Your children won't play with my boys. They will turn to other boys who steal to get what they want. I can already see them behind the bars of their prison instead of behind the bars of my poverty. Or they will turn to the freedom of alcohol or drugs, and find themselves enslaved. And my daughter? At best, there is for her a life like mine.

11   But you say to me, there are schools. Yes, there are schools. My children have no extra books, no magazines, no extra pencils, or crayons, or paper and the most important of all, they do not have health. They have worms, they have infections, they have pink-eye all summer. They do not sleep well on the floor, or with me in my one bed. They do not suffer from hunger, my seventy-eight dollars keeps us alive, but they do suffer from malnutrition. Oh yes, I do remember what I was taught about health in school. It doesn't do much good. In some places there is a surplus commodities program. Not here. The county said it cost too much. There is a school lunch program. But I have two children who will already be damaged by the time they get to school.

12   But, you say to me, there are health clinics. Yes, there are health clinics and they are in the towns. I live out here eight miles from town. I can walk that far (even if it is sixteen miles both ways), but can my little children? My neighbor will take me when he goes; but he expects to get paid, *one way or another*. I bet you know my neighbor. He is that large man who spends his time at the gas station, the barbershop, and the corner store complaining about the government spending money on the immoral mothers of illegitimate children.

13   Poverty is an acid that drips on pride until all pride is worn away. Poverty is a chisel that chips on honor until honor is worn away. Some of you say that you would do *something* in my situation, and maybe you would, for the first week or the first month, but for year after year after year?

Even the poor can dream. A dream of a time when there is money. 14
Money for the right kinds of food, for worm medicine, for iron pills, for
toothbrushes, for hand cream, for a hammer and nails and a bit of
screening, for a shovel, for a bit of paint, for some sheeting, for needles
and thread. Money to pay *in money* for a trip to town. And, oh, money
for hot water and money for soap. A dream of when asking for help
does not eat away the last bit of pride. When the office you visit is as
nice as the offices of other governmental agencies, when there are enough
workers to help you quickly, when workers do not quit in defeat and
despair. When you have to tell your story to only one person, and that
person can send you for other help and you don't have to prove your
poverty over and over and over again.

I have come out of my despair to tell you this. Remember I did not 15
come from another place or another time. Others like me are all around you.
Look at us with an angry heart, anger that will help you help me. Anger
that will let you tell of me. The poor are always silent. Can you be silent too?

TYPES OF WRITING:
cause and effect, definition, description, example/
illustration, personal experience

Topics for Discussion

1. How does the opening paragraph catch the reader's attention and
   establish the relationship between writer and reader?
2. How does the descriptive detail of this piece affect the reader's perception of the writer and of her ability to comment with authority on
   the subject? How do these descriptive details make the essay more
   influential?
3. Who is the projected "you" of the audience? How do you know?
4. This piece might well move readers to pity, but the writer makes a
   point of saying early along that she does not want pity. Do you think
   this assertion is a rhetorical tactic, a simple fact, or both? What is the
   persuasive effect of this assertion?
5. Would Parker's approach in this essay be as effective in an argument
   in favour of specific strategies for fighting poverty?
6. How is this essay vulnerable to rebuttal from someone who feels that
   the poor are partly responsible for their destitution or that there are
   limits to the amount of help that society can offer them?
7. Consider the diction and sentence structure of the piece. What do they
   suggest about the writer? How are they appropriate to the topic?
8. Why, after all the emphatic repetition of the term "poverty" in earlier
   paragraphs, does the writer use the word only once in the last two
   paragraphs? What alternative word or words are repeated for emphasis in the concluding paragraphs? Why?

Topic for Writing

1. Write an essay using definition and descriptive details to promote some social change — for example, more generous student loans, better daycare facilities for students with dependent children, more accommodating library policies, better access to facilities for disabled students — the value of which you can appreciate from your own experience.

American Socio-Cultural Attitudes Towards Death

Therese A. Rando

In order to appreciate our own and others' responses to loss and death, 1
we need to have an understanding of the socio-cultural context within
which they occur. Because death is universal, each culture has had to
develop its own beliefs, mores, norms, standards, and restrictions. Appropriate ways to respond in one culture may be punished in another.
Each society dictates the standards to be followed, supporting or prohib-
iting certain behaviors and determining the repertoire of responses from
which mourners can choose. Any work with people in the areas of loss
and death must take into account their social, cultural, religious/philo-
sophical, and ethnic backgrounds.

Only a brief overview of the dominant American attitude towards 2
death will be presented here, as it would be impossible to discuss the
many rich and varied differences found across the world. Even within
our own culture, though, there will be many differences among individuals depending upon their ethnic, social, and religious backgrounds.

Each society's response to death is a function of how death fits into 3
its teleological view of life. For all societies there seem to be three general
patterns of response: *death-accepting*, *death-defying*, or *death-denying*.

Primitive, nontechnological societies, such as those of the Fiji Island- 4
ers and Trobrianders, are usually death-accepting. The people in these
societies view death as an inevitable and natural part of the life cycle.
Dying and attendant behaviors are integrated into the everyday patterns
of living.

Death-defying societies are those such as in early Egypt. Here the 5
populace refused to believe that death would take anything away. Hence,
pyramids were built to contain all the Pharoah's wives and money and
possessions for the world after death. Death itself would not deprive the
Pharoah; he would vanquish it.

The United States today is an example of a death-denying culture. 6
There is widespread refusal to confront death. There are fewer rituals for
recognizing it, replaced by contrivances for coping with it. The attitude
is that death is antithetical to living and that it is not a natural part of
human existence.

Many Americans go to great lengths to shield themselves from the 7
realities of death. Take for example the fact that the vast majority of
Americans no longer die in their own homes, but are sent to nursing
homes and hospitals to die, away from their own familiar home, family,
and friends. It is true that because of this family members need not be
made uncomfortable by watching their loved one die; but for the dying
individual death becomes lonely, mechanical, and dehumanized. At the
very moment that people most need the comfort of human companionship

and sentiment they are isolated in a hospital room to await death alone and unassisted.

8   Kübler-Ross paints a classic picture of a more natural death in her book *On Death and Dying* (1969):

> I remember as a child the death of a farmer. He fell from a tree and was not expected to live. He asked simply to die at home, a wish that was granted without questioning. He called his daughters into the bedroom and spoke with each one of them alone for a few minutes. He arranged his affairs quietly, though he was in great pain, and distributed his belongings and his land, none of which was to be split until his wife should follow him in death. He also asked each of his children to share in the work, duties, and tasks that he had carried on until the time of the accident. He asked his friends to visit him once more, to bid good-bye to them. Although I was a small child at the time, he did not exclude me or my siblings. We were allowed to share in the prepara-tions of the family just as we were permitted to grieve with them until he died. When he did die, he was left at home in his own beloved home which he had built, and among his friends and neighbors who went to take a last look at him where he lay in the midst of flowers in the place he had lived in and loved so much. In that country today there is still no make-believe slumber room, no embalming, no false makeup to pretend sleep. Only the signs of very disfiguring illnesses are covered up with bandages and only infectious cases are removed from the home prior to the burial.
>
> Why do I describe such "old-fashioned" customs? I think they are an indication of our acceptance of a fatal outcome, and they help the dying patient as well as his family to accept the loss of a loved one. If a patient is allowed to terminate his life in the familiar and beloved envi-ronment, it requires less adjustment. . . . The fact that children are allowed to stay at home where a fatality has stricken and are included in the talk, discussions, and fears gives them the feeling that they are not alone in the grief and gives them the comfort of shared responsibil-ity and shared mourning. It prepares them gradually and helps them view death as part of life. [pp. 5–6]

9   Kübler-Ross is attempting to stress the importance of treating death as a natural part of life. But the death of the farmer in Switzerland she describes would be all too foreign in America. While there has been some progress in recent years in discussing death more openly, for the most part Americans still take great pains to avoid the fact of death. The dying are sent away to institutions at the end of their lives. The dead person resides in the "slumber room." Phrases like "pass on" and "at rest" are used, and there is little open communication about the death. Funerals and mourning rituals are decried as unnecessary and barbaric. In effect, the fact that the individual has died is denied to a large extent. Worse still, that denial is perpetuated in the young by sending them away because they are "too young to understand" or by telling lies such as "Mommy has gone to sleep." Many Americans will go to practically

any extreme to avoid accepting death for what it is — a cessation of life, a natural part of the life cycle.

Herman Feifel, in his essay "The Meaning of Death in American 10 Society: Implications for Education" (1971), traces some of the reasons why it is so difficult for Americans today to accept death. He contrasts today with the Middle Ages, when death was viewed as the emergence into a new life. The Christian idea of death as a continuation of life, albeit changed from before, was prevalent. Death was the reunification with the Creator; death would carry one to a final reward. Today, with the disintegration of family ties and other supportive group interactions, plus the upsurge in technology and its resulting depersonalization and alienation, there is a "waning of providential faith, death no longer signals atonement and redemption as much as man's loneliness and a threat to his pursuit of happiness. Fear of death reveals less concern with judg-ment, and more with total annihilation and loss of identity" (p. 4). Ameri-cans no longer have the sense of continuity or relationship with others that might help them transcend death in a meaningful way, leaving them with existential anxiety.

Lifton, in *Death in Life: Survivors of Hiroshima* (1968), has come to 11 some of the same conclusions as Feifel in delineating what has led Ameri-cans to have increased difficulty in dealing with death. He describes six variables:

- *Urbanization.* Individuals are increasingly removed from nature and witnessing of the life/death cycle. They also have less of a sense of community with others, and have few common rituals to express feelings and guide behavior.
- *Exclusion of the aged and dying.* These people are segregated away from the general populace into nursing homes and hospitals, mak-ing death a foreign experience that elicits the fear of being alone.
- *Movement towards the nuclear family.* With the absence of the extended family comes increased vulnerability to devastation and loss of sup-port following the death of a loved one. There also is no opportunity to see aged relatives die and to experience death as a natural part of the life cycle.
- *Secularization from religion.* Religion used to minimize the impact of physical death by focusing on the hereafter, endow death with a special meaning and purpose, and provide for a future and immor-tality. With the decline in religion there has been a marked loss of these coping mechanisms.
- *Advances in medical technology.* These have given humanity more of a sense of control. There is less of a need for systems of thought that make death meaningful, such as philosophy or religion. Technology has promised immortality through cryonics; however, it also has created torturous bioethical quandaries (e.g., the definition of death, euthanasia). As life can be extended, deaths become more infrequent

occurrences, and terminal illnesses become chronic. All of these advances have compromised the ability to understand death as a natural part of human life.

- *Mass death.* Previously if someone contemplated her own death she could assume that it would cause a ripple in humanity signifying some degree of importance. With today's constant threat of mass death and nuclear destruction, however, this is absent. What good will it do to leave something behind if there is no world left to be aware of it? Additionally, peoples' sensitivities have become blunted to individual death. People learned to feel "good" that only 15 men died in Viet Nam instead of 30 on a particular day. In the past just one death would have been more horrifying.

12   Although advances and changes in Western culture have compounded Americans' struggle to cope with death, there are some systems that can offer comfort in dealing with death and that provide some form of immortality. Lifton (1973) suggests five modes:

- *The biological mode.* We extend ourselves into the future through our children. Our very genes and memories will be carried on in the projection of ourselves through our heirs.
- *The social mode.* Our lives have direction and meaning if we can leave something worthwhile behind us. This usually comes about through our work or creative endeavors.
- *The religious mode.* Religion provides a clear future in an immortal hereafter.
- *The natural mode.* We are part of nature. The decomposition of our bodies will nourish further growth in nature; we will not forever be destroyed because of our spot in the cycle of the chain of life.
- *The experiential transcendence mode.* There are psychological states that are so intense that there is a feeling of being beyond the confines of ordinary daily life. Time and death disappear. They can occur in religious or secular mysticism, in song, dance, battle, sexual love, or in the contemplation of artistic or intellectual creations; there is an extraordinary psychic unity and perceptual intensity in which there is no longer a restriction of the senses, including the awareness of mortality.

13   Some of us may find meaning and solace in one or more of these modes; others may seek alternative ways of coping with natural death anxiety, such as hedonism, existential philosophy, or beliefs in reincarnation.

14   Consideration of all these variables will provide a more complete understanding of the social and cultural framework out of which most patients and their families will operate. An appreciation of this is important because of the strong influence that society and culture will have upon their responses, as well as our own.

TYPES OF WRITING:
cause and effect, classification, comparison, definition

Topics for Discussion

1. In her treatment of American socio-cultural attitudes toward death, Rando's primary aims appear to be clarifying and expanding her readers' understanding of the subject. Yet, while Rando generally avoids overt criticism of the attitudes she explores, she makes it clear that she views them as unhealthy. How?
2. How would the information in this essentially expository essay exert influence on nursing students who encounter it in a course of study? What special influential advantage would this essay derive from reaching its audience as part of such a course?
3. How useful are the explanations and examples of death-accepting, death-defying, and death-denying cultures? Does the classification of all societies into one of these three categories help put Kübler-Ross's view of the American response to death in perspective? Would more contemporary examples of death-accepting and death-defying societies have been more effective?
4. Compare Rando's treatment of the North American denial of the natural fact of death with Jessica Mitford's in "The Story of Service." What are the influential advantages and disadvantages of the two approaches to the topic?
5. In commenting on the dominant American (and, by association, Canadian) attitude toward death, Rando adds: "Even within our own culture . . . there will be many differences among individuals depending upon their ethnic, social, and religious backgrounds." What is your attitude toward death? How does it differ (if at all) from what Rando describes?

Topics for Writing

1. Write an essay encouraging a change in some established social practice by analyzing the attitudes behind it and offering alternatives. Stereotypical roles of the sexes in dating or in responsibility for child care, housework, or financial support would provide good subjects, but you need not feel limited to this area of concern.
2. Rando quotes Elizabeth Kübler-Ross's description of a "good" death. What, in your opinion, would be a good death? Describe such a death from several appropriate points of view such as moral, social, religious, intellectual.
3. In explaining her view that Americans typically "go to great lengths to shield themselves from the realities of death," Rando says nothing of the near obsession with violent death in popular American enter-

tainment forms — fiction, video games, television, and, especially, movies. Does this omission weaken her case or not? Write an essay explaining how the prevalence of violence and death in popular forms of entertainment either supports or undermines Rando's idea that American culture is death-denying.

In the Eye of the Storm

Mordecai Richler

Problems. 1

Do I still enjoy the right to call myself a Quebecer after I actually had 2
the effrontery to criticize *Le Devoir* as well as surface with the scoop that
René Lévesque was a politician, that is to say, a man whose honesty was
suspect? Clearly, the answer is a resounding no, if Pierre Péladeau, publisher of *Le Journal de Montréal*, is to be credited. "[Richler] has the cheek
to call himself a Quebecer," he said recently. "That's a bit as if I were to
consider myself Chinese." Mind you, it has been reliably reported that,
at the time, Péladeau was eating his habitual breakfast: wonton soup,
egg rolls and Lapsang souchong tea.

I was born in Quebec, yes, but certainly the Parti Québécois's onetime 3
cultural ayatollah, Camille Laurin, would have denied me even neo status
for the heinous crime — as he once noted — of thinking of myself as a
Canadian first of all. On the other hand, the current leader of the PQ, an
increasingly blustery "Jock" Parizeau, has assured us that once we are
independent we will still have Canadian passports and bucks. A jolly
good thing, too, as he might say himself, but also baffling. And adding
to my confusion, only a few weeks back federal Constitutional Affairs
Minister Joe Clark drew a line in the sand, as it were, telling those Quebecers who remain staunch federalists that Ottawa can assume no responsibility for us. If Quebec goes, it's bye-bye Canadian citizenship,
unless we are willing to move to Regina or Sudbury or T.O. Following
Hobson's choice, Clark's unappealing invitation.

And so, in the late hours of the night, disqualified as a Quebecer of 4
even impure *laine* by Péladeau, Laurin and Co., and possibly about to be
shorn of my Canadian citizenship, I wonder if I will soon be a man without
a country, condemned to wander the world as retribution — as a pre-
scient *Le Devoir* contributor once put it — for the Jewish crime of deicide.

Meanwhile, perplexed Montrealers previously unknown to me in- 5
troduce themselves as I wait for my luggage by the carousel at one
airport or another. "Montreal's my home. I really like it there," says a
bilingual man in his 30s.

"So do I." 6

"But we've got young children now and I suspect there will be noth- 7
ing for them there."

Another man, this one a property developer who is an old schoolmate 8
of mine, says: "I wouldn't dare invest another penny in Montreal. I
mean, hell, I'm already going to be stuck with plenty I will have to let go
at fire-sale prices."

Many I have spoken to would leave right now, without even waiting 9
for Quebec to pronounce, but they are locked into a dress shop or a
cigar-and-soda that has been in the family for a couple of generations, or
to the only house they have ever owned.

10   Next October's referendum, if there is going to be one, has them frightened. They remember, as I do, how an ill-tempered Lévesque, going into the 1980 referendum on sovereignty-association, pointedly evoked memories of the Sixties. Exploding mailboxes in Westmount. Terrorist bombs in the stock exchange. The October Crisis. "I will not be responsible for what happens," he warned, "if the English continue to oppose the true aspirations of the Québécois."

11   So much for the PQ fiction that anybody who lives in Quebec is a Québécois. In *la belle province*, as on Animal Farm, some voters will be more equal than others come October, and if the referendum result is close, as I anticipate, say only 52 or 53 per cent opting to stay in Canada, things could get hot for Quebecers named Kelly, Lin, Bercovitch or MacNeil. Anybody who suggests otherwise is either a fool or a liar.

12   Forget the whales, never mind the cutesy-poo seal pups. If there is a truly endangered species in Canada, it is the non-francophone population of Quebec. More than 300,000 have grudgingly uprooted themselves from the province since 1976, the year the PQ came to power. The rest, mostly aging survivors — stealthily unloading whatever they anticipate they won't be able to take with them come the crunch — feel increasingly unwelcome here.

13   The mood in non-francophone Montreal, as I read it, is compounded of two parts melancholy and one part anger. True, we still party here, but now it is usually to wish yet another old friend, or one of our children, bon voyage.

VENGEFUL

14 We expect only more broken promises from the provincial Liberals and more vengeful legislation from the PQ. To come clean, we also feel abandoned by the incredibly inept, even panicky, crew that is trying to keep our federal ship of state afloat. Furthermore, we were not amused when its putative, Gucci-clad captain, noting how badly the old tub was listing, lobbied for a job with the United Nations, only to be found wanting there too.

15   Look at it this way: if the PQ's real agenda is to drive as many non-francophones out of Quebec as possible, they are succeeding brilliantly. If, however, this is not the case, would they please stop shedding crocodile tears, telling us how much we are needed, even adored, ho ho ho. We want less tell and more show from both the provincial Liberals and the PQ. Our government could begin by amending the officious Bill 178 — a language law that has made us a laughing stock abroad — and by doing more about English education, which a recent provincial task force described as "a social system under siege." The report went on to state:

16   *"There must be an acceptance by the whole of Quebec society that its English fact is of intrinsic value to Quebec. If the English-speaking commu-*

nity of Quebec is to continue to exist as a contributing component of Quebec's social, cultural and economic makeup, its schools must reflect the distinct character of its aspirations, traditions and potential."

CULTURED

I am a Montrealer born and bred and I do not wish to leave the city or my other home of 15 years in Quebec's Eastern Townships. I enjoy the company of French-Canadians and still consider them among the most cultured people in the country, something I keep repeating to no effect, and I cherish the ethnic diversity (as opposed to the tribalism inherent in the street chant of *"Le Québec aux Québécois!"*) that once made Montreal, my Montreal, the most cosmopolitan city in Canada. And the most fun. 17

I left Montreal in 1950, at the age of 19, a college dropout bound for Paris. Ironies. In those days, much to my amusement, francophone Montrealers (say, Jock Parizeau) headed for London, where nobody would ridicule their accents, and anglophones (like me) sought out Paris, where nobody would wince at *our* accents. Eventually, however, I did settle in London. And when I returned to Montreal, in 1972, with my wife and five children, it wasn't because I was enamored of the climate, or that I was so foolish as to think its cultural advantages rivalled those of London. I came back because it was home. 18

Item: only a couple of weeks ago I was out shopping for food on Laurier Avenue. Laurier, I should explain, was once in the heart of Montreal's Jewish quarter, a street of tacky, dilapidated stores with faded window displays. But in recent years Laurier has been transmogrified with considerable pizzazz by francophones, and now boasts fine-food shops, decent restaurants and fetching boutiques. Anyway, there I was, crossing the street, when a francophone woman, her manner teasing, hailed me. "Hey, Richler, you shouldn't walk down here all alone. This is a French-Canadian district." 19

She was gone before I could tell her that this may be a modish francophone district today, but there was a time when it was my very own neighborhood. Hey, I wanted to tell her, wait a minute, I used to play street hockey here with Morty Pearl and Albert Aaron and Bernie Bloomstone. Only a block away, at the Talmud Torah, I learned modern Hebrew. On Sunday mornings, out on my CCM bicycle, I used to collect butcher bills on these streets. I must have passed here thousands of times, strolling home from Baron Byng High School with Earl Kruger and Eli Weinstein, maybe stopping for a game of Ping-Pong at Joe's or some snooker at the Laurier Billiards. Right there on the corner of Park and Laurier there once stood Jack and Moe's Barbershop, where I made one of my first rites of passage. For years, accompanied to the barbershop by my mother, I had to endure the humiliation of Jack or Moe slipping a board through the silvery arms of the old-fashioned chair, raising me 20 high enough for either one to cut my hair without stooping. Then one hallelujah day, no more board. "Siddown, kid," Jack said, indicating the actual black leather seat, and I understood, for the first time, that things might yet work out for me.

21   There are thousands more like me in Montreal — Jews or WASPs and, more recently, Italians, Greeks, Portuguese, whatever — with their own special memories of growing up in the city, and we are deeply resentful of those xenophobic nationalists who would dismiss us, in the first place, as *les autres*, and, in the second, foster such a linguistically intolerant atmosphere as to force us to leave, if only for the sake of our children.

22   So we are obliged to grasp at straws.

23   Three years after Mayor Jean Doré came out unequivocally for the maintenance of an exclusively French face for Montreal, he has — possibly because he is a *New Yorker* reader — discovered that English is "one of the big international languages," as he recently observed. Furthermore, restrictions against its use, he has learned, hurt the city in the eyes of international investors. Therefore, he has advocated that we be thrown a crumb. He would like to see it possible for businesses with four employees or less to post bilingual signs. Even this was too much for Claude Ryan, Quebec's minister in charge of language matters, who responded, not bloody likely until the constitutional dispute is settled. And so, somewhere down the line, I think we can hope for a break in the officious Bill 178. Next year, or the year after, bilingual outside commercial signs might be permitted in the streets of Montreal between 4 and 6 a.m., or on every second rainy Wednesday.

24   We are living through a farce, but the problem is we are on stage, not in the audience, so our laughter is understandably limited.

TYPES OF WRITING:
direct argument, personal experience

Topics for Discussion

1. In addition to the single word, separate from the text, with which the essay begins, there are two one-word sub-headings. How useful are these words? Do they introduce, summarize, or comment on the material that follows them?

2. What does the apparent antagonism toward the French-speaking majority in Quebec suggest about the audience Richler is attempting to influence? Would this attitude help or hinder Richler in his efforts to influence English-speaking Quebecers? What would the effect of this combative stance be on most Canadians living outside Quebec?

3. In paragraph 11 Richler refers to a passage from George Orwell's novel *Animal Farm*; Barbara Amiel in "Another Threat to Freedom in

Ontario" refers to the same passage from the same novel. Do both authors use Orwell as a means of persuasion? Is there any difference in the way in which they use the passage?

4. "It's bye-bye Canadian citizenship." "Forget the whales, never mind the cutesy-poo seal pups." "Then one hallelujah day, no more board." Such casual, informal language occurs frequently in this essay. How does it serve Richler's persuasive intent? Is the style appropriate to the subject, an affectation peculiar to the writer, or both?

Topics for Writing

1. Both Richler in this essay and Hugh MacLennan in "French is a *Must* for Canadians" write about the difficulties of living in Quebec, although more than thirty years separate their essays. Which of the two do you find the more convincing? Consider not just the subjects of their essays but also their persuasive strategies and techniques.

2. Describe the locality, city, or town you come from. Concentrate on persuading your readers that the surface appearance of the place, however mundane and uninteresting it may appear, hides qualities and characteristics that are well worth attention. To this end, you may want to use the kind of quirky details Richler does in his essay.

One Voice in the Cosmic Fugue

Carl Sagan

Probably all the organic beings which have ever lived on this earth have descended from some one primordial form, into which life was first breathed. . . . There is grandeur in this view of life . . . that, whilst this planet has gone cycling on according to the fixed law of gravity, from so simple a beginning endless forms most beautiful and most wonderful have been, and are being, evolved.

— Charles Darwin, *The Origin of Species,* 1859

1   All my life I have wondered about the possibility of life elsewhere. What would it be like? Of what would it be made? All living things on our planet are constructed of organic molecules — complex microscopic architectures in which the carbon atom plays a central role. There was once a time before life, when the Earth was barren and utterly desolate. Our world is now overflowing with life. How did it come about? How, in the absence of life, were carbon-based organic molecules made? How did the first living things arise? How did life evolve to produce beings as elaborate and complex as we, able to explore the mystery of our own origins?

2   And on the countless other planets that may circle other suns, is there life also? Is extraterrestrial life, if it exists, based on the same organic molecules as life on Earth? Do the beings of other worlds look much like life on Earth? Or are they stunningly different — other adaptations to other environments? What else is possible? The nature of life on Earth and the search for life elsewhere are two sides of the same question — the search for who we are.

3   In the great dark between the stars there are clouds of gas and dust and organic matter. Dozens of different kinds of organic molecules have been found there by radio telescopes. The abundance of these molecules suggests that the stuff of life is everywhere. Perhaps the origin and evolution of life is, given enough time, a cosmic inevitability. On some of the billions of planets in the Milky Way Galaxy, life may never arise. On others, it may arise and die out, or never evolve beyond its simplest forms. And on some small fraction of worlds there may develop intelligences and civilizations more advanced than our own.

4   Occasionally someone remarks on what a lucky coincidence it is that the Earth is perfectly suitable for life — moderate temperatures, liquid water, oxygen atmosphere, and so on. But this is, at least in part, a confusion of cause and effect. We earthlings are supremely well adapted to the environment of the Earth because we grew up here. Those earlier forms of life that were not well adapted died. We are descended from the organisms that did well. Organisms that evolve on a quite different world will doubtless sing its praises too.

5   All life on Earth is closely related. We have a common organic chemistry and a common evolutionary heritage. As a result, our biologists are

profoundly limited. They study only a single kind of biology, one lonely theme in the music of life. Is this faint and reedy tune the only voice for thousands of light-years? Or is there a kind of cosmic fugue, with themes and counterpoints, dissonances and harmonies, a billion different voices playing the life music of the Galaxy?

Let me tell you a story about one little phrase in the music of life on   6 Earth. In the year 1185, the Emperor of Japan was a seven-year-old boy named Antoku. He was the nominal leader of a clan of samurai called the Heike, who were engaged in a long and bloody war with another samurai clan, the Genji. Each asserted a superior ancestral claim to the imperial throne. Their decisive naval encounter, with the Emperor on board ship, occurred at Danno-ura in the Japanese Inland Sea on April 24, 1185. The Heike were outnumbered, and outmaneuvered. Many were killed. The survivors, in massive numbers, threw themselves into the sea and drowned. The Lady Nii, grandmother of the Emperor, resolved that she and Antoku would not be captured by the enemy. What happened next is told in *The Tale of the Heike*:

> The Emperor was seven years old that year but looked much older. He was so lovely that he seemed to shed a brilliant radiance and his long, black hair hung loose far down his back. With a look of surprise and anxiety on his face he asked the Lady Nii, "Where are you to take me?"
>
> She turned to the youthful sovereign, with tears streaming down her cheeks, and . . . comforted him, binding up his long hair in his dove-coloured robe. Blinded with tears, the child sovereign put his beautiful, small hands together. He turned first to the East to say farewell to the god of Ise and then to the West to repeat the Nembutsu [a prayer to the Amida Buddha]. The Lady Nii took him tightly in her arms and with the words "In the depths of the ocean is our capitol," sank with him at last beneath the waves.

The entire Heike battle fleet was destroyed. Only forty-three women   7 survived. These ladies-in-waiting of the imperial court were forced to sell flowers and other favors to the fishermen near the scene of the battle. The Heike almost vanished from history. But a ragtag group of the former ladies-in-waiting and their offspring by the fisherfolk established a festival to commemorate the battle. It takes place on the twenty-fourth of April every year to this day. Fishermen who are the descendants of the Heike dress in hemp and black headgear and proceed to the Akama shrine which contains the mausoleum of the drowned Emperor. There they watch a play portraying the events that followed the Battle of Danno-ura. For centuries after, people imagined that they could discern ghostly samurai armies vainly striving to bail the sea, to cleanse it of blood and defeat and humiliation.

The fishermen say the Heike samurai wander the bottoms of the   8 Inland Sea still — in the form of crabs. There are crabs to be found here with curious markings on their backs, patterns and indentations that disturbingly resemble the face of a samurai. When caught, these crabs are not eaten, but are returned to the sea in commemoration of the dole-ful events at Danno-ura.

9   This legend raises a lovely problem. How does it come about that the face of a warrior is incised on the carapace of a crab? The answer seems to be that humans made the face. The patterns on the crab's shell are inherited. But among crabs, as among people, there are many differ-ent hereditary lines. Suppose that, by chance, among the distant ances-tors of this crab, one arose with a pattern that resembled, even slightly, a human face. Even before the battle of Danno-ura, fishermen may have been reluctant to eat such a crab. In throwing it back, they set in motion an evolutionary process: If you are a crab and your carapace is ordinary, the humans will eat you. Your line will leave fewer descendants. If your carapace looks a little like a face, they will throw you back. You will leave more descendants. Crabs had a substantial investment in the pat-terns on their carapaces. As the generations passed, of crabs and fishermen alike, the crabs with patterns that most resembled a samurai face survived preferentially until eventually there was produced not just a human face, not just a Japanese face, but the visage of a fierce and scowling samurai. All this has nothing to do with what the crabs *want*. Selection is imposed from the outside. The more you look like a samurai, the better are your chances of survival. Eventually, there come to be a great many samurai crabs.

10   This process is called artificial selection. In the case of the Heike crab it was effected more or less unconsciously by the fishermen, and certainly without any serious contemplation by the crabs. But humans have delib-erately selected which plants and animals shall live and which shall die for thousands of years. We are surrounded from babyhood by familiar farm and domestic animals, fruits and trees and vegetables. Where do they come from? Were they once free-living in the wild and then induced to adopt a less strenuous life on the farm? No, the truth is quite different. They are, most of them, made by us.

11   Ten thousand years ago, there were no dairy cows or ferret hounds or large ears of corn. When we domesticated the ancestors of these plants and animals — sometimes creatures who looked quite different — we controlled their breeding. We made sure that certain varieties, having properties we consider desirable, preferentially reproduced. When we wanted a dog to help us care for sheep, we selected breeds that were intelligent, obedient and had some preexisting talent to herd, which is useful for animals who hunt in packs. The enormous distended udders of dairy cattle are the result of a human interest in milk and cheese. Our corn, or maize, has been bred for ten thousand generations to be more tasty and nutritious than its scrawny ancestors; indeed, it is so changed that it cannot even reproduce without human intervention.

12   The essence of artificial selection — for a Heike crab, a dog, a cow or an ear of corn — is this: Many physical and behavioral traits of plants and animals are inherited. They breed true. Humans, for whatever reason,

encourage the reproduction of some varieties and discourage the reproduction of others. The variety selected for preferentially reproduces; it
eventually becomes abundant; the variety selected against becomes rare
and perhaps extinct.

But if humans can make new varieties of plants and animals, must   13
not nature do so also? This related process is called natural selection.
That life has changed fundamentally over the aeons is entirely clear from
the alterations we have made in the beasts and vegetables during the
short tenure of humans on Earth, and from the fossil evidence. The fossil
record speaks to us unambiguously of creatures that once were present
in enormous numbers and that have now vanished utterly.* Far more
species have become extinct in the history of the Earth than exist today;
they are the terminated experiments of evolution.

The genetic changes induced by domestication have occurred very   14
rapidly. The rabbit was not domesticated until early medieval times (it
was bred by French monks in the belief that newborn bunnies were fish
and therefore exempt from the prohibitions against eating meat on certain
days in the Church calendar); coffee in the fifteenth century; the sugar
beet in the nineteenth century; and the mink is still in the earliest stages
of domestication. In less than ten thousand years, domestication has
increased the weight of wool grown by sheep from less than one kilogram
of rough hairs to ten or twenty kilograms of uniform, fine down; or the
volume of milk given by cattle during a lactation period from a few
hundred to a million cubic centimeters. If artificial selection can make
such major changes in so short a period of time, what must natural
selection, working over billions of years, be capable of? The answer is all
the beauty and diversity of the biological world. Evolution is a fact, not a
theory.

That the mechanism of evolution is natural selection is the great   15
discovery associated with the names of Charles Darwin and Alfred Russel
Wallace. More than a century ago, they stressed that nature is prolific,
that many more animals and plants are born than can possibly survive
and that therefore the environment selects those varieties which are, by
accident, better suited for survival. Mutations — sudden changes in heredity — breed true. They provide the raw material of evolution. The
environment selects those few mutations that enhance survival, resulting
in a series of slow transformations of one lifeform into another, the origin
of new species.†

* Although traditional Western religious opinion stoutly maintained the contrary, as for
  example, the 1770 opinion of John Wesley: "Death is never permitted to destroy [even]
  the most inconsiderable species."
† In the Mayan holy book the Popol Vuh, the various forms of life are described as
  unsuccessful attempts by gods with a predilection for experiment to make people. Early
  tries were far off the mark, creating the lower animals; the penultimate attempt, a near
  miss, made the monkeys. In Chinese myth, human beings arose from the body lice of a
  god named P'an Ku. In the eighteenth century, de Buffon proposed that the Earth was
  much older than Scripture suggested, that the forms of life somehow changed slowly

16   Darwin's words in *The Origin of Species* were:

> Man does not actually produce variability; he only unintentionally exposes organic beings to new conditions of life, and then Nature acts on the organisation, and causes variability. But man can and does select the variations given to him by Nature, and thus accumulate them in any desired manner. He thus adapts animals and plants for his own benefit or pleasure. He may do this methodically, or he may do it unconsciously by preserving the individuals most useful to him at the time, without any thought of altering the breed. . . . There is no obvious reason why the principles which have acted so efficiently under domestication should not have acted under Nature. . . . More individuals are born than can possibly survive. . . . The slightest advantage in one being, of any age or during any season, over those with which it comes into competition, or better adaptation in however slight a degree to the surrounding physical conditions, will turn the balance.

17   T. H. Huxley, the most effective nineteenth-century defender and popularizer of evolution, wrote that the publications of Darwin and Wallace were a "flash of light, which to a man who has lost himself in a dark night, suddenly reveals a road which, whether it takes him straight home or not, certainly goes his way. . . . My reflection, when I first made myself master of the central idea of the 'Origin of Species,' was, 'How extremely stupid not to have thought of that! I suppose that Columbus' companions said much the same. . . . The facts of variability, of the struggle for existence, of adaptation to conditions, were notorious enough; but none of us had suspected that the road to the heart of the species problem lay through them, until Darwin and Wallace dispelled the darkness."

18   Many people were scandalized — some still are — at both ideas, evolution and natural selection. Our ancestors looked at the elegance of life on Earth, at how appropriate the structures of organisms are to their functions, and saw evidence for a Great Designer. The simplest one-celled organism is a far more complex machine than the finest pocket watch. And yet pocket watches do not spontaneously self-assemble, or evolve, in slow stages, on their own, from, say, grandfather clocks. A watch implies a watch maker. There seemed to be no way in which atoms and molecules could somehow spontaneously fall together to create organisms of such awesome complexity and subtle functioning as grace every region of the Earth. That each living thing was specially designed, that one species did not become another, were notions perfectly consistent with what our ancestors with their limited historical records knew about life. The idea that every organism was meticulously constructed by a Great Designer provided a significance and order to nature

over the millennia, but that the apes were the forlorn descendants of people. While these notions do not precisely reflect the evolutionary process described by Darwin and Wallace, they are anticipations of it — as are the views of Democritus, Empedocles and other early Ionian scientists.

and an importance to human beings that we crave still. A Designer is a natural, appealing and altogether human explanation of the biological world. But, as Darwin and Wallace showed, there is another way, equally appealing, equally human, and far more compelling: natural selection, which makes the music of life more beautiful as the aeons pass.

The fossil evidence could be consistent with the idea of a Great 19 Designer; perhaps some species are destroyed when the Designer becomes dissatisfied with them, and new experiments are attempted on an improved design. But this notion is a little disconcerting. Each plant and animal is exquisitely made; should not a supremely competent Designer have been able to make the intended variety from the start? The fossil record implies trial and error, an inability to anticipate the future, features inconsistent with an efficient Great Designer (although not with a Designer of a more remote and indirect temperament).

When I was a college undergraduate in the early 1950's, I was fortu- 20 nate enough to work in the laboratory of H. J. Muller, a great geneticist and the man who discovered that radiation produces mutations. Muller was the person who first called my attention to the Heike crab as an example of artificial selection. To learn the practical side of genetics, I spent many months working with fruit flies, *Drosophila melanogaster* (which means the black-bodied dew-lover) — tiny benign beings with two wings and big eyes. We kept them in pint milk bottles. We would cross two varieties to see what new forms emerged from the rearrangement of the parental genes, and from natural and induced mutations. The females would deposit their eggs on a kind of molasses the technicians placed inside the bottles; the bottles were stoppered; and we would wait two weeks for the fertilized eggs to become larvae, the larvae pupae, and the pupae to emerge as new adult fruit flies.

One day I was looking through a low-power binocular microscope 21 at a newly arrived batch of adult *Drosophila* immobilized with a little ether, and was busily separating the different varieties with a camel's-hair brush. To my astonishment, I came upon something very different: not a small variation such as red eyes instead of white, or neck bristles instead of no neck bristles. This was another, and very well-functioning, kind of creature with much more prominent wings and long feathery antennae. Fate had arranged, I concluded, that an example of a major evolutionary change in a single generation, the very thing Muller had said could never happen, should take place in his own laboratory. It was my unhappy task to explain it to him.

With heavy heart I knocked on his office door. "Come in," came the 22 muffled cry. I entered to discover the room darkened except for a single small lamp illuminating the stage of the microscope at which he was working. In these gloomy surroundings I stumbled through my explanation. I had found a very different kind of fly. I was sure it had emerged from one of the pupae in the molasses. I didn't mean to disturb Muller but ..."Does it look more like Lepidoptera than Diptera?" he asked, his face illuminated from below. I didn't know what this meant, so he had to explain: "Does it have big wings? Does it have feathery antennae?" I glumly nodded assent.

23   Muller switched on the overhead light and smiled benignly. It was an old story. There was a kind of moth that had adapted to *Drosophila* genetics laboratories. It was nothing like a fruit fly and wanted nothing to do with fruit flies. What it wanted was the fruit flies' molasses. In the brief time that the laboratory technician took to unstopper and stopper the milk bottle — for example, to add fruit flies — the mother moth made a dive-bombing pass, dropping her eggs on the run into the tasty molasses. I had not discovered a macro-mutation. I had merely stumbled upon another lovely adaptation in nature, itself the product of micromutation and natural selection.

24   The secrets of evolution are death and time — the deaths of enormous numbers of lifeforms that were imperfectly adapted to the environment; and time for a long succession of small mutations that were *by accident* adaptive, time for the slow accumulation of patterns of favorable mutations. Part of the resistance to Darwin and Wallace derives from our difficulty in imagining the passage of the millennia, much less the aeons. What does seventy million years mean to beings who live only one-millionth as long? We are like butterflies who flutter for a day and think it is forever.

TYPES OF WRITING:
analysis, cause and effect, example/illustration,
narration, personal experience

Topics for Discussion

1. In his first two paragraphs Sagan asks eleven questions, but without answering any of them. Do you find this an effective way of opening an essay? Why, or why not?
2. The legend about the Heike and their seven-year-old Emperor, Antoku, is charming, but does it really help Sagan to advance his thesis? If so, how? If not, why not? Ask yourself the same questions concerning the story Sagan tells about when he was an undergraduate working in the laboratory of H. J. Muller.
3. Compare Sagan's essay with Anne Brennan's "The Creationism Controversy: The Religious Issues." Which do you consider the more persuasive? Why? In dealing with this second question, you should consider both intellectual and emotional appeal.
4. "We are like butterflies who flutter for a day and think it is forever." Consider the advantages of using a poetic conclusion like this one as opposed to a clear, direct statement about the importance of natural selection.

Topics for Writing

1. "All my life I have wondered about the possibility of life elsewhere." Write an essay expressing your personal views on this subject. Keep in mind as you write that science is not the only area of human inquiry that may be relevant in a consideration such as this.
2. Write an essay arguing for or against the premise that UFO's are real and of extra-terrestrial origin.

On Not Seeing: Vincent van Gogh and the Birth of Cloisonism

Donna E. Smyth

Note: The word cloisonism *derives from* cloissoné, *described in the* Oxford Companion to the Decorative Arts *(1975) as follows:*

> *In cloisonné enamelling cells, or cloisons, are built up on a thin sheet of metal by attaching metal wire or fine strips of metal fixed edgewise. These cells are filled with finely powdered glass paste, which is then fused to the metal in a furnace. As the enamel shrinks on melting and cools with a concave surface, more has to be poured in and the process repeated. Finally the surface is levelled and the whole is smoothed and polished.*

1   Two images on the TV screen. One is a reporter in a white shirt and tie, dark suit. He is young middle-aged with fleshy cheeks, glasses, hair cut short. He is standing in front of the other image: Van Gogh's last self-portrait, with the floppy hat, the vulnerable hands. The painter's haunted face looks over the reporter's shoulder at us. The eyes are intense, fierce; the face drawn with suffering.

2   This is the national news coverage of the preview of the exhibition opening the next day at the Art Gallery of Ontario. It includes an interview with Bogamila Welsh, the art historian who arranged the show, and a few shots of the most famous pictures. We're informed about the fabulous cost of insuring these 'priceless' paintings whose value skyrocketed again recently at art auctions in distant cities. We're told we are lucky to have them gathered together in Toronto for what may be 'the last of the big Internationals' (exhibitions) because of the huge costs of setting up such a show. We are shown the turnstiles the viewers will file through and the carefully marked path they will have to follow. Security has been increased at all points in the gallery.

3   In short, we are set up for an event. The paintings are advertised as treasures; perhaps not on the scale of Tutankhamun's, but worth a lot of money and therefore worthy of our attention. It is also being marketed as an educational experience: an initiation into High Culture for those who feel that such things are the prerogative of highbrows and university professors.

4   In the *Globe and Mail* the next morning, there is a picture of Princess Juliana of the Netherlands peering intently at a painting. She is accompanied by the formally dressed director of the Rijksmuseum in Amsterdam, who is looking equally intense but somewhat anxious. Both persons reveal the nature of the occasion. High culture is serious business perhaps best understood by those of royal birth and/or great wealth.

5   In the same paper appears a laudatory review of the show complete with colour reproductions.* The reviewer suggests that the open-

---

* John Bentley Mays, "Visionaries of the Soul," *Globe and Mail*, January 24, 1981, p. E.1.

ing of the show 'is ample grounds for fireworks, and champagne all round.' Clearly, on such an occasion, *vin ordinaire* or cold beer would not do. After much discussion of the exhibition, the critic eventually tells us something of van Gogh's life, his poverty, his suffering, his madness.

I think again of the self-portrait and those eyes watching hundreds of us filing past in dutiful order.   6

What is going on here?   7

To begin with, we have the mystique, conscious and unconscious, that surrounds and informs Great Art in our society. None of us, with the possible exception of young children, can view these paintings as if for the first time. And even the children, absorbing the pseudoreligious atmosphere will know that certain responses are more acceptable than others. Adults may dimly remember popular reproductions on post cards, posters, and in books. But even if previous contact has been minimal, the way the paintings are presented (which we all know by now cost a lot of money) influences our perception.   8

Some will approach with strained hesitation. What if we aren't up to Great Art? What does *cloisonism* mean anyhow? Suppose we stand in front of a famous painting and nothing happens to us. No great revelation, no illumination. Does that mean we are incapable of appreciating the finer things in life? Are we trapped in a Canadian parochialism born of too much weather and waiting in airports? But then, there is a familiar foreign feel to the whole exhibition. It's from over there, where Great Art tends to happen more often than right here.   9

No doubt some will be intrigued by the price tags, and the idea that investing in art (particularly if it turns out to be Great Art) can be a hedge against inflation on a par with purchasing hockey teams.   10

Some will attend as a kind of social obligation commensurate with their position on the corporate/professional ladder.   11

Curious, maybe, or sulky, but there we are mutable and variable, filing past that face which does not change because it is a work of art. Through painting, van Gogh turned himself into swirls of colour which did not die when he did. In fact, at the time of his death, few people cared about the man or his paintings. He was not a good neighbour or brother, he threatened his friends, if he was alive today he would not get a credit rating.   12

What we discover is the further removed the living reality of the man is from us, the more valuable his paintings become. The more valuable the paintings become, the more they are likely to be hailed as Great Art. As in matters of social class, market value confers prestige. Critics, art scholars and historians protest that *they* are not swayed by such vulgar considerations, but we don't find many of them arranging prestigious shows for artists not yet admitted to the charmed circle. Aesthetic merit alone does not make a big International. Great Art always carries a big price tag.   13

14   Moreover, it is obvious that the gallery does not trust the masses to behave themselves when they come into contact with Great Art. Coming in out of a grey Toronto winter day, it just might happen that, for brief seconds, the crowds would be so dazzled by brilliant colours, flowers burning like the sun, that they'd run amok — people might rush from painting to painting with undue speed, talking loudly to each other, or to themselves. Someone might actually stand rooted to the spot in front of a particular painting for a while, ignoring the milling crowd and the harassed men in blue talking into black boxes.

15   Standing there with our sweaty feet in winter boots, we might want to hold hands in front of that self-portrait, not because we're moved to romantic tenderness, but because that man is so alone, he makes us aware of our own separateness, makes us want to touch human flesh quickly before we die too.

16   We might want to react this way, to experience these things. But we won't. More likely, we'll pay our money and file, like docile sheep, past the paintings. There is a way into the exhibition and a way out.

17   As we reclaim our winter coats, we're aware that in five minutes our feet will be freezing. Passing again the video booth set up outside the exhibition ticket office, we stop for a lingering look. The story of van Gogh's life plays over and over. Is there something we missed?

18   But we're tired, hungry, have appointments with dentists and lovers. It's getting late. Vaguely uneasy we leave the gallery. It is as though we've paid our dues to High Culture and it feels uncomfortably like going to church on Sunday to please someone else. For the Aesthetic Experience is infused with vague moral platitudes. We will be better people for this experience (as if the paintings ooze a kind of spiritual uplift). Critics and pundits assure us that van Gogh speaks to a common humanity transcending time and place. This may be so. Yet some of the Chinese housewives and shoppers out on Dundas Street must remember wistfully a different tradition, another way of looking with a single brush stroke rather than all that paint. Most of them will not come to this exhibition. Nor will thousands of Torontonians who know in their bones that Great Art is no more for them than the York Club is their stomping ground. Nor will thousands of Canadians who do not live in this centre of English-Canadian power and wealth. Such an exhibition will not travel to Trois Rivières, or to small prairie cities where the kids throw snowballs and the sunset looks like a painting.

19   The pictures themselves are portable but the exhibition is not. It's too expensive — only major galleries in large cities such as Amsterdam and New York can afford it. Within this framework, the paintings of van Gogh and his contemporaries become selectively available commodities subject to the same kinds of market forces as coffee beans. But coffee beans are not surrounded by the cultural mystique which obscures Great Art.

20   When we see this exhibition, we're not seeing van Gogh, we're seeing this mystique. It comes between us and the paintings as surely as

frost on the window pane. It makes works of art into Great Art with its solemn face and cultural *avoirdupois*. It takes the joy and pain out of the encounter between us and the artist's work and substitutes a spurious and deadening decorum instead.

If van Gogh 'illuminated the inner self'* in these paintings, then 21 someone, somewhere has turned out the lights.

* Mays, "Visionaries of the Soul."

TYPES OF WRITING:
analysis, description, personal experience

Topics for Discussion

1. Does the title of this essay make you want to read it? Why or why not?
2. How relevant is Smyth's title to the body of her essay?
3. In the course of dealing with her essential subject, Smyth criticizes various aspects of Canadian society. Identify as many of these as you can. Do these secondary concerns contribute to the effect of her main point or not?
4. Smyth's essay concentrates on the limitations and incongruities of exhibitions like the one she describes but it says little about alternatives. Would her essay be more likely to promote change if she had added constructive suggestions to her criticism?
5. What influential advantage does Smyth gain from working gradually toward her insights into the limitations of "Great Art" exhibitions rather than making her point at the beginning and then defending it?

Topics for Writing

1. Write an essay analyzing the unfortunate side-effects of studying literature for college credits.
2. Write an essay exploring what is lost or gained by fans when a sport becomes big business. Although you may want to refer to developments in several sports, focus your essay on one sport that you know well.

The Pain of Animals

David Suzuki

1   Medical technology has taken us beyond the normal barriers of life and death and thereby created unprecedented choices in *human* lives. Until recently, we have taken for granted our right to use other species in any way we see fit. Food, clothing, muscle power have been a few of the benefits we've derived from this exploitation. This tradition has continued into scientific research where animals are studied and "sacrificed" for human benefit. Now serious questions are being asked about our right to do this.

2   Modern biological research is based on a shared evolutionary history of organisms that enables us to extrapolate from one organism to another. Thus, most fundamental concepts in heredity were first shown in fruit flies, molecular genetics began using bacteria and viruses and much of physiology and psychology has been based on studies in mice and rats. But today, as extinction rates have multiplied as a result of human activity, we have begun to ask what right we have to use all other animate forms simply to increase human knowledge or for profit or entertainment. Underlying the "animal rights" movement is the troubling question of where we fit in the rest of the natural world.

3   When I was young, one of my prized possessions was a BB gun. Dad taught me how to use it safely and I spent many hours wandering through the woods in search of prey. It's not easy to get close enough to a wild animal to kill it with a BB gun, but I did hit a few pigeons and starlings. I ate everything I shot. Then as a teenager, I graduated to a .22 rifle and with it, I killed rabbits and even shot a pheasant once.

4   One year I saw an ad for a metal slingshot in a comic book. I ordered it, and when it arrived, I practised for weeks shooting marbles at a target. I got to be a pretty good shot and decided to go after something live. Off I went to the woods and soon spotted a squirrel minding its own business doing whatever squirrels do. I gave chase and began peppering marbles at it until finally it jumped onto a tree, ran to the top and found itself trapped. I kept blasting away and grazed it a couple of times so it was only a matter of time before I would knock it down. Suddenly, the squirrel began to cry — a piercing shriek of terror and anguish. That animal's wail shook me to the core and I was overwhelmed with horror and shame at what I was doing — for no other reason than conceit with my prowess with a slingshot, I was going to *kill* another being. I threw away the slingshot and my guns and have never hunted again.

5   All my life, I have been an avid fisherman. Fish have always been the main source of meat protein in my family, and I have never considered fishing a sport. But there is no denying that it is exciting to reel in a struggling fish. We call it "playing" the fish, as if the wild animal's desperate struggle for survival is some kind of game.

6   I did "pleasure-fish" once while filming for a television report on the

science of fly fishing. We fished a famous trout stream in the Catskill Mountains of New York state where all fish had to be caught and released. The fish I caught had mouths gouged and pocked by previous encounters with hooks. I found no pleasure in it because to me fish are to be caught for consumption. Today, I continue to fish for food, but I do so with a profound awareness that I am a predator of animals possessing well-developed nervous systems that detect pain. Fishing and hunting have forced me to confront the way we exploit other animals.

I studied the genetics of fruit flies for twenty-five years and during 7 that time probably raised and killed tens of millions of them without a thought. In the early seventies, my lab discovered a series of mutations affecting behaviour of flies, and this find led us into an investigation of nerves and muscles. I applied for and received research funds to study behaviour in flies on the basis of the *similarity* of their neuromuscular systems to ours. In fact, psychologists and neurobiologists analyse behaviour, physiology and neuroanatomy of guinea pigs, rats, mice and other animals as *models* for human behaviour. So our nervous systems must closely resemble those of other mammals.

These personal anecdotes raise uncomfortable questions. What gives 8 us the right to exploit other living organisms as we see fit? How do we know that these other creatures don't feel pain or anguish just as we do? Perhaps there's no problem with fruit flies, but where do we draw the line? I used to rationalize angling because fish are cold blooded, as if warm-bloodedness indicates some kind of demarcation of brain development or greater sensitivity to pain. But anyone who has watched a fish's frantic fight to escape knows that it exhibits all the manifestations of pain and fear.

I've been thinking about these questions again after spending a week- 9 end in the Queen Charlotte Islands watching grey whales close up. The majesty and freedom of these magnificent mammals contrasted strikingly with the appearance of whales imprisoned in aquariums. Currently, the Vancouver Public Aquarium is building a bigger pool for some of its whales. In a radio interview, an aquarium representative was asked whether even the biggest pool can be adequate for animals that normally have the entire ocean to rove. Part of her answer was that if we watched porpoises in the pool, we'd see that "they are quite happy."

That woman was projecting human perceptions and emotions on the 10 porpoises. Our ability to empathize with other people and living things is one of our endearing qualities. Just watch someone with a beloved pet, an avid gardener with plants or, for that matter, even an owner of a new car and you will see how readily we can personalize and identify with another living organism or an object. But are we justified in our inferences about captive animals in their cages?

Most wild animals have evolved with a built-in need to move freely 11 over vast distances, fly in the air or swim through the ocean. Can a wild animal imprisoned in a small cage or pool, removed from its habitat and forced to conform to the impositions of our demands, ever be considered "happy"?

12   Animal rights activists are questioning our right to exploit animals, especially in scientific research. Scientists are understandably defensive, especially after labs have been broken into, experiments ruined and animals "liberated." But just as I have had to question my hunting and fishing, scientists cannot avoid confronting the issues raised, especially in relation to our closest relatives, the primates.

13   People love to watch monkeys in a circus or zoo and a great deal of the amusement comes from the recognition of ourselves in them. But our relationship with them is closer than just superficial similarities. When doctors at Loma Linda hospital in California implanted the heart of a baboon into the chest of Baby Fae, they were exploiting our close *biological* relationship.

14   Any reports on experimentation with familiar mammals like cats and dogs are sure to raise alarm among the lay public. But the use of primates is most controversial. In September 1987, at the Wildlife Film Festival in Bath, England, I watched a film shot on December 7, 1986, by a group of animal liberationists who had broken into SEMA, a biomedical research facility in Maryland. It was such a horrifying document that many in the audience rushed out after a few minutes. There were many scenes that I could not watch. As the intruders entered the facility, the camera followed to peer past cage doors, opened to reveal the animals inside. I am not ashamed to admit that I wept as baby monkeys deprived of any contact with other animals seized the fingers of their liberators and clung to them as our babies would to us. Older animals cowered in their tiny prisons, shaking from fear at the sudden appearance of people.

15   The famous chimpanzee expert, Jane Goodall, also screened the same film and as a result asked for permission to visit the SEMA facility. This is what she saw (*American Scientist*, November-December 1987):

> Room after room was lined with small, bare cages, stacked one above the other, in which monkeys circled round and round and chimpanzees sat huddled, far gone in depression and despair.
>
> Young chimpanzees, three or four years old, were crammed, two together into tiny cages measuring 57 cm by 57 cm and only 61 cm high. They could hardly turn around. Not yet part of any experiment, they had been confined in these cages for more than three months.
>
> The chimps had each other for comfort, but they would not remain together for long. Once they are infected, probably with hepatitis, they will be separated and placed in another cage. And there they will remain, living in conditions of severe sensory deprivation, for the next several years. During that time they will become insane.

16   Goodall's horror sprang from an intimate knowledge of chimpanzees in their native habitat. There, she has learned, chimps are nothing like the captive animals that we know. In the wild, they are highly social, requiring constant interaction and physical contact. They travel long distances, and they rest in soft beds they make in the trees. Laboratory

cages do not provide the conditions needed to fulfill the needs of these social, emotional and highly intelligent animals.

Ian Redmond (*BBC Wildlife*, April 1988) gives us a way to under- 17 stand the horror of what lab conditions do to chimps:

> Imagine locking a two- or three-year-old child in a metal box the size of an isolette — solid walls, floor and ceiling, and a glass door that clamps shut, blotting out most external sounds — and then leaving him or her for months, the only contact, apart from feeding, being when the door swings open and masked figures reach in and take samples of blood or tissue before shoving him back and clamping the door shut again. Over the past 10 years, 94 young chimps at SEMA have endured this procedure.

Chimpanzees, along with the gorilla, are our closest relatives, shar- 18 ing ninety-nine per cent of our genes. And it's that biological proximity that makes them so useful for research — we can try out experiments, study infections and test vaccines on them as models for people. And although there are only about 40,000 chimps left in the wild, compared to millions a few decades ago, the scientific demand for more has increased with the discovery of AIDS.

No chimpanzee has ever contracted AIDS, but the virus grows in 19 them, so scientists argue that chimps will be invaluable for testing vaccines. On February 19, 1988, the National Institute of Health in the U.S. co-sponsored a meeting to discuss the use of chimpanzees in research. Dr. Maurice Hilleman, Director of the Merck Institute for Therapeutic Research, reported:

> We need more chimps. . . . The chimpanzee is certainly a threatened species and there have been bans on importing the animal into the United States and into other countries, even though . . . the chimpanzee is considered to be an agricultural pest in many parts of the world where it exists. And secondly, it's being destroyed by virtue of environmental encroachment — that is, destroying the natural habitat. So these chimpanzees are being eliminated by virtue of their being an agricultural pest and by the fact that their habitat is being destroyed. So why not rescue them? The number of chimpanzees for AIDS research in the United States [is] somewhere in the hundreds and certainly, we need thousands.

Our capacity to rationalize our behaviour and needs is remarkable. 20 Chimpanzees have occupied their niche over tens of millennia of biological evolution. *We* are newcomers who have encroached on *their* territory, yet by defining them as *pests* we render them expendable. As Redmond says, "The fact that the chimpanzee is our nearest zoological relative makes it perhaps the unluckiest animal on earth, because what the kinship has come to mean is that we feel free to do most of the things to a chimp that we mercifully refrain from doing to each other."

And so the impending epidemic of AIDS confronts us not only with 21 our inhumanity to each other but to other species.

TYPES OF WRITING:
description, example/illustration, personal experience

Topics for Discussion

1. What do the first two paragraphs of this essay do? Would the essay work as well if these two paragraphs were deleted?
2. Although Suzuki's topic is the pain that animals suffer, the word "pain" does not appear until near the end of paragraph 6. What other words or expressions does he use instead? Does he appear to be deliberately withholding this word? If so, what effect would he achieve by doing so?
3. In the first part of his essay Suzuki recounts three anecdotes from his personal life. How do these stories help to emphasize his key point? Are they all equally effective?

Topics for Writing

1. "What gives us the right to exploit other living organisms as we see fit?" asks Suzuki in paragraph 8. Write an essay in response to this question as it applies to some area of "exploitation" with which you are familiar. Although you may want to address areas such as hunting, fishing, and medical research, with which Suzuki's essay deals, you may find it easier to concentrate on some other human use of animals, such as farming, horse riding or racing, training animals to perform tricks, or even keeping animals in zoos or as pets.
2. Using "the pain of animals" as your topic, write an essay in which you describe the experiences you have had with animals that appeared to be suffering.

Late Night Thoughts on Listening to Mahler's Ninth Symphony

Lewis Thomas

I cannot listen to Mahler's Ninth Symphony with anything like the old 1
melancholy mixed with the high pleasure I used to take from this music.
There was a time, not long ago, when what I heard, especially in the
final movement, was an open acknowledgment of death and at the same
time a quiet celebration of the tranquillity connected to the process. I
took this music as a metaphor for reassurance, confirming my own strong
hunch that the dying of every living creature, the most natural of all
experiences, has to be a peaceful experience. I rely on nature. The long
passages on all the strings at the end, as close as music can come to
expressing silence itself, I used to hear as Mahler's idea of leave-taking at
its best. But always, I have heard this music as a solitary, private listener,
thinking about death.

Now I hear it differently. I cannot listen to the last movement of the 2
Mahler Ninth without the door-smashing intrusion of a huge new thought:
death everywhere, the dying of everything, the end of humanity. The
easy sadness expressed with such gentleness and delicacy by that repeated
phrase on faded strings, over and over again, no longer comes to me as
old, familiar news of the cycle of living and dying. All through the last
notes my mind swarms with images of a world in which the thermo-
nuclear bombs have begun to explode, in New York and San Francisco,
in Moscow and Leningrad, in Paris, in Paris, in Paris. In Oxford and
Cambridge, in Edinburgh. I cannot push away the thought of a cloud of
radioactivity drifting along the Engadin, from the Moloja Pass to Ftan,
killing off the part of the earth I love more than any other part.

I am old enough by this time to be used to the notion of dying, 3
saddened by the glimpse when it has occurred but only transiently
knocked down, able to regain my feet quickly at the thought of continuity, any day. I have acquired and held in affection until very recently
another sideline of an idea which serves me well at dark times: the life of
the earth is the same as the life of an organism: the great round being
possesses a mind: the mind contains an infinite number of thoughts and
memories: when I reach my time I may find myself still hanging around
in some sort of midair, one of those small thoughts, drawn back into the
memory of the earth: in that peculiar sense I will be alive.

Now all that has changed. I cannot think that way anymore. Not 4
while those things are still in place, aimed everywhere, ready for
launching.

This is a bad enough thing for the people in my generation. We can 5
put up with it, I suppose, since we must. We are moving along anyway,
like it or not. I can even set aside my private fancy about hanging around,
in midair.

6   What I cannot imagine, what I cannot put up with, the thought that keeps grinding its way into my mind, making the Mahler into a hideous noise close to killing me, is what it would be like to be young. How do the young stand it? How can they keep their sanity? If I were very young, sixteen or seventeen years old, I think I would begin, perhaps very slowly and imperceptibly, to go crazy.

7   There is a short passage near the very end of the Mahler in which the almost vanishing violins, all engaged in a sustained backward glance, are edged aside for a few bars by the cellos. Those lower notes pick up fragments from the first movement, as though prepared to begin everything all over again, and then the cellos subside and disappear, like an exhalation. I used to hear this as a wonderful few seconds of encouragement: we'll be back, we're still here, keep going, keep going.

8   Now, with a pamphlet in front of me on a corner of my desk, published by the Congressional Office of Technology Assessment, entitled *MX Basing*, an analysis of all the alternative strategies for placement and protection of hundreds of these missiles, each capable of creating artificial suns to vaporize a hundred Hiroshimas, collectively capable of destroying the life of any continent, I cannot hear the same Mahler. Now, those cellos sound in my mind like the opening of all the hatches and the instant before ignition.

9   If I were sixteen or seventeen years old, I would not feel the cracking of my own brain, but I would know for sure that the whole world was coming unhinged. I can remember with some clarity what it was like to be sixteen. I had discovered the Brahms symphonies. I knew that there was something going on in the late Beethoven quartets that I would have to figure out, and I knew that there was plenty of time ahead for all the figuring I would ever have to do. I had never heard of Mahler. I was in no hurry. I was a college sophomore and had decided that Wallace Stevens and I possessed a comprehensive understanding of everything needed for a life. The years stretched away forever ahead, forever. My great-great grandfather had come from Wales, leaving his signature in the family Bible on the same page that carried, a century later, my father's signature. It never crossed my mind to wonder about the twenty-first century; it was just there, given, somewhere in the sure distance.

10   The man on television, Sunday midday, middle-aged and solid, nice-looking chap, all the facts at his fingertips, more dependable looking than most high-school principals, is talking about civilian defense, his responsibility in Washington. It can make an enormous difference, he is saying. Instead of the outright death of eighty million American citizens in twenty minutes, he says, we can, by careful planning and practice, get that number down to only forty million, maybe even twenty. The thing to do, he says, is to evacuate the cities quickly and have everyone get under shelter in the countryside. That way we can recover, and meanwhile we will have retaliated, incinerating all of Soviet society, he says. What about radioactive fallout? he is asked. Well, he says. Anyway, he says, if

the Russians know they can only destroy forty million of us instead of eighty million, this will deter them. Of course, he adds, they have the capacity to kill all two hundred and twenty million of us if they were to try real hard, but they know we can do the same to them. If the figure is only forty million this will deter them, not worth the trouble, not worth the risk. Eighty million would be another matter, we should guard ourselves against losing that many all at once, he says.

If I were sixteen or seventeen years old and had to listen to that, or 11 read things like that, I would want to give up listening and reading. I would begin thinking up new kinds of sounds, different from any music heard before, and I would be twisting and turning to rid myself of human language.

TYPES OF WRITING:
description, personal experience

Topics for Discussion

1. Would Thomas's characterization of himself at sixteen encourage identification in contemporary sixteen-year-olds?
2. Is this essay written for a particular audience? If so, what is this primary audience? How can you tell?
3. Why does Thomas approach the contemporary acceptance of nuclear capability using American examples rather than focusing on the Soviets?

Topics for Writing

1. Concentrating on your own impressions of the future, characterize the attitude of your generation as it looks toward the twenty-first century.
2. Write a response to Thomas's questions, "How do the young stand it?" and "How can they keep their sanity?"
3. Use your subjective reactions to a story, a piece of music, or a movie as a starting point for an essay on an aspect of human nature you consider important.

Nurses

Lewis Thomas

1   When my mother became a registered nurse at Roosevelt Hospital, in 1903, there was no question in anyone's mind about what nurses did as professionals. They did what the doctors ordered. The attending physician would arrive for his ward rounds in the early morning, and when he arrived at the ward office the head nurse would be waiting for him, ready to take his hat and coat, and his cane, and she would stand while he had his cup of tea before starting. Entering the ward, she would hold the door for him to go first, then his entourage of interns and medical students, then she followed. At each bedside, after he had conducted his examination and reviewed the patient's progress, he would tell the nurse what needed doing that day, and she would write it down on the part of the chart reserved for nursing notes. An hour or two later he would be gone from the ward, and the work of the rest of the day and the night to follow was the nurse's frenetic occupation. In addition to the stipulated orders, she had an endless list of routine things to do, all learned in her two years of nursing school: the beds had to be changed and made up with fresh sheets by an exact geometric design of folding and tucking impossible for anyone but a trained nurse; the patients had to be washed head to foot; bedpans had to be brought, used, emptied, and washed; temperatures had to be taken every four hours and meticulously recorded on the chart; enemas were to be given; urine and stool samples collected, labeled, and sent off to the laboratory; throughout the day and night, medications of all sorts, usually pills and various vegetable extracts and tinctures, had to be carried on trays from bed to bed. At most times of the year about half of the forty or so patients on the ward had typhoid fever, which meant that the nurse couldn't simply move from bed to bed in the performance of her duties; each typhoid case was screened from the other patients, and the nurse was required to put on a new gown and wash her hands in disinfectant before approaching the bedside. Patients with high fevers were sponged with cold alcohol at frequent intervals. The late-evening back rub was the rite of passage into sleep.

2   In addition to the routine, workaday schedule, the nurse was responsible for responding to all calls from the patients, and it was expected that she would do so on the run. Her rounds, scheduled as methodical progressions around the ward, were continually interrupted by these calls. It was up to her to evaluate each situation quickly: a sudden abdominal pain in a typhoid patient might signify intestinal perforation; the abrupt onset of weakness, thirst, and pallor meant intestinal hemorrhage; the coughing up of gross blood by a tuberculous patient was an emergency. Some of the calls came from neighboring patients on the way to recovery; patients on open wards always kept close eye on each other: the man in the next bed might slip into coma or seem to be dying, or be indeed dead. For such emergencies the nurse had to get word

immediately to the doctor on call, usually the intern assigned to the ward, who might be off in the outpatient department or working in the diagnostic laboratory (interns of that day did all the laboratory work themselves; technicians had not yet been invented) or in his room. Nurses were not allowed to give injections or to do such emergency procedures as spinal punctures or chest taps, but they were expected to know when such maneuvers were indicated and to be ready with appropriate trays of instruments when the intern arrived on the ward.

It was an exhausting business, but by my mother's accounts it was 3 the most satisfying and rewarding kind of work. As a nurse she was a low person in the professional hierarchy, always running from place to place on orders from the doctors, subject as well to strict discipline from her own administrative superiors on the nursing staff, but none of this came through in her recollections. What she remembered was her usefulness.

Whenever my father talked to me about nurses and their work, he 4 spoke with high regard for them as professionals. Although it was clear in his view that the task of the nurses was to do what the doctor told them to, it was also clear that he admired them for being able to do a lot of things he couldn't possibly do, had never been trained to do. On his own rounds later on, when he became an attending physician himself, he consulted the ward nurse for her opinion about problem cases and paid careful attention to her observations and chart notes. In his own days of intern training (perhaps partly under my mother's strong influence, I don't know) he developed a deep and lasting respect for the whole nursing profession.

I have spent all of my professional career in close association with, 5 and close dependency on, nurses, and like many of my faculty colleagues, I've done a lot of worrying about the relationship between medicine and nursing. During most of this century the nursing profession has been having a hard time of it. It has been largely, although not entirely, an occupation for women, and sensitive issues of professional status, complicated by the special issue of the changing role of women in modern society, have led to a standoffish, often adversarial relationship between nurses and doctors. Already swamped by an increasing load of routine duties, nurses have been obliged to take on more and more purely administrative tasks: keeping the records in order; making sure the supplies are on hand for every sort of ward emergency; supervising the activities of the new paraprofessional group called LPNs (licensed practical nurses), who now perform much of the bedside work once done by RNs (registered nurses); overseeing ward maids, porters, and cleaners; seeing to it that patients scheduled for X rays are on their way to the X-ray department on time. Therefore, they have to spend more of their time at desks in the ward office and less time at the bedsides. Too late maybe, the nurses have begun to realize that they are gradually being excluded from the one duty which had previously been their most important reward but which had been so taken for granted that nobody mentioned it in listing the duties of a nurse: close personal contact with patients. Along with everything else nurses did in the long day's work, making up for all the tough and sometimes demeaning jobs assigned to them, they had the matchless opportunity to be useful friends to great numbers of human beings in trouble. They listened to their patients all day long and through the night, they gave comfort and reassurance to the patients and their families, they got to know them as friends, they were depended on. To contemplate the loss of this part of their work has been the deepest worry for nurses at large, and for the faculties responsible for the curricula of the nation's new and expanding nursing schools. The issue lies at the center of the running argument between medical school and nursing school administrators, but it is never clearly stated. Nursing education has been upgraded in recent years. Almost all the former hospital schools, which took in high-school graduates and provided an RN certificate after two or three years, have been replaced by schools attached to colleges and universities, with a four-year curriculum leading simultaneously to a bachelor's degree and an RN certificate.

6   The doctors worry that nurses are trying to move away from their historical responsibilities to medicine (meaning, really, to the doctors' orders). The nurses assert that they are their own profession, responsible for their own standards, coequal colleagues with physicians, and they do not wish to become mere ward administrators or technicians (although some of them, carrying the new and prestigious title of "nurse practitioner," are being trained within nursing schools to perform some of the most complex technological responsibilities in hospital emergency rooms and intensive care units). The doctors claim that what the nurses really want is to become substitute psychiatrists. The nurses reply that they have unavoidable responsibilities for the mental health and well-being of their patients, and that these are different from the doctors' tasks. Eventually the arguments will work themselves out, and some sort of agreement will be reached, but if it is to be settled intelligently, some way will have to be found to preserve and strengthen the traditional and highly personal nurse-patient relationship.

7   I have had a fair amount of firsthand experience with the issue, having been an apprehensive patient myself off and on over a three-year period on the wards of the hospital for which I work. I am one up on most of my physician friends because of this experience. I know some things they do not know about what nurses do.

8   One thing the nurses do is to hold the place together. It is an astonishment, which every patient feels from time to time, observing the affairs of a large, complex hospital from the vantage point of his bed, that the whole institution doesn't fly to pieces. A hospital operates by the constant interplay of powerful forces pulling away at each other in different directions, each force essential for getting necessary things done, but always at odds with each other. The intern staff is an almost irresistible force in

itself, learning medicine by doing medicine, assuming all the responsi- bility within reach, pushing against an immovable attending and admin- istrative staff, and frequently at odds with the nurses. The attending physicians are individual entrepreneurs trying to run small cottage in- dustries at each bedside. The diagnostic laboratories are feudal fiefdoms, prospering from the insatiable demands for their services from the interns and residents. The medical students are all over the place, learning as best they can and complaining that they are not, as they believe they should be, at the epicenter of everyone's concern. Each individual worker in the place, from the chiefs of surgery to the dieticians to the ward maids, porters, and elevator operators, lives and works in the conviction that the whole apparatus would come to a standstill without his or her individual contribution, and in one sense or another each of them is right.

My discovery, as a patient first on the medical service and later in surgery, is that the institution is held together, *glued* together, enabled to function as an organism, by the nurses and by nobody else.   9

The nurses, the good ones anyway (and all the ones on my floor were good), make it their business to know everything that is going on. They spot errors before errors can be launched. They know everything written on the chart. Most important of all, they know their patients as unique human beings, and they soon get to know the close relatives and friends. Because of this knowledge, they are quick to sense apprehensions and act on them. The average sick person in a large hospital feels at risk of getting lost, with no identity left beyond a name and a string of numbers on a plastic wristband, in danger always of being whisked off on a litter to the wrong place to have the wrong procedure done, or worse still, not being whisked off at the right time. The attending physician or the house officer, on rounds and usually in a hurry, can murmur a few reassuring words on his way out the door, but it takes a confident, competent, and cheerful nurse, there all day long and in and out of the room on one chore or another through the night, to bolster one's confi- dence that the situation is indeed manageable and not about to get out of hand.   10

Knowing what I know, I am all for the nurses. If they are to continue their professional feud with the doctors, if they want their professional status enhanced and their pay increased, if they infuriate the doctors by their claims to be equal professionals, if they ask for the moon, I am on their side.   11

TYPES OF WRITING:
comparison, description, example/illustration, personal experience

Topics for Discussion

1. Thomas draws from a wealth of experience in forming his opinion of nurses — his experience with his parents, his own experience during many years as a doctor, and his experience as a patient. Why, given his laudatory approach to the nursing profession in this essay, does he draw less on his experience as a doctor than on what he learned from his parents and from his experience as a patient?

2. While Thomas's virtually unqualified praise of nurses would no doubt be welcome within the nursing profession, resolving the contemporary conflicts he notes regarding the role of nurses would require support from doctors and hospital administrators, too. Would his support for nurses be more likely to influence a knowledgeable, unconvinced audience if he had concerned himself more with analyzing particular issues and less with general praise?

3. How appropriate is Thomas's approach in this essay for winning assent from persons who are not professionally involved in health care?

Topics for Writing

1. Write an essay commenting on the way some social institution — a hospital, or perhaps a school, a university, or some government department — deals with individuals, basing your views on personal experience.

2. Concentrating on the details of the work involved, write an essay revealing the value of some occupation in which you have worked or hope to work.

The Shame of Hunger

Elie Wiesel

I have been obsessed with the idea of hunger for years and years because 1
I have seen what hunger can do to human beings. It is the easiest way
for a tormenter to dehumanize another human being. When I think of
hunger, I see images: emaciated bodies, swollen bellies, long bony arms
pleading for mercy, motionless skeletons. How can one look at these
images without losing sleep?

And eyes, my God, eyes. Eyes that pierce your consciousness and 2
tear your heart. How can one run away from those eyes? The eyes of a
mother who carries her dead child in her arms, not knowing where to
go, or where to stop. At one moment you think that she would keep on
going, going, going — to the end of the world. Except she wouldn't go
very far, for the end of the world, for her, is there. Or the eyes of the old
grandfather, who probably wonders where creation had gone wrong,
and whether it was all worthwhile to create a family, to have faith in the
future, to transmit misery from generation to generation, whether it was
worth it to wager on humankind.

And then, the eyes of all eyes, the eyes of children, so dark, so 3
immense, so deep, so focused and yet at the same time, so wide and so
vague. What do they see? What do hungry children's eyes see? Death?
Nothingness? God? And what if they saw us, all of us, in our complacency
if not complicity? And what if their eyes are the eyes of our judges?

Hunger and death, death and starvation, starvation and shame. Poor 4
men and women who yesterday were proud members of their tribes,
bearers of ancient culture and lore, and who are now wandering among
corpses. What is so horrifying in hunger is that it makes the individual
death an anonymous death. In times of hunger, the individual death has
lost its uniqueness. Scores of hungry people die daily, and those who
mourn for them will die the next day, and the others will have no strength
left to mourn.

Hunger in ancient times represented the ultimate malediction to so- 5
ciety. Rich and poor, young and old, kings and servants, lived in fear of
drought. They joined the priests in prayer for rain. Rain meant harvest,
harvest meant food, food meant life, just as lack of food meant death. It
still does.

Hunger and humiliation. A hungry person experiences an over- 6
whelming feeling of shame. All desires, all aspirations, all dreams lose
their lofty qualities and relate to food alone. I may testify to something
that I have witnessed, in certain places at certain times, those people
who were reduced by hunger, diminished by hunger, they did not think
about theology, nor did they think about God or philosophy or literature.
They thought of a piece of bread. A piece of bread was, to them, God,
because a piece of bread then filled one's universe. Diminished by hun-

ger, man's spirit is diminished as well. His fantasy wanders in quest of bread. His prayer rises toward a bowl of milk.

7   Thus the shame.

8   In Hebrew, the word hunger is linked to shame. The prophet Ezekiel speaks about "Kherpat raav," the shame of hunger. Of all the diseases, of all the natural diseases and catastrophes, the only one that is linked to shame in Scripture is hunger — the shame of hunger. Shame is associated neither with sickness nor even with death, only with hunger. For man can live with pain, but no man ought to endure hunger.

9   Hunger means torture, the worst kind of torture. The hungry person is tortured by more than one sadist alone. He or she is tortured, every minute, by all men, by all women. And by all the elements surrounding him or her. The wind. The sun. The stars. By the rustling of trees and the silence of night. The minutes that pass so slowly, so slowly. Can you imagine time, can you image time, when you are hungry?

10   And to condone hunger means to accept torture, someone else's torture.

11   Hunger is isolating; it may not and cannot be experienced vicariously. He who never felt hunger can never know its real effects, both tangible and intangible. Hunger defies imagination; it even defies memory. Hunger is felt only in the present.

12   There is a story about the great French-Jewish composer Daniel Halevy who met a poor poet: "Is it true," he asked, "that you endured hunger in your youth?" "Yes," said the poet. "I envy you," said the composer. "I never felt hunger."

13   And Gaston Bachelard, the famous philosopher, voiced his view on the matter, saying, "My prayer to heaven is not, 'Oh God, give us our daily bread, but give us our daily hunger.'"

14   I don't find these anecdotes funny. These anecdotes were told about and by people who were not hungry. There is no romanticism in hunger, there is no beauty in hunger, no creativity in hunger. There is no inspiration in hunger. Only shame. And solitude. Hunger creates its own prison walls; it is impossible to demolish them, to avoid them, to ignore them.

15   Thus, if hunger inspires anything at all, it is, and must be, only the war against hunger.

16   Hunger is not a matter of choice. Of course, you may say, but what about the hunger striker? Haven't they chosen to deprive themselves of nourishment, aren't they hungry? Yes, but not the same way. First, they alone suffer, those around them do not. Second, they are given the possibility to stop any time they so choose, any time they win, any time their cause is attained. Not so the people in Africa. Not so the people in Asia. Their hunger is irrevocable. And last, hunger strikers confer a meaning, a purpose, upon their ordeal. Not so the victims in Ethiopia or Sudan. Their hunger is senseless. And implacable.

17   The worst stage in hunger is to see its reflection in one's brother,

one's father, one's child. Hunger renders powerless those who suffer its consequences. Can you imagine a mother unable, helpless, to alleviate her child's agony? There is the abyss in shame. There, suffering and hunger and shame multiply.

In times of hunger, family relations break down. The father is impo- 18 tent, his authority gone, the mother is desperate, and the children, the children, under the weight of accumulated suffering and hunger, grow older and older, and soon, they will be older than their grandparents.

But then, on the other hand, perhaps of all of the woes that threaten 19 and plague the human condition, hunger alone can be curtailed, attenuated, appeased, and ultimately vanquished, not by destiny, nor by the heavens, but by human beings. We cannot fight earthquakes, but we can fight hunger. Hence our responsibility for its victims. Responsibility is the key word. Our tradition emphasizes the question, rather than the answer. For there is a "quest" in question, but there is "response" in responsibility. And this responsibility is what makes us human, or the lack of it, inhuman.

Hunger differs from other cataclysms such as floods in that it can be 20 prevented or stopped so easily. One gesture of generosity, one act of humanity, may put an end to it, at least for one person. A piece of bread, a bowl of rice or soup makes a difference. And I wonder, what would happen, just imagine, what would happen, if every nation, every industrialized or non-industrialized nation, would simply decide to sell one aircraft, and for the money, feed the hungry. Why shouldn't they? Why shouldn't the next economic summit, which includes the wealthiest, most powerful, the richest nations in the world, why shouldn't they decide that since there are so many aircrafts, why shouldn't they say, "Let's sell just one, just one, to take care of the shame and the hunger and the suffering of millions of people."

So the prophet's expression, "the shame of hunger," must be under- 21 stood differently. When we speak of our responsibility for the hungry, we must go to the next step and say that the expression "shame of hunger" does not apply to the hungry. It applies to those who refuse to help the hungry. Shame on those who could feed the hungry, but are too busy to do so.

Millions of human beings constantly are threatened in Africa and 22 Asia, and even in our own country, the homeless and the hungry. Many are going to die of starvation, and it will be our fault. For we could save them, and if we do not, we had better have a good reason why we don't.

If we could airlift food and sustenance and toothpaste to Berlin in 23 1948, surely we could do as much for all the countries, Ethiopia and Sudan and Mozambique and Bangladesh, in the year 1990. Nations capable of sending and retrieving vehicles in space must be able to save human lives on earth.

Let our country, and then other countries, see in hunger an emergency 24 that must be dealt with *right now*. Others, our allies, will follow. Private relief often has been mobilized in the past: Jews and Christians, Moslems and Buddhists have responded to dramatic appeals from the African desert. One of my most rewarding moments was when I went to the Cambodian border 10 years ago and saw there the misery, the weakness, the despair, the resignation, of the victims.

25   But I also saw the extraordinary international community motivated by global solidarity to help them. And who were they? They represented humankind at its best: there were Jews and Christians and Moslems and Buddhists from all over the world. And if ever I felt proud of the human condition, it was then. It is possible to help, but private help is insufficient. Government-organized help is required; only governments can really help solve this tragedy that has cosmic repercussions.

26   We must save the victims of hunger simply because they *can* be saved. We look therefore at the horror-filled pictures, when we dare to look, day after day. And I cannot help but remember those who had surrounded us elsewhere, years and years ago. Oh, I do not wish to make comparisons. I never do. But I do have the right to invoke the past, not as a point of analogy, but as a term of reference. I refuse to draw analogies with the Jewish tragedy during the era of darkness; I still believe and will always believe that no event ought to be compared to that event. But I do believe that human tragedies, all human tragedies, are and must be related to it. In other words, it is because one people has been singled out for extinction that others were marked for slavery. It is because entire communities were wiped out then that others were condemned to die later in other parts of the planet. All events are intertwined.

27   And it is because we have known hunger that we now must eliminate hunger. It is because we have been subjected to shame that we must now oppose shame. It is because we have witnessed humanity at its worst that we now must appeal to humanity at its best.

TYPES OF WRITING:
definition, description, personal experience

Topics for Discussion

1. What is unusual about the transition between the first and second paragraphs? Where else does Wiesel use this kind of transition? Do you believe that this is an effective stylistic device? Why or why not?
2. No reader needs to be persuaded that starvation is evil. What, then, is the author trying to persuade the reader of?
3. How does the structure of the concluding paragraph and of its individual sentences emphasize meaning?

Topics for Writing

1. In paragraph 1 Wiesel says: "When I think of hunger, I see images: emaciated bodies, swollen bellies, long bony arms pleading for mercy, motionless skeletons." What images of hunger are there in your own experience? Your essay need not follow the structure used by Wiesel.

2. "Hunger in ancient times represented the ultimate malediction to society." What, in your opinion, represents the "ultimate malediction" to society in our time? The society you deal with will likely be Canadian, although you may choose another if you know it well.

The Tyranny of the Clock

George Woodcock

1 In no characteristic is existing society in the West so sharply distinguished from the earlier societies, whether of Europe or of the East, as in its conception of time. To the ancient Chinese or Greek, to the Arab herdsman or the Mexican peon of today, time is represented by the cyclic processes of nature, the alternation of day and night, the passage from season to season. The nomads and the farmers measured and still measure their day from sunrise to sunset, and their year in terms of seed-time and harvest, of the falling leaf and the ice thawing on the lakes and rivers. The farmer worked according to the elements, the craftsman for as long as he felt it necessary to perfect his product. Time was seen as a process of natural change, and men were not concerned in its exact measurement. For this reason civilizations highly developed in other respects had the most primitive means of measuring time: the hourglass with its trickling sand or dripping water, the sundial, useless on a dull day, and the candle or lamp whose unburnt remnant of oil or wax indicated the hours. All these devices were approximate and inexact, and were often rendered unreliable by the weather or the personal laziness of the tender. Nowhere in the ancient or the mediaeval world were more than a tiny minority of men concerned with time in the terms of mathematical exactitude.

2 Modern, western man, however, lives in a world which runs according to the mechanical and mathematical symbols of clock time. The clock dictates his movements and inhibits his actions. The clock turns time from a process of nature into a commodity that can be measured and bought and sold like soap or sultanas. And because, without some means of exact timekeeping, industrial capitalism could never have developed and could not continue to exploit the workers, the clock represents an element of mechanical tyranny in the lives of modern men more potent than any individual exploiter or than any other machine. It is therefore valuable to trace the historical process by which the clock influenced the social development of modern European civilization.

3 It is a frequent circumstance of history that a culture or a civilization develops the device that will later be used for its destruction. The ancient Chinese, for example, invented gunpowder, which was developed by the military experts of the West and eventually led to the Chinese civilization itself being destroyed by the high explosives of modern warfare. Similarly, the supreme achievement of the craftsmen of the mediaeval cities of Europe was the invention of the clock, which, with its revolutionary alteration of the concept of time, materially assisted the growth of the Middle Ages.

4 There is a tradition that the clock appeared in the eleventh century, as a device for ringing bells at regular intervals in the monasteries, which, with the regimented life they imposed on their inmates, were the closest

258

social approximation in the Middle Ages to the factory of today. The first authenticated clock, however, appeared in the thirteenth century, and it was not until the fourteenth century that clocks became common as ornaments of the public buildings in German cities.

These early clocks, operated by weights, were not particularly accurate, and it was not until the sixteenth century that any great reliability was attained. In England, for instance, the clock at Hampton Court, made in 1540, is said to have been the first accurate clock in the country. And even the accuracy of the sixteenth-century clocks is relative, for they were equipped only with hour-hands. The idea of measuring time in minutes and seconds had been thought out by the early mathematicians as far back as the fourteenth century, but it was not until the invention of the pendulum in 1657 that sufficient accuracy was attained to permit the addition of a minute-hand, and the second-hand did not appear until the eighteenth century. These two centuries, it should be observed, were those in which capitalism grew to such an extent that it was able to take advantage of the techniques of the Industrial Revolution to establish its economic domination over society.

The clock, as Lewis Mumford has pointed out, is the key machine of the machine age, both for its influence on technics and for its influence on the habits of men. Technically, the clock was the first really automatic machine that attained any importance in the life of man. Previous to its invention, the common machines were of such a nature that their operation depended on some external and unreliable force, such as human or animal muscles, water, or wind. It is true that the Greeks had invented a number of primitive automatic machines, but these were used, like Hero's steam engine, either for obtaining "supernatural" effects in the temples or for amusing the tyrants of Levantine cities. But the clock was the first automatic machine that attained public importance and a social function. Clock-making became the industry from which men learnt the elements of machine-making and gained the technical skill that was to produce the complicated machinery of the Industrial Revolution.

Socially the clock had a more radical influence than any other machine, in that it was the means by which the regularization and regimentation of life necessary for an exploiting system of industry could best be assured. The clock provided a means by which time — a category so elusive that no philosophy has yet determined its nature — could be measured concretely in the more tangible terms of space provided by the circumference of a clock dial. Time as duration became disregarded, and men began to talk and think always of "lengths" of time, just as if they were talking of lengths of calico. And time, being now measurable in mathematical symbols, was regarded as a commodity that could be bought and sold in the same way as any other commodity.

The new capitalists, in particular, became rabidly time-conscious. Time, here symbolizing the labour of the workers, was regarded by them almost as if it were the chief raw material of industry. "Time is money" was one of the key slogans of capitalist ideology, and the timekeeper was the most significant of the new types of official introduced by the capitalist dispensation.

9   In the early factories the employers went so far as to manipulate their clocks or sound their factory whistles at the wrong times in order to defraud the workers of a little of this valuable new commodity. Later such practices became less frequent, but the influence of the clock imposed regularity on the lives of the majority of men that had previously been known only in the monasteries. Men actually became like clocks, acting with a repetitive regularity which had no resemblance to the rhythmic life of a natural being. They became, as the Victorian phrase put it, "as regular as clockwork." Only in the country districts where the natural lives of animals and plants and the elements still dominated existence did any large proportion of the population fail to succumb to the deadly tick of monotony.

10   At first this new attitude to time, this new regularity of life, was imposed by the clock-owning masters on the unwilling poor. The factory slave reacted in his spare time by living with a chaotic irregularity which characterized the gin-sodden slums of early-nineteenth-century industrialism. Men fled to the timeless worlds of drink or Methodist inspiration. But gradually the idea of regularity spread downwards and among the workers. Nineteenth-century religion and morality played their part by proclaiming the sin of "wasting time." The introduction of mass-produced watches and clocks in the 1850s spread time-consciousness among those who had previously merely reacted to the stimulus of the knocker-up or the factory whistle. In the church and the school, in the office and the workshop, punctuality was held up as the greatest of the virtues.

11   Out of this slavish dependence on mechanical time which spread insidiously into every class in the nineteenth century, there grew up the demoralizing regimentation which today still characterizes factory life. The man who fails to conform faces social disapproval and economic ruin — unless he drops out into a nonconformist way of life in which time ceases to be of prime importance. Hurried meals, the regular morning and evening scramble for trains or buses, the strain of having to work to time schedules, all contribute, by digestive and nervous disturbance, to ruin health and shorten life.

12   Nor does the financial imposition of regularity tend, in the long run, to greater efficiency. Indeed, the quality of the product is usually much poorer, because the employer, regarding time as a commodity which he has to pay for, forces the operative to maintain such a speed that his work must necessarily be skimped. Quantity rather than quality becoming the criterion, the enjoyment is taken out of the work itself, and the worker in his turn becomes a "clock-watcher," concerned only with when he will be able to escape to the scanty and monotonous leisure of industrial society, in which he "kills time" by cramming in as much time-scheduled and mechanical enjoyment of cinema, radio, and newspaper as his wage

packet and his tiredness will allow. Only if he is willing to accept the hazards of living by his faith or his wits can the man without money avoid living as a slave to the clock.

The problem of the clock is, in general, similar to that of the machine. 13
Mechanized time is valuable as a means of co-ordinating activities in a highly developed society, just as the machine is valuable as a means of reducing unnecessary labour to a minimum. Both are valuable for the contribution they make to the smooth running of society, and should be used in so far as they assist men to co-operate efficiently and to eliminate monotonous toil and social confusion. But neither should be allowed to dominate men's lives as they do today.

Now the movement of the clock sets the tempo of men's lives — 14
they become the servants of the concept of time which they themselves have made, and are held in fear, like Frankenstein by his own monster. In a sane and free society such an arbitrary domination of man's functions by either clock or machine would obviously be out of the question. The domination of man by man-made machines is even more ridiculous than the domination of man by man. Mechanical time would be relegated to its true function of a means of reference and coordination, and men would return again to a balanced view of life no longer dominated by time-regulation and the worship of the clock. Complete liberty implies freedom from the tyranny of abstractions as well as from the rule of men.

TYPES OF WRITING:
cause and effect, description

Topics for Discussion

1. Do the title and the opening sentence of this essay make you want to read on? Why?
2. Consider the pattern of development in Woodcock's opening paragraph. How does the structure of this paragraph help Woodcock make his point clearly and emphatically?
3. In the final sentence of paragraph 13, Woodcock insists that neither clock nor machine "should be allowed to dominate men's lives as they do today." Does he explain his proposed alternative clearly and convincingly? What exactly is his alternative?
4. The clock obviously exercises a certain amount of control over any person living in civilized society today. But does this control amount to "tyranny"? Does the clock exercise a tyrannical effect in your own life?

Topics for Writing

1. Write an essay arguing that the generalization in Woodcock's opening sentence exaggerates the importance of time. Support your view by explaining how some other conception such as space, personal property, gender roles, is even more significant in our society than time.

2. Write an essay about the influence some technological innovation other than the clock exerts in contemporary life. Possible examples would be the automobile, the television, or the computer, but there are many others to choose from. Do not feel obligated to follow Woodcock's lead in emphasizing the negative aspects of the influence you explore.

Appendix 1:
Guiding Questions

QUESTIONING INFLUENCE IN YOUR OWN WRITING

Titles

In general, titles should generate interest but should not do so at the expense of threatening or offending any segment of the audience you are attempting to reach.

1. Will your title lead your audience to read what you have written? Can the title be revised to enhance interest?
2. Experiment with the title you have chosen: change the order of the words; compress your title into a much shorter form; change a declaration into a question, or vice versa. What results have you achieved?
3. Is your position on the subject clear in the title? If it is, will this forthrightness cause you to alienate an audience you want to reach? Is there a way of revising the title that will allow you to maintain interest while diminishing a potential threat to those who will disagree with your position?

Opening Paragraphs

Opening paragraphs should seize the readers' interest and make them eager to read on. They should lead readers to accept the writer, not as an opponent, but as a collaborator in their efforts to review and improve their thinking about the subject.

1. Is your position on the subject clear in the first part of your essay? Do you make it plain that you are thoroughly convinced that you are right? Or do you leave open the possibility of change on your part? What incentives does your opening provide for readers to keep on reading when they disagree with your position?
2. How do your opening paragraphs make the topic seem interesting or important: Do you challenge readers? Do you present an unusual idea or image? Do you question a commonly accepted belief? Do you make an outrageous statement? Do you promise to provide useful insights

or information? Would presenting a bare statement of the topic be valuable?

3. Do your opening paragraphs demonstrate knowledge and understanding of the topic? Do they make your authority to address the subject as convincing as possible?

4. Do you identify your primary audience for the piece in your opening paragraph? If you do, are you implicitly excluding important secondary audiences?

The Body of the Essay

The body of your essay should offer readers an original perspective or new information about the topic. It should also approach the topic in a way that will cause readers to continue reading; for instance, they may want to see how you will uphold beliefs they already hold, they may want to see how you will challenge their beliefs, or they may be interested in you as a writer.

1. Is your audience informed, entertained, and challenged directly?

2. If the body of your essay influences by informing, how does the structure of the essay shape understanding? Are opposing views given adequate coverage? Does your case become stronger at the end? Would re-ordering your main points make your conclusion more forceful?

3. Is your stance on the subject appropriate for your intended audience? Would tact or restraint at any point avoid alienating readers?

4. Is your vocabulary suited to your audience?

5. What is your tone: angry? conciliatory? detached? humorous? outraged? defensive? reflective? sarcastic? Would a change in tone help or hinder your attempt at persuasion? Would changing tone part way through your essay be an effective strategy?

6. To what emotions in your reader will your approach appeal: compassion? pride? anger? fear? Will the emotional effect of your essay reinforce its persuasive goal?

Ending and Total Effect

However complex the body of the essay may have been, the ending should pull all the material together so that your readers are left with a clear impression of one or two main points that will provide a direction for their future thinking about the subject.

1. Has writing the piece caused you to adjust your thinking on the subject? Have you added to your knowledge or understanding of the subject, with regard either to details or to major points? Does the essay need revision to reflect your final view? Will such revision affect the body of your essay?

2. Is your essay intended to change the views of your audience in the

short or the long term, or in both? (If you see your essay as part of a long-term campaign for change, you will be wise to make notes about possibilities for future reinforcement.)

3. What audience would your essay fail to influence? Why? Could you revise the essay to reach this audience without diminishing its success with other target groups? Or would a separate essay with a different approach be required?

QUESTIONING INFLUENCE IN YOUR READING

The questions below can be asked of any essay you read, although not all of them will apply to any one essay.

1. To what audience is this essay directed? How do you know?
2. How helpful (if at all) is the title in attracting the reader's interest? Does it help prepare readers to accept the writer's position?
3. When an essay appears to be based on logic, is there an underlying appeal to emotion? Which emotions are appealed to? How can you tell?
4. In your opinion, is any appeal to emotions successful?
5. What methods does the writer use to interest the reader?
6. After you have read the first two or three paragraphs, has the writer won your confidence? Explain why, or why not.
7. Does the writer assume that you are on her side? How is this assumption of agreement implied?
8. At what point do you realize where the writer stands on the issue? Once you know for certain, review the essay to see if you can find evidence of foreshadowing that might prepare readers to accept this position.
9. How does the writer deal with objections to her position? Can you think of any objections that the writer has not mentioned?
10. In an essay that is clearly narrative (or descriptive or expository or humorous, etc.) is there a hidden persuasive objective? What is it? How is the persuasive implication suggested?
11. In an essay that presents an overt argument, outline the main points and consider why they appear in the order they do. Could the persuasive force of the argument be strengthened by reorganization?
12. When a writer reveals that he is aware of counter-arguments to his position, how complete and objective is his presentation of these opposing views?
13. If a persuasive essay seems to be directed at a fairly specific audience, how does the writer go about engaging the interest of this audience?
14. If a writer claims to have examined both sides of an issue with care, are you convinced? Is there any evidence that the writer has, in fact, weighted one side more heavily than the other?

15. In which paragraph does the writer most clearly state the nature of the problem he wishes to discuss? Where in the essay does the writer most clearly state the solution to that problem?
16. Does the concluding paragraph of the essay have a persuasive point? If not, why not? If so, how effectively does this point serve as a conclusion to the whole essay?
17. Has reading this essay changed your mind about the subject? In what ways? If not, how has the writer failed?
18. Do you believe that the writer has succeeded in influencing you in the way that she intended? Why, specifically, has the writer succeeded or failed?

LOGICAL THINKING

There are many other ways of influencing readers besides logical argument, but writers cannot afford to ignore the conventions of argument. Many readers will recognize the more common flaws in reasoning — called fallacies. Readers do not need to know the term "logical fallacy" to recognize that something is wrong with an argument.

Formal argument is based on two fundamental lines of reasoning. **Deductive reasoning** builds on a standard pattern called a syllogism. There are several forms of syllogism, but the most common is the categorical syllogism, which works like basic algebra:

$$
\begin{array}{ll}
\text{if} & a = b \\
\text{and} & b = c \\
\text{then} & a = c
\end{array}
$$

or

Major Premise:	All men are mortal.
Minor Premise:	Donald is a man.
Conclusion:	Therefore, Donald is mortal.

In the categorical syllogism we can substitute a number of concepts — "greater than" or "less than," for example — for "equals," but the result is still the same: within the structure of the syllogism, proof, like a basic algebraic equation, is absolute.

In syllogistic reasoning, correct form is termed "valid." There are a number of ways that a syllogism can fail to be valid and a number of ways of representing validity, but validity is usually less of a problem than the more fundamental question of whether the premises upon which the syllogism depends are in fact true. What if a does not equal b? Or what if b does not equal c?

How do we determine the truth of premises on which deductive reasoning depends?

We test the truth of general assumptions by means of the other basic line of reasoning, called **inductive reasoning**. While deductive reasoning works from general premises to a definite, specific conclusion, inductive reasoning works from observed particulars toward general conclusions — toward the sorts of general conclusions that work in deductive reasoning: b_1, b_2, b_3, and b_4 all equal a, so b_5 very probably equals a too, particularly when observations run to b_{126} or b_{127}, but not certainly.

In a society where there are many generally accepted truths, such as the mediaeval idea that kings were destined by God to rule, deduction works well. But in our society, where scepticism has become a habit of mind and testing general ideas and assumptions, often using extremely sophisticated and rigorous scientific methods, is standard practice, arguments based largely on deduction prove much less convincing. Any syllogism, correctly structured though it may be, is only as true as the premises upon which it is based, and these depend on inductive proof. Recognition of this fundamental dependency is why logical arguments today generally rely more heavily on inductive reasoning — working whenever possible from specific, verifiable instances toward a generalization — than on deduction.

Among the most useful insights provided by the traditions of logical argument are the fallacies of reasoning, which amount to breaking the rules of pure logic. On the one hand, an argument that depends on fallacious reasoning will be vulnerable to attack on logical grounds; on the other, particularly where emotionally charged issues, such as abortion, capital punishment, or the environment are involved, fallacies can become potent tools for influence.

TESTING LOGIC

1. *Personal Attacks.* Are attacks on the character or competence of those who disagree with your views relevant to the matter under consideration? Will noting the faults of individuals or groups lend credibility to your position? Or will it distract readers from the issues? Will a personal attack arouse sympathy for your opponents?
2. *False Authority.* Are those you cite as sharing or supporting your position recognized authorities of your subject?
3. *Popularity.* Have you simply taken for granted that the popularity of your position strengthens it? Have you explained why your position is or is becoming popular?
4. *Jumping to Conclusions.* Have you formed generalizations on the basis of inadequate evidence? Have you assumed that your personal experience is typical? If you are basing a conclusion on a limited number of sample instances, have you given fair consideration to alternative interpretations?
5. *Assumed Cause and Effect.* Are you leaping to the conclusion that an event or development that follows another is caused by it? Have you explained how the causal relationship works? Have you considered other possible interpretations fairly?

6. *Appeal to Pity.* Is an emotional appeal relevant to your subject? Is it exaggerated? Is an appeal to pity based on generalizations or, even better, on particular representative instances described in detail? If you have focused an appeal to pity on one person or group, for example, the family of a person condemned to prison, have you adequately considered the claim to pity by others involved, for example, the victim of the crime?

7. *False Analogy.* Is your analogy (extended comparison for the purpose of illustration) appropriate? Your analogy may be extremely useful in explaining a concept, but are you assuming that it amounts to proof?

Appendix 2:
Biographical Notes

Barbara Amiel
Barbara Amiel is a Canadian journalist who has worked in films, for the CBC, and as Editor of the *Toronto Sun*. She is now a regular columnist for both *Maclean's* and the *Sunday Times*. She published *Confessions* in 1990.

Margaret Atwood
Margaret Atwood is one of Canada's most respected writers of poetry, fiction, and literary and social criticism. She won the Governor General's Award for poetry in 1966, when she was only twenty-seven, and again, for fiction, in 1985. She has earned an international reputation with such novels as *Lady Oracle* (1976), *Life Before Man* (1979), and *The Handmaid's Tale* (1985).

Russell Baker
An American journalist who writes, often humorously, on social and political issues, Russell Baker won the Pulitzer Prize for journalism in 1979. He has published ten books, and his column in the *New York Times* has been carried by hundreds of newspapers across North America.

Sissela Bok
Sissela Bok has published three books, the titles of which indicate her principal concerns: *Moral Choice in Public and Private Life, Secrets: On the Ethics of Concealment and Revelations,* and *A Strategy for Peace: Human Values and the Threat of War*. She teaches medical ethics at Harvard University.

Anne Brennan
Anne Brennan is an American writer who has served as Director of the Institute for Academic Knowledge and Public Policy in Florida.

Harry Bruce
A Canadian journalist, Harry Bruce has published six books on a wide variety of subjects, including a history of the Central Trust Company, and *"You've Got Ten Minutes to Get That Flag Down,"* the proceedings of the 1986 Halifax conference on Canadian cultural policy.

Robertson Davies
One of Canada's most respected writers, Robertson Davies has been publishing books since the 1940s. In addition to the novels for which he is best known, his work includes journalism, humour, literary and social criticism, and plays. He won the Governor General's Award in 1973 for his novel *The Manticore*.

Nora Ephron
Nora Ephron is a widely known American journalist and columnist. She published three books of essays and a novel, *Heartburn* (1983), before turning her talent increasingly to screenplays. She has scripted such successful films as *Silkwood* (1983), *When Harry Met Sally* (1989), and *Sleepless in Seattle* (1993).

Northrop Frye
The author of some twenty books and hundreds of essays, articles, and reviews, Northrop Frye is one of the most important literary theorists and critics of the twentieth century. As a teacher at the University of Toronto for many years, and as a social commentator, he had an enormous influence on Canadian writers and culture in general.

Robert Fulford
Formerly a journalist with the *Toronto Star*, and later editor of *Maclean's*, Robert Fulford then became editor of the magazine *Saturday Night*. In his long tenure in this position, Fulford had considerable influence on Canadian literature and the fine arts. He has written several books on Canadian culture, arts, and politics, and (under the pseudonym of Marshall Delaney) has been an influential film reviewer.

Bil Gilbert
An American journalist whose articles have appeared in such magazines as *Sports Illustrated, Audubon,* and *The Smithsonian*, Bil Gilbert has published a number of books on such widely differing subjects as *How Animals Communicate* (1966), *The Trailblazers* (1973), and *Westering Man: The Life of Joseph Walker* (1983).

Linda Goyette
Linda Goyette is a Canadian journalist who has worked for the CBC, the *Ottawa Citizen*, and the *London Free Press*. She now writes for the *Edmonton Journal*, where she has been a member of the editorial board for several years.

Pico Iyer
A journalist and travel writer, Pico Iyer has published essays and reviews in such periodicals as *Time, The Village Voice,* and *Partisan Review*. He is also the author of several books, including the popular *Video Night in*

Kathmandu (1980) and *Falling Off the Map: Some Lonely Places of the World* (1993).

Paulette Jiles
An American-born poet, novelist, and journalist who came to Canada in 1969, Paulette Jiles won the Governor General's Award for poetry in 1985 for her *Celestial Navigation*. She has published a number of other books, among which the best known is her novel *Sitting in the Club Car Drinking Rum and Karma Cola* (1986).

George Jonas
George Jonas has worked as a radio and television producer for the CBC, and he has also done much investigative journalism, producing books such as *Vengeance: The True Story of an Israeli Counter-Terrorist Team* (1984). He has also published the libretti for two operas, a novel, poetry, and a collection of his journalism, *Crocodiles in the Bathtub and Other Perils* (1987).

Martin Luther King, Jr.
An American Baptist minister, author, orator, and civil rights leader, the internationally renowned Martin Luther King, Jr., was one of the most important leaders of the anti-segregationist movement in the southern United States in the 1950s and 1960s. A strong advocate of nonviolent protest, he won the Nobel Prize for peace in 1964. He was assassinated in 1968.

Edward I. Koch
An American lawyer and Member of Congress, Edward I. Koch served as mayor of New York City from 1978 to 1989. He is the author of four books about politics and his experience in public life.

Carolyn Leitch
Carolyn Leitch is a Canadian journalist who has worked for the *Cornwall Standard Freeholder* and as a freelance journalist reporting from Asia. She now reports on technology and on the travel industry for the "Report on Business" section of the *Globe and Mail*.

Norma Lundberg
A Toronto writer who has been active in the women's movement, Norma Lundberg holds a Ph.D. in Library and Information Science from the University of Western Ontario. She has published essays and book reviews and is now working on a novel and several short stories.

Hugh MacLennan
The author of such important novels as *Barometer Rising, Two Solitudes, The Watch That Ends the Night,* and *Voices in Time,* Hugh MacLennan was also widely admired for his essays, which ranged over Canadian culture and

political and social affairs. He has received five Governor General's Awards, three for fiction and two for non-fiction.

Christina McCall
Christina McCall is a Canadian journalist and author who has published extensively in such periodicals as *Chatelaine* and *Maclean's*. She is the author of *Grits: An Intimate Portrait of the Liberal Party* (1982), and, with Stephen Clarkson, of a two-volume biography of Pierre Trudeau: *The Magnificent Obsession* (1990), and *The Heroic Delusion* (1994).

Nellie L. McClung
A journalist, fiction writer, and popular speaker throughout the United States and Canada, Nellie McClung was influential as a political activist and, especially, as a feminist. She fought to win voting rights for women in Manitoba and played a leading role in persuading the British Privy Council to recognize the legal status of women as persons in 1929.

E. J. McCullough
A Canadian philosopher who specializes in ethics and life issues, E. J. McCullough has been a member of the Department of Philosophy at Saint Thomas More College, Saskatoon, since 1968.

Ovide Mercredi
A Cree lawyer, Ovide Mercredi has been involved with the Assembly of First Nations, initially as the Manitoba Regional Chief, and, since 1991, as its leader. His *In the Rapids: Navigating the Future of First Nations* was published in 1993.

Jessica Mitford
The author of ten books, Jessica Mitford is an English social critic. The range of her interests can be seen in the titles of some of her books: *The American Way of Death, Kind and Usual Punishment: The Prison Business, Poison Penmanship: The Gentle Art of Muckraking,* and *The American Way of Birth.*

Ruth Morris
Ruth Morris has long worked on the problem of finding alternatives to prisons. She is the author of such books as *The Risk of Loving, Seeds of Abolitions, Street People Speak,* and, her latest, *Crumbling Walls: Why Prisons Fail* (1989).

Farley Mowat
Having published nearly thirty books since *People of the Deer* (1952), Farley Mowat has long been one of Canada's most widely read authors; his books have been published in nearly forty other countries. Topics to which he has devoted books include his youth, his experiences during

the Second World War, his eight years spent in Newfoundland, the behaviour of animals, and the survival of endangered species.

Joyce Nelson
Joyce Nelson is a journalist and social critic whose essays have appeared in a large number of journals and magazines. She has published four books, the latest of which is *Sign Crimes/Road Kill: From Mediascape to Landscape* (1992).

Peter C. Newman
In addition to having served as Editor-in-Chief of the *Toronto Star* and *Maclean's*, for which he still writes a regular column, Peter Newman is widely known for his numerous books on Canadian history and politics. Among the most popular of these are *Renegade in Power: The Diefenbaker Years* (1963), *The Distemper of Our Times (1968)*, and *The Canadian Establishment* (1981). He has also published a three-volume history of the Hudson's Bay Company.

Patrick Nowell-Smith
A historian who has taught at York University, Patrick Nowell-Smith is the author of a number of influential historical essays, as well as of *What Actually Happened* (1971), a book concerned with the nature of historical accuracy.

George Orwell
One of the most widely read political writers of the twentieth century, Orwell's first book, *Down and Out in Paris and London* (1933), describes his life among the poor in France and England. His two most influential books, which record his passionate hatred of totalitarianism, are *Animal Farm* (1945) and *1984* (1949).

Camille Paglia
Camille Paglia is Professor of Humanities at the University of the Arts in Philadelphia. Her two books, *Sexual Personae* (1990), and *Sex, Art, and American Culture* (1992), have been the subjects of considerable controversy in North America and Britain because of her radical views. Her latest book, *Vamps and Tramps*, promises to be just as controversial.

Jo Goodwin Parker
"What Is Poverty?" by Jo Goodwin Parker is from an unpublished speech that she gave in Deland, Florida, on December 27, 1965. She has requested that no biographical information be provided.

Therese A. Rando
Therese Rando is an American clinical psychologist who specializes in areas related to grief and death. Among the several books she has pub-

lished are *Grief, Dying, and Death: Clinical Interventions for Caregivers* (1984), and *Loss and Anticipatory Grief* (1986).

Mordecai Richler
A native of Montreal, Mordecai Richler is a controversial critic of Canadian culture, society, and politics. It is, however, as a novelist that he has achieved an international reputation, based on such works as *The Apprenticeship of Duddy Kravitz* (1959), *The Incomparable Atuk* (1963), *Joshua Then and Now* (1980), and *Solomon Gursky Was Here* (1990).

Carl Sagan
Carl Sagan is an astronomer, author, and space scientist, as well as a popular lecturer and television personality. He has published many books, including *Atmospheres of Mars and Venus* (1961), *Other Worlds* (1975), and *Cosmos* (1980), as well as *The Dragons of Eden*, for which he won a Pulitzer Prize in 1970.

Donna E. Smyth
Donna Smyth is an environmental activist who teaches creative writing and English at Acadia University. In addition to plays, numerous short stories, and articles on art and the uranium industry, she has published three books: *Quilt* (1982), *Subversive Elements* (1986), and *No Place Like Home* (1988).

David Suzuki
A geneticist by training, David Suzuki became a very popular television commentator with his series *Suzuki on Science*, which began in 1971. He also hosted CBC-TV's *The Nature of Things* for ten years. He has published several books, including an autobiography, *Metamorphosis* (1987).

Lewis Thomas
A physician and scientist who specialized in cancer research, Lewis Thomas was President for several years of the Memorial Sloan-Kettering Cancer Center in New York. His books, which deal with such matters as science, society, language, and music, include *Lives of a Cell* (1973), *Late Night Thoughts on Listening to Mahler's Ninth Symphony* (1983), and *Et Cetera, Et Cetera: Notes of a Word Watcher* (1990).

Elie Wiesel
A writer and educator, Elie Wiesel has frequently been honoured for his involvement in international Jewish affairs and the welfare of the Jewish people. Among his books are *The Jews of Silence* (1966), *The Trial of God* (1979), and *From the Kingdom of Memory* (1990).

George Woodcock
Essayist, man of letters, literary journalist, historian, literary critic, and anarchist, George Woodcock has published over one hundred books on

politics, history, travel, and literary criticism. He founded the periodical *Canadian Literature* in 1959. Among his books are *Anarchism* (1962), *Gandhi* (1971), *Gabriel Dumont* (1975), *The Canadians* (1979), and *Caves in the Desert* (1988).

STUDENT REPLY CARD

In order to improve future editions, we are seeking your comments on

Influential Writing, by Connor and Legris.

Please answer the following questions and return this form via Business Reply Mail. Your opinions matter. Thank you in advance for sharing them with us!

Name of your college or university: _____

Major program of study: _____

Course title: _____

Were you required to buy this book? _____ yes _____ no

Did you buy this book new or used? _____ new _____ used ($_____)

Do you plan to keep or sell this book? _____ keep _____ sell

Is the order of topic coverage consistent with what was taught in your course?

Are there chapters or sections of this text that were not assigned for your course? Please specify:

Were there topics covered in your course that are not included in the text? Please specify:

What did you like most about this text?

What did you like least?

If you would like to say more, we would appreciate hearing from you. Please write to us at the address shown on the reverse of this page.

- - - - - - - - - - - - - - *cut here* - - - - - - - - - - - - ┐
                                                              ╎
                                                              ╎ *cut here*
                                                              ╎

- - - - - - - - - - - - - *fold here* - - - - - - - - - - - -

Postage will be paid by

MAIL ⇒ POSTE

Canada Post Corporation / Société canadienne des postes

| Postage paid
If mailed in Canada | Port payé
si posté en Canada |

Business Reply   **Réponse d'affaires**

0183560299   01

0183560299-L1N9B6-BR01

Attn.: Sponsoring Editor
College Division

MCGRAW-HILL RYERSON LIMITED
300 WATER ST
WHITBY ON   L1N 9Z9

tape shut